PERSIAN NATIVITIES III:

ON SOLAR REVOLUTIONS

Abū Ma'shar's
*On the Revolutions of the
Years of Nativities*

TRANSLATED AND EDITED BY
BENJAMIN N. DYKES, PHD

The Cazimi Press
Minneapolis, Minnesota
2010

Published and printed in the United States of America
by The Cazimi Press, Minneapolis, MN 55414

© 2010 by Benjamin N. Dykes, Ph.D.

All rights reserved. No part of this publication may be reproduced, stored in or introduced into a retrieval system, or transmitted, in any form or by any means (electronic, mechanical, photocopying, recording or otherwise), without the prior written permission of both the copyright owner and the above publisher of this book.

The scanning, uploading, and distribution of this book via the Internet or via any other means without the permission of the publisher is illegal and punishable by law. Please do not participate in or encourage the electronic piracy of copyrighted materials. Your support of the author's rights is appreciated.

ISBN-13: 978-1-934586-13-6

Acknowledgments

I would like to thank Chris Brennan, Frank Clifford, Andy Gehrz, and Robert Schmidt for making this book possible.

TABLE OF CONTENTS

Book Abbreviations v
Table of Figures vi
INTRODUCTION 1
   §1: Abū Ma'shar 1
   §2: The Persian annual predictive system 4
   §3: Approaching the chart: stages and principles 7
   §4: Benefic-malefic considerations 14
   §5: A few points on timing 16
   §6: Profections 17
   §7: The Ascendant of the year and its Lord 27
   §8: Distributors and partners 29
   §9: The Moon 34
   §10: Lots 36
   §11: The *firdārīyyāt* 37
   §12: Transits 41
   §13: Ninth-parts 47
   §14: Monthly, weekly, daily, and hourly rulers and periods 48
   §15: Superior squares, overcoming, decimation 48
   §16: Vocabulary and terms 51
BOOK I: DEFENSE & DEFINITIONS 53
   I.1: On the revolutions of nativities 53
   I.2: On the usefulness of the revolution 53
   I.3: Against those who would not accept revolutions 54
   I.4: How much the ancients used revolutions 57
   I.5: On the arrangement of the figure of the revolution 58
   I.6: On the horoscope of the year and the dispositions of the planets in the revolution 60
   I.7: On the fact that an astrologer should know beforehand the age of him whose revolution it is 61
   I.8: On the disposition of the planets in the nativity and in the revolution 64
   I.9: On those things which an astrologer should know beforehand 65
BOOK II: PROFECTIONS 69
   II.1: On the number of the significators of the year 69
   II.2: On the significations of the soul and body, from revolutions 72
   II.3: On the sign of the revolution and its Lord 74
   II.4: On Saturn, when he is the Lord of the Year and is made fortunate .. 77
   II.5: On the significations of Saturn when he is the Lord of the Year and would be of a bad condition 80
   II.6: On the signification of Saturn when he is the Lord of the Year, concerning the places in which he is 87

II.7: On the signification of Jupiter, if he were the Lord of the Year and he were of a good condition 90
II.8: On the significations of Jupiter if he were the Lord of the Year, and were of a bad condition 93
II.9: On the signification of Jupiter if he were the Lord of the Year, from the places in which he is 98
II.10: On the significations of Mars if he were the Lord of the Year and of a good condition 100
II.11: On the signification of Mars, if he were the Lord of the Year and was of a bad condition 102
II.12: On the signification of Mars from his places, if he were the Lord of the Year 106
II.13: On the signification of the Sun if he were the Lord of the Year and he were of a good condition 108
II.14: On the signification of the Sun if he were the Lord of the Year and were of a bad condition 110
II.15: On the signification of the Sun from the places in which he was, [while] appearing as the Lord of the Year 111
II.16: On the signification of Venus if she were the Lady of the Year, and she were of a good condition 113
II.17: On the signification of Venus as the Lady of the Year, if she were impeded 114
II.18: On Venus if she were the Lady of the Year, namely from the places in which she were found 116
II.19: On the signification of Mercury if he were the Lord of the Year and were of a good condition 118
II.20: On Mercury if he were the Lord of the Year and were of a bad condition 119
II.21: On the signification of Mercury if he were the Lord of the Year, from the place in which he was found 120
II.22: On the Moon, if she were the Lady of the Year and were of a good condition 121
II.23: On the signification of the Ascendant of the revolution 123
II.24: Notable profection-revolution positions 125

BOOK III: DIRECTIONS IN REVOLUTIONS 132
III.1: On undertaking directions in revolutions 132
III.2: On the signification of the good and bad planets appearing as the Lords of the bounds, and of those who partner with them, whether by body or by rays 137
III.3: On the signification of Saturn if he were the dispositor by distribution, and on the signification of the partnership of the planets in the distribution 146
III.4: On the signification of Jupiter by his disposition, and on the planets partnering [with him] 148

III.5: On the signification of the disposition of Mars and of those planets partnering with him 149
III.6: On the signification of Venus and of the planets partnering with her 151
III.7: On the distribution of Mercury and of the planets partnering with him 153
III.8: On the partnership of the Lord of the Year and its distribution, [with] the distributor and the Ascendant according to [their combined] signification..156
III.9: On the ninth-parts and their direction, and the third of their distribution, according to the opinions of the Indians................................162
III.10: On the knowledge of the Lord of the Year from the ninth-parts, according to the opinion of the Indians...168

BOOK IV: ON THE *FIRDĀRIYYĀT* 170
IV.1: On the *firdārīyyah* of the Sun..170
IV.2: On the *firdārīyyah* of Venus...174
IV.3: On the *firdārīyyah* of Mercury..176
IV.4: On the *firdārīyyah* of the Moon..178
IV.5: On the *firdārīyyah* of Saturn..180
IV.6: On the *firdārīyyah* of Jupiter...182
IV.7: On the *firdārīyyah* of Mars..184
IV.8: On the *firdārīyyāt* of the Nodes..185

BOOK V: ON INGRESSES 187
V.1: On the ingress of the planets 187
V.2: On the ingress of Saturn to his own places and those of the rest of the planets 190
V.3: On the ingress of Jupiter to his own and to the places of the rest of the planets 191
V.4: On the ingress of Mars 193
V.5: On the signification of the Sun in the individual signs....................194
V.6: On the ingress of Venus into her own place and that of the other planets...195
V.7: On the signification of Mercury when he enters into the places 196
V.8: On the signification of the ingress of the Moon 197
V.9: General comments on transits 199
V.10: Miscellaneous considerations..200

BOOK IX: DIVISIONS OF MONTHS, DAYS, HOURS..................203
IX.7: On the indicators of the days and hours 203
APPENDIX A: ALTERNATIVE TEXT FOR THE *FIRDĀRIYYĀT* OF THE NODES..207
APPENDIX B: TABLE OF EGYPTIAN BOUNDS FOR DISTRIBUTORS 208
APPENDIX C: APHORISMS ON REVOLUTIONS 209
APPENDIX D: STUDY GUIDE TO PERSIAN NATIVITIES........................214
APPENDIX E: THE ESSENTIAL MEDIEVAL ASTROLOGY CYCLE 221

BIBLIOGRAPHY **223**
INDEX **226**

BOOK ABBREVIATIONS

Abū 'Ali al-Khayyāt:	*The Judgments of Nativities*	*JN*
Abū Ma'shar:	*Liber Introductorii Maioris ad Scientiam Iudiciorum Astrorum (Great Introduction to the Knowledge of the Judgments of the Stars)*	*Gr. Intr.*
	On the Revolutions of Nativities	*On Rev. Nat.*
Bonatti, Guido	*Book of Astronomy*	*BOA*
Dorotheus of Sidon:	*Carmen Astrologicum*	*Carmen*
Māshā'allāh:	*On the Significations of the Planets in a Nativity*	*On Sig. Planet*
	Book of Aristotle	*BA*
Ptolemy	*Tetrabiblos*	*Tet.*
Sahl bin Bishr:	*The Introduction*	*Introduct.*
'Umar al-Tabarī	*Three Books on Nativities*	*TBN*
Vettius Valens:	*The Anthology*	*Anth.*

TABLE OF FIGURES

Figure 1: Planetary *firdārīyyāt* 39
Figure 2: Transit template 47
Figure 3: Abū Ma'shar's nativity 134
Figure 4: Ninth-parts 163
Figure 5: Subdivisions of the ninth-parts 165

INTRODUCTION

This is the third and probably final volume of *Persian Nativities*, the natal installment of my *Essential Medieval Astrology*, a projected series of translations which will redefine the contours of traditional astrology.[1] It contains *On the Revolutions of the Years of Nativities* (*On Rev. Nat.*) by Abū Ma'shar, one of the most famous of medieval astrologers. Later in 2010 I will begin to release horary works and new translations of introductory works such as al-Qabīsī's *Introduction to Astrology* and Abū Ma'shar's *Abbreviation of the Introduction*.

Please note: readers new to the vocabulary of profections, distributions, and so on, may find it best to begin with §§1-2, then to familiarize themselves with the particular techniques in §§6-14, finally returning to the delineation principles in §§3-5 and the final remarks in §§15-16.

§1: Abū Ma'shar

Abū Ma'shar Ja'far bin Muhammad al-Balkhi was born around 10:00 p.m. on August 10, 787, near Balkh, Afghanistan.[2] He was initially an astrology skeptic, but around the age of 47 he is said to have been introduced to astrology by the famous Arab polymath, al-Kindī. From that point on, Abū Ma'shar became a prolific astrological writer and wielded great influence in both the Arabic and Latin astrological worlds. Several important works of his were translated into Latin by the mid-1100s, but many more still exist in Arabic alone. His work may even have been instrumental in introducing Aristotelian philosophy into the Latin West, courtesy of his *Great Introduction to the Knowledge of the Judgments of the Stars* (*Gr. Intr.*), a large work defending astrology as a science and presenting all aspects of astrology's basic concepts and ways of looking at signs, houses, planets, and Lots. He died on March 8 or 9, 886.

On Rev. Nat. presents Abū Ma'shar's version of what had by his time become a standard suite of annual predictive techniques. Most of these techniques had been described by earlier Greek-speaking astrologers, though not always in the same books or as techniques to be used together.[3] But by

---

[1] See Appendix E.
[2] See his nativity (established as such by Pingree) in III.1 below.
[3] Based on a comparison of Abū Ma'shar with 'Umar's *Carmen* and parallel texts on transits in Schmidt 1995 (p. 5), it is evident that Abū Ma'shar had access to a different edition of Dorotheus—perhaps Māshā'allāh's text or even a Greek version. See below, §8.

the mid-7th Century (at the latest), Persian astrologers had worked these techniques into a package which fell under the general scheme of the "cycle" or "revolution" or "change-over" of the year. Nowadays we often refer to solar "returns," but traditionally the cycle or revolution was a time to re-appraise the nativity in light of several overlapping techniques, some of which lasted more than a year and were not strictly related to the Sun's annual return. The revolution was also a time at which certain planets were said to hand over responsibility for the native's life to other planets, which "took turns" at "steering" the native's life in various respects—hence it was sometimes spoken of as the "handing over" of the year.

The current translation does not represent all of *On Rev. Nat.* By the time Pingree wrote his 1968 critical edition of the medieval Greek version, at least four complete Arabic manuscripts were known to exist, along with an epitome by one of Abū Ma'shar's students in the 10th Century (al-Sijzi). There may be more yet. But these complete and epitomized Arabic versions have never been translated: instead, in the late 10th Century it was partially translated into Greek, and that work was the basis of a Latin version in about 1262 AD. *Persian Nativities III* is based on this Latin version, with references to Pingree's Greek.

The fact that *On Rev. Nat.* was never fully translated, and that it only appeared in Latin in the 1260s, is significant for medieval astrology. For the majority of the key Latin translations of Perso-Arabic astrology had been completed in the 1100s, with others by people such as Salio of Padua in the early 1200s. Māshā'allāh's own briefer but similar account of the Persian methods had indeed been translated by Hugo of Santalla in 1140 or 1141 as Book IV of the Latin *Book of Aristotle*; but as I mentioned in my introduction to it in *Persian Nativities I*, Hugo's style was difficult and unpopular: thus an early opportunity for Western astrologers to practice the Persian methods was largely lost. So it was that influential astrologers and encyclopediasts such as Guido Bonatti did not have robust versions of this material, but instead had to rely on the thumbnail sketches found in the translations of 'Umar al-Tabarī, Abū Bakr, and al-Qabīsī.[4]

Modern people interested in and practicing traditional astrology still feel this lack of a complete translation, because much material pertaining to

---

[4] I have translated the material by 'Umar and Abū Bakr in *Persian Nativities II*, and will publish my own translation of al-Qabīsī in 2010. Abū Bakr did write his own short work on revolutions which contains much of the basic material, but it does not seem to have been popular in its Latin incarnation, and I do not know when it was originally translated.

techniques such as transits and profections is still unavailable. To give the reader a sense of what is missing from this translation, consider the following table of contents originally in Arabic, which represents the missing portions (except for the italicized IX.7, which does appear in this work):

VI. On the Conditions of the Planets and Signs
    VI.1: On the Lord of the period
    VI.2. On the periods of the signs in the nativity, and on the assigning of degrees
    VI.3: On the significations of the sign of the year or of the horoscope of the revolution
    VI.4: On the significations of the arrival of the year in a sign
    VI.5: On the significations of the planets in the pivots of the nativity
    VI.6: On the significations of the Lords of the places

VII. On the Motion of the Planets through the Signs of the Year
    VII.1: On the significations of the planets from the signs and places
    VII.2-9: On the significations of the planets and Nodes transiting the twelve places

VIII. On the Conditions of the Planets in the Parts of the Signs
    VIII.1-7: On the significations of the planets in the domiciles of the planets
    VIII.8-14: On the significations of the planets in the bounds of the planets
    VIII.15: On the significations of the planets in the wells of the signs

IX. On the Knowledge of the Conditions of Men in the Months, Days, and Hours
    IX.1: On the knowledge of the indicators of the months
    IX.2: On the knowledge of the condition of the first month
    IX.3: On constructing the chart of the revolution of the month
    IX.4: On temperaments[5]
    IX.5: On investigation the significations of the [other] eleven months

---

[5] Or perhaps, the "proper interpretive mixtures" of different parts of the chart.

IX.6: On the significations of the planets with respect to stable matters
IX.7: On the indicators of the days and hours
IX.8: On things breaking up[6]
IX.9: On the special indicators

It is easy to see that plenty of valuable material (and indeed the entire book) still needs to be translated from the Arabic.

§2: The Persian annual predictive system

On Rev. Nat. exemplifies well the suite of predictive techniques which we already saw in Book IV of Māshā'allāh's *BA*. But whereas *BA*'s treatment was often compressed and brief (especially given the style of Hugo's Latin), *On Rev. Nat.* bursts with details and interpretive hints despite the large amount of missing material. Following are the main stages in a complete version of the annual predictive system according to *On Rev. Nat.*:[7]

1. The Ptolemaic Ages of Man.[8]
2. The profected Ascendant and its Lord (called the Lord of the Year or the *sālkhudāy*).
3. The distributor and its partner. The distributor is the bound Lord of the directed Ascendant (here called the *jārbakhtār*),[9] while the partner is any planet or ray encountered by the directed Ascendant.
4. The solar revolution (or solar "return"), noting especially where the calculated Ascendant of the year falls in the nativity, what its Lord is, and planets transiting in it. One also notes the prominence of the Lots in the revolutionary chart, according to both their natal and annually recalculated positions.
5. The Lords of the *firdārīyyāt* or "periods," and their sub-Lords.

---

[6] *Interrumpentibus*.
[7] These will all be described in some detail below.
[8] Described by Ptolemy in *Tet*. IV.10.
[9] Māshā'allāh restricted the use of "*jārbakhtār*" to the bound Lord of the directed *hīlāj*. In III.3, Abū Ma'shar does include the directions of all of these *hīlāj*es, with their own *jārbakhtār*s and partners, but he seems not to emphasize them as much as he does the Ascendant. On the other hand, perhaps Abū Ma'shar means his delineation texts for the Ascendant's distributors and partners to be templates applicable to the other *hīlāj*es.

6. Transits at and throughout the solar revolution, particularly if a planet returns to its natal sign.
7. The Moon at and throughout the solar revolution.[10]
8. Directions of points within the charts of the annual and monthly revolutions, around the entire chart for that particular period. The effects will primarily hold only for that period.
9. The "Indian" ninth-parts.

For easy reference, the following table gives the locations of the major treatments of this material across *Persian Nativities* and al-Qabīsī. In the last rows I have included passages which describe the monthly and daily rulers, as well as natal directions generally (i.e., not strictly as part of the distributor-partner technique):

	BA	*TBN*	*Abū Bakr*	*On Rev. Nat.*	*Al-Qabīsī*
1. Ages of Man				I.7-8	
2. Profection	IV.1-7	II.4-6		II.1-22, II.24	IV.8
3. Distributor-partner	III.1.10, IV.8-13	II.2	I.17	III.1-8	IV.14
4. Solar revolution	IV.14-15			I.6, II.23	
5. *Firdāriyyāt*	III.17-25		I.16	IV.1-8	IV.20
6. Ingresses, returns	IV *passim*			V.1-9	IV.21
7. Moon	IV.1			II.22, III.8, V.10	
8. Directions in the revolution		II.3, II.5-6		II.1, III.1	IV.13

---

[10] This material is mostly missing in the Greek and Latin versions.

9. Ninth-parts				III.9-10	IV.16-17
10. Monthly, daily, hourly rulers	IV.16			IX.7	
11. Natal directions	II.17, III.1.10	I.4, II.1, II.5-6	I.15		IV.11-12

Much of the rest of my Introduction will be devoted to Abū Ma'shar's instructions and method, with occasional references to Māshā'allāh. But first I would like to get a few technical points out of the way.

First of all, Abū Ma'shar goes further than *BA* in its treatment of the revolutionary chart and house systems. In *BA* there were no explicit instructions to erect a separate revolutionary chart. Rather, Māshā'allāh gave the impression that the revolution should be considered as a set of annual transits, as though marked around the edges of the natal chart, with the calculated Ascendant of the year as a special point. In *On Rev. Nat.* we have the opposite: not only are we instructed to erect a separate chart, but in I.5 Abū Ma'shar practically suggests that natal positions should be marked around the edges of the revolutionary chart! Likewise, Māshā'allāh did not explicitly suggest or seem to use any house cusps in the revolution, apart from noting the location of the calculated Ascendant of the year (or "east of the year"). Abū Ma'shar explicitly endorses the use of quadrant-style house cusps. I do not know whether Abū Ma'shar himself decided upon these changes, or whether he was drawing upon older authors: the translation of more works from Arabic may help us here. But the difference between these two approaches is significant, both in the theoretical emphasis on the revolutionary chart and in the actual interpretations of houses.

Second, although Abū Ma'shar concentrates on the profection of the Ascendant, he does also profect the Lot of Fortune and other key areas of the figure, just as in Hellenistic astrology. In addition, like 'Umar al-Tabarī but unlike Māshā'allāh, Abū Ma'shar explicitly profects in 30° increments.[11]

Third, in III.7 he mentions briefly, but otherwise does not emphasize, the use of ascensional times in combination with the planetary years. This too is Hellenistic and can be found throughout Vettius Valens. Perhaps the missing Arabic chapters contain more information on them.

---

[11] IX.7.

Fourth, in I.9 Abū Ma'shar does allow the possibility of using a dead native's chart to continue speaking about his or her children, as a "second report"; and one may use a dead native's chart to continue speaking about his or her still-living father. One occasionally reads cryptic comments along these lines in medieval natal astrology, but rarely with such explicitness.

Fifth, *On Rev. Nat.* gives advice on how to differentiate between public and private expressions of the planets,[12] as well as the source of the effects. As to their public nature, the angularity of a planet (especially if in both the nativity and the revolution) makes the effects not only stronger, but more public and evident; cadence (especially if cadent in both) diminishes evils and makes them less public, even if they are still evident to those close to the native. If the planets are in aversion to the Ascendant,[13] they are more clandestine. But if the planets are in aversion and yet aspected by an angular planet, something of the effect will be public over time; if the planet in aversion is actually conjoined with the angular planet, then the native will be the one to disclose it.[14]

As to the sources of the effects, this is often a function of dignities:[15] if the planet (usually the Lord of the Year)[16] is in one of its own dignities, the effects will come from some known direction or a friend; but if in a peregrine or alien sign, from a stranger or an unexpected or unknown direction, or while in a foreign land. However, other classifications are useful: if in a watery sign, while on or near water; if in a four-footed sign, from animals.[17]

§3: *Approaching the chart: stages and principles*

In the first part of Book I, Abū Ma'shar provides a general way of approaching the chart during any given year. The first step is to determine the native's age according to the Ptolemaic Ages of Man, and to analyze the

---

[12] See I.3.
[13] That is, in signs which cannot aspect the rising sign (whether in the nativity or the revolution): the twelfth, eighth, sixth, and second, but with emphasis on the first three.
[14] This must assume that the planet in aversion represents the native—either by being the profected Lord of the Year or the distributor.
[15] See for example II.4 and *BA* IV.2.
[16] In II.4 he uses the Lord of the Year in an example with the Lot of Fortune: if the Lord of the Year aspects or rules the Lot, then the Lord's own dignities where it is will show the source, just as described here.
[17] II.5.

planet ruling that age, both natally and by transit.[18] Then, one should analyze the empirical circumstances of the native's life, such as his social status, habits, character, capacities—which, one supposes, might simply involve asking the native. This provides us an opportunity to emphasize that astrology is not a form of psychism, but is a consulting profession akin to medicine or law. For doctors do not simply look at charts and perform tests, but they interview patients in order to obtain the context for the consultation: this allows doctors to diagnose and offer advice. Likewise, attorneys cannot simply predict how a case will unfold, or how to argue their case, until they can go beyond affidavits and documents and interview actual witnesses. Astrologers too must ask questions and obtain biographical information which may not be strictly contained in the chart, and sometimes one needs to know how a given feature of the chart has actually manifested. For instance, a chart may show someone of higher status, but status is often relative to one's own community and not absolute. Thus a nativity might show someone actually middle-class or of average influence, but astrologically there is evidence of being very influential *within* one's own middle-class group. Or, some predictive techniques make it difficult to know whether someone is sick, or dead, or just having a disastrous year: it helps to know how the native is actually doing, in order to provide a general context for delineation and prediction.

After establishing the general context, Abū Ma'shar divides the various significators into three groups, in order to help the astrologer identify how the native will be affected by each feature of the charts.[19] The first group identifies significators of the native's body: all of these are places receiving aspects and influences, just as matter is traditionally thought to be passive and receptive of other things, without being active on its own. These significators allegedly show such influences and therefore effects on bodily health. The second group identifies significators of the native's soul and attitudes, and they are especially the Lords of the aforementioned places: they are understood to be more active, just as reason and spirit are active as compared to passive matter. If all or many of the significators of the body and soul are in good places or unharmed, then there will not only be a favorable concord between body and soul for that time, but they will have

---

[18] I.7, I.9. I will not describe the Ages of Man in this Introduction. Readers are directed to the chapters in *On Rev. Nat.* and *Tet.* IV.10.
[19] See II.2.

durability and a good bearing in life.[20] The third group identifies significators pertaining to "movements and operations," which could refer to combinations of the first two types of effects, or rather how the mind and body cooperate together to produce actions.

Although this threefold classification is intriguing and has precedents in other medieval material, I am skeptical of its use simply because the delineations given later by Abū Ma'shar often deal indiscriminately with effects on the body, soul, actions, other people, and so on. Of course, it is also possible that some of these delineations are simply archetypal, and one may use the threefold classification to distinguish the bodily from the mental effects within the range of possibilities listed.

Nevertheless, one might reasonably ask how to tell which significations matter or are more likely to manifest. For especially if we are dealing with two separate charts (the nativity and the revolution), we will have dozens of different aspects, placements, planetary conditions, and so on—how can we sort the wheat from the chaff? A close reading of *On Rev. Nat.* and other sources yields three basic delineation principles, which I will illustrate with examples:

1. The priority of the nativity. The nativity provides the basic pattern for life, setting the tone for general goods and evils. Any feature of the revolution shows variations, occasional and temporary trends, and intensifications or slackenings of what is *already* signified or possible in the nativity, not only for absolute issues such as having children or not, but for the changes in ongoing matters such as wealth and reputation. So, if a planet signifies something in both the nativity and the revolution, it will perfect that signification in a great way, and it might be *inevitable and unchangeable*.[21] If however a planet signifies something in the nativity, but the indications in the revolution prevent it (or vice versa), one should go with the chart with the stronger signification, but its influence will still be moderated:[22] for "the signification of the nativity does not become inactive on account of a revolution."[23] If the nativity seems to deny the possibility of children but a revolution indicates it, then perhaps the native will adopt; or if the nativity denies a spouse, perhaps at a revolution indicating marriage he will take on a

---

[20] II.2.
[21] II.5.
[22] II.5.
[23] I.3.

concubine.²⁴ Māshā'allāh provides the example that if the Lord of the Year and/or the distributor are in a bad condition in the nativity but in a good one in the revolution, there will still be some good even though the nativity for the most part does not signify it.²⁵ Let me draw this out a bit with a few examples:

- If the Ascendant of the revolution (or the sign of the profection) falls on a *natal* configuration (especially on an important one), then what it indicates will be activated in a more lasting and powerful way than if there were only a planet there *by transit* at the revolution.²⁶ So, the Ascendant on a natal configuration involving Mars will activate that Mars more strongly than if Mars only happened to be transiting on the Ascendant of the revolution.
- Likewise, if the Ascendant of the year (or the sign of the profection) is on a natal planet, then that planet can (possibly) act more powerfully as a substitute Lord of the Ascendant of the year precisely because it is a natal planet.²⁷
- Remember that in a revolution there are *three* Ascendants to watch: the natal Ascendant, the sign of the profected Ascendant, and the Ascendant of the year. While the sign of the profection and the Ascendant of the year are each relevant to how the year as a whole goes, the Ascendant of the year and its Lord are *partners* to the profection because the profection is more closely tied to the original meaning of the nativity.

This notion of the revolution as a temporary variation on the nativity also provides Abū Ma'shar a model for criticizing other approaches to the revolution—in this case, I believe he is criticizing 'Umar al-Tabarī²⁸ and Māshā'allāh.²⁹ Now, Abū Ma'shar recommends³⁰ that we direct many points *within* and *around* the revolutionary chart, both in that of the annual revolution and that of monthly revolutions: for example, one should direct the

---

²⁴ I.9.
²⁵ *BA* IV.14.
²⁶ Extrapolating from many statements in II.24.
²⁷ III.8.
²⁸ See *TBN* II.
²⁹ See *BA* IV.1.
³⁰ III.1.

Ascendant of the year around the whole circle for that year, noting what planets or aspects are encountered, and converting those encounters into dates throughout the year; or, one might do the same for a monthly revolution, directing the Ascendant around the whole circle in one month. The first method of directing around the annual revolution is in fact endorsed by both 'Umar and Māshā'allāh. However, Abū Ma'shar criticizes this approach for its incompleteness, since it treats the annual revolution as dispositive for everything in the whole year, without going down to the detail of the monthly revolutions. Let me reconstruct his argument as follows:

> "The nativity is a basic plan for life, establishing its basic themes and possibilities. Now, natal configurations are not all equally active at any given time, so we must apply predictive techniques to show when each is activated. Still, even important techniques like annual profections are rather static variants on the nativity (which never changes). Therefore, in order to track the changes in the native's life more fully, we must use a variety of techniques such as revolutions, which track changes at important symbolic times. The annual revolution is essentially a set of *ongoing* transits measured once a year, and we can use directions and transits within the revolutionary chart to examine trends throughout the year. *However*, some authorities want to use these transits and directions only at the annual revolution, as though the positions at the revolution and the directions in the annual chart will be dispositive for all actions and events throughout the year. And this makes the same mistake as someone who believes that the nativity alone can provide the timing for everything. If we only used the chart of the annual revolution, then it would be as though only one kind of thing (signified by a planet at that moment) was possible throughout that year. But that is contrary to experience. So even though directions and transits within the annual revolution are important, in order to identify the most important events and their timing, we must do similar things in smaller units of time such as in monthly revolutions."

Abū Ma'shar's approach requires that two interpretive elements be interrelated: the *likelihood* of an event, and *when* it will happen. For on the one hand, an event becomes more likely if it is reinforced by repetition: say, a feature in the nativity being repeated in the revolution. But on the other hand, the reason for the event's likelihood is the very reason for predicting *when* it will happen: since the revolution takes place at a certain time, the reinforcement of its likelihood coincides with the reason for it happening at *that* time. So, *what* happens is inextricably linked to *when* it happens.

However, this interrelation may also be a source of problems. For there is no rationale given for stopping at monthly revolutions and not going further, nor for the extent to which the planets and configurations in the smaller units of time need to mirror the larger ones. For instance, if some direction in the annual revolution is mirrored in the monthly revolution, is that enough to be certain that it will happen? Or must we go to weekly and daily rulers to be sure of its likelihood, not to mention when it will transpire? And if so, is it in every case, or only in some, and why? Perhaps experimentation will supply some guidelines.

On the other hand, although multiple charts and smaller units of time would lead to greater certainty and accuracy, it would also imply that the world is more thoroughly deterministic. For even if the world and human affairs are *in fact* determined down to the smallest detail, our *astrological* understanding of that would remain only somewhat general if we had to predict from the nativity alone. If the nativity indicated a Martial-type action or event (say, by an annual profection), there would still be great variety in the possible outcomes: in other words, we could still believe that there is great power to choose otherwise or for events to be highly varied, so long as they were still Martial. But the use of many layers of charts and techniques would imply that determinism is more widespread and deep, and would require *astrological* recognition of that fact. For we would not only be more certain of an event's likelihood, not to mention its timing, but each successive chart or technique would lead to even greater descriptive detail in *how* it would come about, greatly restricting alternative outcomes.

2. Reinforcement by repetition, across charts and across techniques. In these methods, indications will be more powerful the more they are repeated, whether across charts or techniques. Thus, similar indications in the nativity and in the revolution will be emphasized, but so will similar indications in both the current profection and the current *firdārīyyah*. So for instance, a planet which signifies something in both the nativity and the revolution will produce it to the greatest extent it can; and if a planet signifies something bad in both charts—even if joined by a good aspect to a benefic—it accentuates failure and difficulty.³¹ Likewise, a planet which is aspecting a benefic in both times will strengthen the significations of good.³² On the other hand, if two planets are in a bad condition but only joined in one of the times, then the evils will be lesser due to the lack of repetition.³³ Let me provide some further examples:

- If the natal, profected, and revolutionary Ascendants are the same sign, with both a natal and transiting malefic in them, then the indications for the year as a whole are very negative, especially if the Lord of the Year and the Lord of the Ascendant of the year are in poor condition.³⁴
- Malefics transiting in the sign of the profection and also squaring the Ascendant of the year, is a very bad indication.³⁵
- If Venus is the distributor, and also happens to be the Lady of the Year (or if the profected Ascendant comes to the Lot of Marriage), then Venusian and particularly marital indications will be more certain and powerful.³⁶
- If a natal malefic harms some planet, then that harm will be especially activated when (a) the Ascendant of the year is on that natal malefic, and (b) the harmed planet happens to be the distributor or Lord of the Year at that time.³⁷
- If some planet impeded the nativity,³⁸ it will be especially bad for the year if it also did any of the following: transited in the natal Ascendant, or in the Ascendant of the year, or the place of the distribution, or it were with the Lords of these. The same is true for good indications if a benefic were helping the nativity and in one of these places.³⁹

---

³¹ I.3, II.5.
³² II.4.
³³ II.5.
³⁴ II.23. This is an extreme example of duplicating significations, but underscores that these Ascendants set the tone for the whole year.
³⁵ II.24.
³⁶ III.6.
³⁷ III.8.
³⁸ An example might be a contrary-to-sect malefic in the tenth sign, squaring the natal Ascendant by degree.
³⁹ III.8.

- The whole year will be especially good if all of the following were benefics: the distributor, the Lord of the Ascendant of the year, and the dispositor of the transiting Moon.[40]
- Compare the following: (a) the natal house of the annual profection, and (b) the derived position of the natal Ascendant from the Ascendant of the year. If they are the same, it will emphasize those matters strongly.[41] For example, let the natal Ascendant be Aries, and let the annual profection reach the 5th house (Leo). If the Ascendant of the year falls in Sagittarius, then the natal Ascendant will be in the 5th from it, emphasizing 5th house matters.
- The Lord of the Year will have repetitive emphasis if it transits: (a) through the same natal house, or (b) in that house as derived from the Ascendant of the year, or (c) transiting in that house as derived from the sign of the profection.

3. Activation by key significators and key places. Just as we prioritize the nativity and whatever is reinforced by repetition, so certain places and Lords are emphasized: *not every place or planet is equally important at any given time.* Below I will mention places specific to every technique, but generally: natal configurations will be activated when the planets involved are time-lords, or when certain planets (especially time-lords) transit those places or their whole-sign angles, or when planets are stationing or retrograding on key places, or if a natal or transiting planet is in the angles of the nativity or of the revolution, or if planets transit the place of a distribution—there are others mentioned here and there, but the basic idea should be clear.

§4: Benefic-malefic considerations

Abū Ma'shar spends a great deal of time discussing the conditions and combinations of benefics and malefics, especially in the material on distributors and partners (Book III). However, these conditions and combinations are not something special to distribution, but are relevant to profections, *firdārīyyāt*, and other techniques. Therefore in this section I will present his basic approach as something applying more broadly across the revolution as a whole.[42]

---

[40] *BA* IV.14.
[41] *BA* IV.15.
[42] A few of these rules could have been used above as example of repetitive emphasis.

When looking at planets individually, a planet in a good condition will have the strongest signification for consistent benefic effects. But a benefic planet in a bad condition will have weakened significations for benefic effects.[43] And if it is also configured[44] to a malefic, it will even receive some operations to the bad, and may even perform some of those bad things itself due to their commingling.[45]

On the other hand, a malefic in a good condition can signify good things consistent with its nature, especially if it is with another planet in a good condition, and through a good aspect.[46] If however it is in a bad condition by itself, it will show even worse problems and losses than usual; and if configured to another planet in a bad condition, it increases the harm.[47] But if a malefic in a bad condition is configured to a planet in a good condition, the other planet will at least not contribute additional harm; and if the malefic is configured to a benefic, it will also diminish its malice.[48]

From this we can move to Abū Ma'shar's thorough list of combinations for distributors and partners from Ch. III.2. In distributions, the distributor is considered the primary planet and the partner as the secondary one: we can let these stand as proxies for any other planetary combinations which focus on a primary planet and those aspecting it. The combinations will be given in the order of *primary-secondary*:

Benefic. If a benefic planet is alone or considered in itself, and is in a good condition in both charts, it indicates manifest prosperities; but if it is alone and in a bad condition in both, then it will manifest the contrary things. If it is good in the nativity but bad in the revolution, the goods will be moderate but they will still be firm and certain because of the priority of the nativity; while if it is bad in the nativity and good in the revolution, the goods will be both moderate and somewhat uncertain or transitory.

Malefic. Similarly, a malefic alone and in a good condition in both charts shows victory and triumph and prosperity (according to its planetary nature);

---

[43] II.4.
[44] It is unclear to me whether Abū Ma'shar really draws a clear distinction in *On Rev. Nat.* between configurations by sign and aspects by degrees/orbs, since we are reading him in translation. We should be cautious about preferring one or the other when seeing the words "configure" or "aspect."
[45] II.4.
[46] II.4.
[47] II.4.
[48] II.4.

but if in a bad condition in both, the native may even die.[49] For the other combinations, compare with the previous paragraph.

Malefic-benefic. A malefic primary planet will expose the native to dangers and have a mixed condition, but the benefic will rescue the native from the worst things if it is strong enough—but if not very strong, or if there are many bad indications, it will not rescue. So for instance, a Saturn-Venus combination is not normally favorable for relationships and sexuality: if they were both in a good condition, it will be favorable for such things; but if they and especially Venus were of only a moderate or poor condition, the quality of the relationships will suffer and decline more towards the Saturnian.[50]

Benefic-malefic. This is similar to the previous paragraph in its mixed circumstances; there may be adversities because of the malefic secondary planet, but the primary emphasis will be on prosperity and goodness.

Malefic-malefic. This combination brings greater misfortune, depending upon the overall context of the revolution and what features these planets affect. And with such a situation, Abū Ma'shar says that a benevolent which happens to aspect in addition will not rescue the native, but it will at least make him *honorable and upright* while he suffers; but if a malefic does so, it will add compulsion and suffering.[51]

Benefic-benefic. Two benefic planets in a good condition in the two times will obviously indicate prosperity and other good effects; in a mixed condition, mixed ones. But if a malefic is involved by aspect, it will add some *confusion* and make the delight less secure.[52]

§5: A few points on timing

Below I will add more details about timing, depending on the technique involved. But I would like to add four perspectives on timing from *On Rev. Nat.* here:

---

[49] The delineation assumes the planet is the distributor, and so a proxy for the native himself and his life.

[50] II.4, II.5.

[51] I hasten to add that this delineation draws on the particular features of distribution, and may not fit all circumstances. As I will mention below, Abū Ma'shar indicates that planets transiting the distributor and partner will provide commentary on the *mental state* of the native at the time.

[52] Again, this statement about the native's mental state is drawn from the material on distribution.

- If a planet is configured to the Lord of the Year,[53] it will manifest its signification when (*a*) it governs some part of the year,[54] and (*b*) especially if it is associated to the Lord of the Year by transit at that part of the year; or (*c*) it is configured to the sign where the Lord of the Year is, either in the nativity or revolution, or (*d*) it is configured to (*e*) the sign of the profection or to (*f*) the Ascendant of the year or its Lord, or (*g*) the Lord of the day.[55]
- The quadruplicities of a planet, both natally and by transit, affect a planet's actions in a given time: fixed signs show more unchangeable effects, common ones a tensing and relaxing pattern, movable signs will be more unpredictable and casual.[56]
- Placements by quadrant at the revolution will indicate broadly when the effects will manifest during the year—this affects the Lord of the Year, the distributor in particular, but also the benefics and malefics in their general meanings of good and bad. Thus for planets in the eastern quadrant (from the Ascendant to the Midheaven), the effects are near the beginning; in the southern one (from the Midheaven to the Descendant), toward the middle; and so on.[57]
- The significations of angular planets will manifest faster than those of cadent ones; succeedents are somewhere in the middle.[58]

§6: Profections

Profections are among the most important predictive techniques in traditional astrology. Although one may make reliable predictions with them using only the nativity, the full Persian method combines natal profections, the solar revolution, and transits. In this section I will outline a general approach to profections based on statements by Abū Ma'shar throughout *On Rev. Nat.*[59]

---

[53] I presume this means at the nativity.
[54] Perhaps by being the Lord of the Ascendant of the year, or that of one of the monthly revolutions.
[55] II.5. I confess this seems like too many possibilities, with few specifics or ways of telling which is more powerful than the others.
[56] III.7. Abū Ma'shar also makes comments about matching the quadruplicities to ascensional times, but I do not understand it fully.
[57] III.8.
[58] III.8.
[59] The reader should note that the standardly accepted profection method differs somewhat from that presented by Vettius Valens in *Anth.* IV.

Profections are "advancements" of some natal place around the chart, standardly at a rate of one house per year. By "house," I mean a whole-sign house, that is, a sign. For it seems that the older, Hellenistic approach to profections used whole-sign houses. But by the Arabic period, astrologers such as 'Umar al-Tabarī and Abū Ma'shar advocated equal houses: thus, instead of moving from sign to sign, they moved in 30° increments.

The general theory is this: whatever is profected will have its natal meaning modified year by year, depending on what natal houses and planets it encounters, and that matter will be governed or "steered" by the domicile Lord of whatever house it lands on. The domicile Lord is called the "Lord of the Year," which sometimes appears in medieval texts under its earlier Pahlavi name, the *sālkhudāy*.

The most common profection is that of the Ascendant: the native's Ascendant is on itself or the 1st house when he or she is born, at age 0; at age 1, the Ascendant advances to the 2nd house; at age 2, to the 3rd house, and so on. Thus anything which is profected will return to itself in increments of 12: the Ascendant will return to itself and reinforce the original natal meaning at ages 12, 24, 36, and so on.

So if we profect the Ascendant, we are dealing with the year-to-year changes in the native's life as a whole; if we profect the tenth, we are dealing with the annual changes in the native's actions and reputation and profession; if the 2nd, money and possessions. Every place begins on its own natal position at age 0, and advances one sign or house thereafter. So, at age 6 anyone's Ascendant will profect to the 7th house; but anyone's 3rd will profect to the 9th house, and so on. If the Ascendant profects to a natal place with a natal benefic in good condition, with a benefic Lord of the Year, then the standard assumption is that the native's life (the Ascendant) will go well that year, and be conditioned by the type of natal house the profected Ascendant has encountered. But we must also see what planets are transiting through that place at the solar revolution, as well as how the Lord of the Year is doing by transit: the nativity may promise good things, but these will be modified if malefic planets are transiting through the sign of the profection, or if the Lord of the Year happens to be in a terrible condition at that time. Thus again, the nativity is given priority, but it is conditioned annually by how the sign of the profection and the Lord of the Year are doing.[60]

---

[60] See §14 below for information on monthly and daily profections.

On Rev. Nat. does not have a unified treatment of advice for profections, but scatters important information throughout the work, sometimes combining advice about profections with advice about transits or distributions. In this section I will try to organize the material in a way helpful for students. In all cases, we are assuming the profection of the Ascendant rather than any other place: this is an extension of the fact that the profected natal Ascendant is most important because it is based on the nativity, and because the Ascendant in particular represents the native. But these rules could in theory be applied to a profection of the Midheaven, of the 2nd house, and so on.

1. *Interpreting the sign of the profection.* First, (*a*) analyze the sign of the profection according to its nature in the nativity. What is the natal *house* and *angularity* of that sign, and is its Lord benefic or malefic—and generally, what is its Lord like?[61] Obviously good houses, angular or succeedent, with benefic Lords, will indicate more positive experiences and outcomes. Also, is there a natal planet or Lot in that sign,[62] and what rays are being cast into it, and from where?[63] Again, a benefic planet in a good condition in it, or with natal benefics casting trines into the sign, will be more positive than malefics in bad condition in it, or malefics casting squares into it.

(*b*) Look at the sign according to the transits at the solar revolution: is there a transiting planet in it, or any rays being cast into it, and from where?[64] The nature of that planet or aspect, and its condition, will modify what is indicated by the nativity: a transiting benefic can relieve some of the problems shown by a troubling natal configuration.

(*c*) Identify what derived house the sign of the profection is, from the Ascendant of the year: not only will the sign of the profection have its own natal meaning, but by derived houses from the Ascendant of the year it will have indications for that topic. Thus if the sign of the profection is the sixth from the Ascendant of the year, it will have indications for illness and stress.[65]

---

[61] II.3.
[62] Abū Ma'shar also instructs us to see if that sign corresponds to the twelfth-part of any planet; but this plays such a minor role in the text as we have it, that I omit it here.
[63] II.1, II.3.
[64] II.3.
[65] This is Abū Ma'shar's example (II.24). He also implies that being in a bad house of the revolution will have adverse effects on the sign of the profection as a whole. But as with other areas, he does not really explain how much weight we should grant this.

(*d*) Compare the natal and revolutionary analyses in order to appraise the overall benefit, harm, success, or failure of the native's condition in that year.[66]

2. *General comments on the profected sign.* Remember that, because the sign of the profection is the profected *natal Ascendant*, it has special significance for the year as a whole—even though the calculated Ascendant of the revolution will also be important. Following are some of the cautions and examples Abū Ma'shar offers with respect to the year as a whole:

- A profection to a natal malefic signifies harm;[67] but it will be made worse if there are also angular or succeedent malefics in the revolution itself.[68] So the profection to the malefic means something fundamentally malefic for the year due to the priority of the nativity, but it will be worse if this is reinforced by powerful malefics in the revolution.
- A profection to a natal malefic, with that malefic harming that same place by transit in the revolution, makes it bad for *that area of life* in that year.[69]
- A profection to the natal Midheaven, with a malevolent there, harms the native's work.[70]
- If the sign of the profection is in a good condition in both charts, and likewise its Lord (by sect, dignities, *etc.*), and that Lord is in a good place from the natal Ascendant *and* the profected sign *and* the Ascendant of the year, it signifies health, goodness, pleasantness, and conventional goods, according to whatever the Lord of the Year signifies.[71]
- Profections of the Ascendant to itself[72] are important because they renew the whole chart—so good and bad influences are more important at that time.[73]

---

[66] II.3.
[67] II.23.
[68] II.24.
[69] II.24.
[70] II.23. Abū Ma'shar does not specify whether the malefic must be there natally or by transit.
[71] II.3.
[72] Again, this happens for any profection at ages 12, 24, 36, and so on.
[73] III.8.

- If the sign of the profection is in a good condition but the Lord of the Year is not (or *vice versa*), it indicates mediocre harms and benefits.[74]
- The year will be harmed if transiting malefics aspect the sign of the profection with no benefic aspecting. But what will be harmed, or the type of harm, will derive from the Lord of the Year or the distributor.[75]

3. Analyzing the Lord of the Year. The sign of the year provides a general context for the positive or negative character of the year. But as a planet, the Lord of the Year has the task of managing the year and indicating people and actions and events. Abū Ma'shar often seems to treat the Lord of the Year as a proxy for the native, and the planets to which it is configured as indicating people and events: the other planets' conditions show such people's good or bad condition, and the aspect indicates whether their relation to him is positive or negative—*provided that we remember the natural affinity of the planets themselves.*[76] Some examples should illustrate this.[77] If Saturn is the Lord of the Year, and Venus is in a good condition, aspecting him by a trine in both times,[78] then the native (Saturn) will have good relations (trine, good condition) with women (Venus), and will enjoy art (Venus). But if she trines him in only one of the trines, then the good experiences will be more modest, and something of the normal antagonism between Saturn and Venus will manifest: for instance, becoming sad on the occasion of women. But if the aspect were a square, perhaps there will be some conflict with women. And if they were of a poor condition and in a square, it could show him suffering evils with respect to women; but in a poor condition and a good aspect, then he mixes readily with, or befriends (trine), low-class prostitutes (poor condition). But I hasten to add that in some cases the differences between aspects will not be as conceptually clear as in this example: good aspects might only show that the difficulties are narrowly contained, whereas bad aspects show they are more widespread and complete.[79]

---

[74] II.23.
[75] III.8.
[76] II.4.
[77] II.5.
[78] That is, at the nativity and at the revolution.
[79] II.5.

Again, if the Lord of the Year is in a bad condition, it will affect the nature of the year adversely. Similarly, if the Lord of the Year is a malefic, with its natal place being transited by a malefic (i.e., transiting in the sign of the profection), this is particularly bad;[80] but if a malefic Lord of the Year is being aspected by benefics, then it will have some of its harm removed,[81] especially if that Lord of the Year is in a good sect condition.[82] An impeded Lord of the Year (or distributor) can also show *inactivity* and not just troubling outcomes,[83] as well as anxieties and worries about the matters it indicates, especially by house.[84]

One ought to examine the condition and aspects of the Lord of the Year, both in the nativity and in the revolution, including aspects to Lots.[85] If it is aspected, the Lord of the Year will bring in the significations of the houses those other planets rule: thus if the Lord of the 2nd aspects it, then wealth will be connected to its significations.[86] The aspecting planets can show sources of the good or bad indicated.[87] And generally speaking, see if the Lord of the Year is transiting in a place and with planets reinforcing its natal rulerships—this follows the principle of reinforcement by repetition.[88] But planets aspecting the Lord of the Year in only one of the times bring less advantage and harm than if the aspect were present in both times.[89] And aspects which are concordant are more conducive to luckiness *in the things which they signify*; but discordant aspects are more conducive to unluckiness.[90]

4. *Comparing the Lord of the Year in the two times.* Comparing the natal and revolutionary significations follows the usual pattern: (*a1*) if the Lord of the Year is in a good condition and in good places in both times, then (*a2*) if it is also with benefics, it shows the possession and usefulness of goods;[91] but (*a3*) without any benefics aspecting, the goods are less and gradually re-

---

[80] II.24.
[81] III.8.
[82] II.5.
[83] III.8.
[84] II.6.
[85] II.3. See also Hephaistio II.27.
[86] II.24.
[87] III.8.
[88] II.24.
[89] II.4.
[90] II.5. By "concordant" and "discordant," I take Abū Ma'shar to mean positive (sextile, trine) and negative (square, opposition) aspects.
[91] II.3.

duced;[92] but if (*a4*) with an impeded planet, the goods will be produced only with labor, particularly if the aspect is a square or opposition.[93]

If it is (*b1*) impeded and cadent in both times, it generally shows an intensity of the harm in the things it usually signifies;[94] but if (*b2*) with benefics, then it shows some goods and usefulness, but only in small matters and low-quality ones;[95] but if (*b3*) impeded in both but angular in only one, and in the conjunction, square or opposition of a malefic, it shows adversities and dangers—though if the malefic is retrograde or under the rays, there is some irrational compulsion or necessity which will appear;[96] and if impeded in both but angular in both, there will be more adversities.[97] So, one can see that the angularity of a planet will intensify and make the problems involved more obvious.

If it is (*c*) good in the nativity but bad in the revolution, then the operations promised by the nativity will be infirm and obscure, in accordance with how bad its condition is[98]—but the negativity of the revolution will be reduced because of the positive promise of the nativity.[99]

If it is (*d*) bad in the nativity but good in the revolution, then the evils are mediocre,[100] and it shows a moderated good due to the fact that the Lord of the Year is powerful at least for outcomes that only last a year.[101]

5. *The place of the Lord of the Year.* Abū Ma'shar does include a number of considerations for the place of the Lord of the Year. Some of these are uncontroversial, given the principle of reinforcement by repetition: of course the Lord of the Year will produce good or bad things in relation both to its natural significations and where it is;[102] but if it is in the same house in both the nativity and by transit at the revolution, it will emphasize that house's topics—and Abū Ma'shar includes *both* transiting in that place relative to the Ascendant of the year *and* relative to the sign of the profection.[103] So if the Lord of the Year were in the 3rd of the nativity, but were also transiting in the

---

[92] II.3.
[93] II.5.
[94] II.3.
[95] II.3, II.5.
[96] II.3.
[97] II.3.
[98] II.3.
[99] II.5.
[100] II.5.
[101] II.3.
[102] II.6.
[103] II.6, II.12.

3rd of the revolution or in the 3rd from the sign of the profection, it would emphasize 3rd house matters. I myself don't see why it couldn't be the same if it were transiting in the natal 3rd as well, and indeed he generally does allow planets to be interpreted as derived from *any* of these three Ascendants: the natal, the profected, and the calculated Ascendant of the year.[104] Unfortunately, he does not differentiate meaningfully between these options. If the Lord of the Year is in a different house in the two times, Abū Ma'shar unhelpfully recommends that we mix the significations.[105]

Following are some additional points regarding the place of the Lord of the Year:

- A Lord of the Year can produce good things even in bad houses, and even if it is a malefic, provided that it is in a good condition[106]—at the worst, it will indicate only moderately negative things.[107] For example, a good Saturn as the Lord of the Year but in the 12th can show victory over enemies, or at least enmity will decrease or the enemies will even praise the native; in the 6th, especially with a good Lord of the 6th, it can show illnesses which will later be healed.[108]
- A malefic Lord of the Year, making a return by transit in the revolution, and transited by another malefic in the revolution, will harm according to that natal house.[109]
- Abū Ma'shar also makes some important comments about being in aversion to the Ascendant:[110] in general, being in aversion shows a kind of wandering, being disconnected to the main flow of events: if such a Lord of the Ascendant is impeded in such a place, it shows indifference and idleness and anxiety;[111] if it is oriental and in one of its dignities, it will still show wandering and idleness, but the native

---

[104] II.24.
[105] II.6.
[106] II.6, II.12.
[107] II.6.
[108] II.6.
[109] II.24.
[110] Being in aversion means being in a place which does not aspect the Ascendant: in the 12th, 8th, 6th, and 2nd. But Abū Ma'shar does not specify whether this is aversion to the natal Ascendant or that of the revolution.
[111] II.6, II.9.

will at least be involved in some productive activities;[112] it shows that he is *inconspicuous* in that year;[113] and not only will some advantageous things not connect with him, but he may not even care much for them.[114]

6. Alternative Lords of the Year. Abū Ma'shar does also allow for three exceptions in choosing the Lord of the Year: the first has to do with the profected Ascendant or the calculated Ascendant of the year falling on a natal planet; the other two come into play if the Sun or Moon are Lords of the Year.

If the Ascendant of the solar revolution, or the sign of the profection, fall on a natal planet, then that malefic can be taken as a substitute Lord of the Year.[115] Abū Ma'shar adds that this will be especially so if the normally-expected Lord of the Year or Lord of the Ascendant of the revolution does not aspect its own Lord, but to my mind this should read, "especially if it does not aspect its own domicile." At any rate, I have my doubts about the value of this rule: surely it would mean that we would have substitute Lords of the Year or of the Ascendant of the year about half the time. It probably means we may observe the *aspects* and *transits* of such a natal planet, not that it should actually be preferred as the Lord of the Year.

Now we come to some more difficult rules, if a luminary is the Lord of the Year: this will be the case whenever the profected Ascendant falls on Cancer or Leo. The difficulty lies not only in the fact that the texts leave us with competing options, but Abū Ma'shar nevertheless provides delineations for the Sun and Moon as Lords of the Year, and in two places says that while the luminary should not be the *principal* Lord of the Year, but should be taken as secondary.[116] The notion that the luminaries cannot act as sole or primary Lords of the Year does go back at least to al-Andarzaghar, since Māshā'allāh states this clearly in *BA* IV.7. But Abū Ma'shar and Māshā'allāh do not completely agree on what the alternatives are, and Māshā'allāh does not state that the luminary can be a secondary significator. Following is the list of alternatives provided by both Abū Ma'shar and Māshā'allāh.

---

[112] II.6.
[113] II.9.
[114] II.9.
[115] II.24, III.8.
[116] II.13, II.22.

Sun	**Moon**
1. Domicile Lord of the directed *hīlāj*[117]	1. Domicile Lord of the directed *hīlāj*[118]
2. A planet configured with the Sun[119]	2. A planet conjoined to the Moon[120]
3. The distributor[121]	3. The distributor[122]
4. The sign the luminary is in[123]	4. The sign the luminary is in[124]
5. The domicile Lord of the luminary[125]	5. The domicile Lord of the luminary[126]
	6. A planet which was in Cancer, either natally or in the revolution.[127]
	7. The sign in which the Moon is at the revolution, and its Lord—as equals to the Ascendant of the year.[128]

Abū Ma'shar adds that if the Moon is the assumed Lord of the Year but is void in course, we may look to the condition and nature of her domicile Lord to determine the types of success and failure.[129]

A final suggestion by Abū Ma'shar is that, for the Moon, we take the various planets we have identified, and divide the year equally among them.[130] This does not make sense to me.

---

[117] II.13, II.14.
[118] II.22.
[119] II.13, II.14; *BA* IV.7. Note that he does not specify whether to use the nativity or the revolution for this; I can imagine arguments for both.
[120] II.22, *BA* IV.7. But Abū Ma'shar has this planet being in the same sign as the Moon, whereas Māshā'allāh allows aspects.
[121] I.14.
[122] II.22.
[123] *BA* IV.7.
[124] *BA* IV.7.
[125] *BA* IV.7.
[126] *BA* IV.7.
[127] II.22.
[128] II.22.
[129] II.22.
[130] II.22.

In the end, my own feeling is that if we adopt some version of these alternative Lords of the Year for the luminaries, we should favor planets configured or conjoined to them (in the nativity or in the revolution), and the signs and Lords of their natal locations, *even though* we ought still to pay attention to them by condition and transit at the revolution.

§7: The Ascendant of the year and its Lord

Recall that in a revolution we are dealing with three Ascendants: the natal, the profected, and the calculated. The calculated Ascendant of the year (or "east of the year" in *BA*) not only identifies natal themes which will arise in that year, and establishes new angles for the year, but as an Ascendant, it and its Lord will also provide commentary on the general condition of the native's life as a whole that year. Unfortunately, although Abū Ma'shar treats the Ascendant of the year and its Lord as having a "partnership" with the sign of the profection and the Lord of the Year,[131] there is little in the text as it stands to distinguish their relative importance.

1. Analyzing the Ascendant of the year. At any rate, some of the elements for analyzing the Ascendant of the year are as follows: (1) what natal house does it fall in;[132] (2) treat it as a 1st house and see where the natal Ascendant falls as derived from it;[133] (3) what is its natal angularity;[134] (4) what planets were in it natally, and by transit at the revolution;[135] (5) what Lots and twelfth-parts were in it natally.[136] Following are some additional guidelines:

- A malefic in the Ascendant of the year will impede the year in general, especially if the malefic also impedes the Moon or the Lord of the Year.[137]
- One malefic in the Ascendant of the year, and the other in the natal Ascendant,[138] will also make the year very difficult; but if one of them is in a good condition, the harm is made easier.[139]

---

[131] II.13. Cf. also II.23.
[132] *BA* IV.14.
[133] *BA* IV.15.
[134] I.6.
[135] I.6.
[136] I.6.
[137] II.23; *BA* IV.14.
[138] This would probably also hold true if it were the same malefic.

- A natal malefic in the Ascendant of the year, with that malefic also there by transit at the revolution, is also very bad; but the year would be very good with a natal benefic and transiting benefic, without any aspect of the malefics.[140]
- Malefics in the angles of the revolution will show adversities for the year as well; but if the Lord of the Ascendant of the year is in a good condition and aspects the Ascendant of the year, it will take the problems away.[141]
- Malefics in the Midheaven of the revolution indicate a lack of success, idle actions, and waste; but if a benefic helps,[142] it will at least be easier to obtain good, even if it is lost later.[143]
- If the Ascendant of the year is on a natal malefic which itself harms the natal Ascendant, then that natal signification of harm will be activated for that year.[144] But if there is only a malefic there by transit at the revolution, its harm will be easier and more transitory.[145]
- If a planet impedes the Ascendant of the year, see if it rules any Lots: those matters (marriage, children, *etc.*) will be relevant for the sources of problems in that year.[146]

2. The Lord of the Ascendant of the year. Analyzing the Lord of the Ascendant of the year is partly a matter of the usual planetary analysis, and partly that of taking it as a representative of the year. For normal planetary analysis, Abū Ma'shar recommends looking at the following, both in the nativity and in the revolution: (*a*) what place the Lord is in, by houses relative the Ascendant of the year;[147] (*b*) formal considerations like its dignities, direct or forward motion, sect status, orientality/occidentality, and so on;[148] (*c*) whether it

---

[139] II.23.
[140] *BA* IV.14.
[141] II.23.
[142] Probably either by location there, or by making a strong aspect.
[143] II.23.
[144] This underscores the notion that the Ascendant of the year identifies what natal matters will be "arising" in that year, but *particularly* if natal planets indicating those natal matters are closely related to the *natal* Ascendant.
[145] II.24.
[146] III.8.
[147] I.6, II.23. This is the same as with any Lord-domicile relation. If the Lord is in the 5th relative to the Ascendant of the year, it would probably affect children or pleasures—but my sense is that it might do so *relative to the natal house on which the Ascendant of the year falls*. See below.
[148] I.6.

aspects its own domicile;[149] and (*d*) its other aspects.[150] A strong Lord of the Ascendant of the year, in a good condition, will affect well the areas signified by its location.[151]

But as I mentioned before, what is the role of the Lord of the Ascendant of the year, relative to that of the profected Lord of the Year? Does the Lord of the Ascendant of the year have jurisdiction over the year as a whole in the way the Lord of the Year does? Or does it perhaps only steer the matters pertaining to the natal house the Ascendant of the year falls on? My sense is that Abū Ma'shar intends it to signify two things primarily: the matters of the *natal house* on which the Ascendant of the year falls, and those of its location in the *revolutionary* chart. For example, suppose a native has Scorpio rising. If the Ascendant of the year fell on the natal 12th, Libra, then it would show that 12th house matters are arising that year. Venus, the Lady of Libra, would indicate how those matters go, and her place in the revolution would show what matters are connected with them: if in the 5th house of the revolution (Aquarius), then she would connect the 12th house to children or pleasures. But it is also possible that she would connect 12th house matters to whatever *natal* house she happened to be transiting. So although Aquarius is the 5th house of the revolution, it is the 4th house of the nativity: perhaps she would connect the 12th house to parents and land, as well.

§8: Distributors and partners

Distribution is a technique well attested to in Hellenistic astrology, occupying the whole of *Carmen* III. It is closely connected to longevity prediction, and employs primary directions and bounds. The basic idea is this: identify a natal point which you want to release, from the usual list of potential "releasers" or *hīlājes*—typically the Sun, Moon, Ascendant, or Lot of Fortune.[152] Then, direct this point through the bounds by ascensions.[153] The

---

[149] I.6. Planets which can aspect their own signs by whole-sign aspects show more direct control and consistency and knowledge in their effects.
[150] II.23. This is probably by transit at the revolution.
[151] II.23.
[152] Māshā'allāh releases the *hīlāj* discovered through the longevity analysis, which is not necessarily the Ascendant. My sense is that Māshā'allāh is probably correct or at least closer to his Hellenistic sources. In *Carmen* III.1 and III.2, the *hīlāj* just happens to be the Ascendant in both examples: since Abū Ma'shar has us direct the Ascendant in every case, my guess is that he conflated the *hīlāj* itself with the Ascendant. It is true that he recommends directing other releasers in the same way, but he does not emphasize them.

Lord of the bound is called the "distributor" or *jārbakhtār*, and any planetary body in or aspecting the bound is its "partner." As the released point or *hīlāj* represents the native's life, so the bound Lord steers the life for a certain number of years according to its own nature and natal configurations and transits, and the bodies or aspects which are encountered by the releaser will cooperate or partner with the distributor.[154] However, in terms of the length of the periods involved, the distributor and partner differ in one important way: the distributor's term of governing is restricted to the period of the bound itself, while partners work across bounds; and the Persians stated that a partner may become active upon a releaser entering the bound and not only when it reaches the partner by degree.

It is easiest to provide an example.[155] Let us suppose that the Ascendant is the releaser or *hīlāj*, and it is at 10° Sagittarius. This bound is ruled by Jupiter up to 12° in the Egyptian system of bounds,[156] so from birth up to about 2 years later,[157] Jupiter will be the distributor or *jārbakhtār*. After that, the Ascendant will move into the bound of Venus (from 12°-17°), and she will be the distributor for approximately 5 years of life—and so on through the bounds until the native dies. But suppose that the body of Mars is at 13° Sagittarius, just 1° into the bound of Venus. That means that while Venus will distribute for the whole period of the bound, Mars will be her partner once the Ascendant directs to 13° Sagittarius, and Mars will continue to be the partner of *any distributor henceforth* until the Ascendant encounters the body

---

[153] Ascensions are an ancient way of making predictions, by converting zodiacal degrees into equatorial ones, treating each sign as a unit. Different signs rise at different rates, and these rates will be longer and shorter depending upon the birth latitude. The rate by sign and latitude is converted into a number of years, so that the 30° zodiacal degrees of each sign will be equated to years of life, which may be more or less than 30°. Thus, if a zodiacal bound is 5°, it may be more or less than 5 years of time, depending on the birth latitude and type of sign. Some astrology programs can do some or all of these ascensional directions: currently, Delphic Oracle includes a choice of releasers and includes the partners; Janus directs only the Ascendant and omits the partners; I am told that Solar Fire will soon offer the complete distribution technique. To calculate your own ascensions, refer to the Project Hindsight table at: www.projecthindsight.com/images/TablesPDFs/Tb2-AscensionTimes.pdf.

[154] In III.2, Abū Ma'shar states that distributors and partners are more effective and powerful than profections, because they signify things over longer periods of times, whereas profections only work for one year.

[155] Abū Ma'shar's own example in III.1 uses Lots in an unusual way, so I will construct my own example here.

[156] A table of Egyptian bounds is included in Appendix B.

[157] Again, the years for each bound will depend on the ascensional times for that sign and birth latitude. See the footnote above.

or ray *of another planet*. So, there is an overlap between distributors and partners: the distributors change from bound to bound, but the partners change from body/ray to body/ray. If the sextile of the natal Moon were at 14° Sagittarius, then the partnership of Mars comes to an end at that point, and the Moon would be the partner to Venus so long as the Ascendant is in that bound. If there were no other bodies or rays in Venus's bound, then the Moon would continue to partner with the next bound Lord or distributor, Mercury (17°-21°), until the Ascendant reached the body or ray of the next partner. Moreover, although these trends are calculated in the nativity, we are also supposed to monitor the transits of and to the distributor at the revolution. Thus, just as we track the transits of and to the sign of the profection and the Lord of the Year, so too with the distributor and partner. (This distributor-partner technique is also used when directing points around the whole circle of the revolutionary chart for a single year.)

1. Distinguishing the distributor and partner. Abū Ma'shar distinguishes distributors and partners in the following ways:

(*a*) The distributor provides the fundamental tone and character of the period, and what the various events eventually get resolved into (and a sense it represents the native himself); the partner shows more temporary circumstances, as well as particular situations and types of people the native encounters.[158] For example, if Jupiter is the distributor and Saturn the partner, then while the native will encounter troubles and Saturnian people and situations, they will eventually be resolved and improved due to Jupiter's setting the fundamental tone.[159]

(*b*) The distributor indicates any fundamental problems during the period, and of what type they are; the partner indicates the source of the problems (especially if it is in a bad condition).[160]

(*c*) Planets aspecting the distributor show the *state of mind* of the native as these events unfold, even if the aspecting planet is the partner;[161] but planets aspecting the partner enhance or alleviate the good or bad qualities relative to the types of events.[162] In a related way, planets transiting in or aspecting the

---

[158] III.4, III.6. But Abū Ma'shar says that when Mercury is the distributor, he will take on more of the character of the partner.
[159] III.4. Of course a lot depends on what condition Jupiter and Saturn are in.
[160] III.2, III.5, III.6. Presumably the same goes for good trends and their sources.
[161] III.2, III.6.
[162] III.6, III.7.

current bound at the revolution, will add confidence or confusion to situations, and are rather secondary.[163]

(*d*) Just as with some of the other benefic-malefic combinations we have seen with profections (and also with *firdārīyyāt*), benefic partners can enhance good distributors or rescue the native from the problems of bad ones; malefic partners reduce the benefit of or show excesses in good distributors, and enhance the malice of bad ones,[164] A benefic partner in a poor condition, however, cannot offer much help, and may be a source of problems.[165]

2. *Analyzing the distribution.* Some of Abū Ma'shar's advice is not very helpful, or at least adds too much information: for example, he recommends that we include an analysis of both the domicile and exaltation Lords of the place of the distribution, not to mention the triplicity and decan/face Lords.[166] In my view that would simply create a murky soup of indications. On the other hand, he does also recommend analyzing both the natal and revolutionary condition of the distributor and partner, as well as their rulerships: this is rather standard.[167] Following is a list of other things to note:

- Note the house position of the bound, relative to the Ascendant of the year: this will identify topics of note for that year.[168]
- See if the distributor or partner had a relationship by aspect in the nativity: that natal configuration will be activated at this time.[169]
- Note the planets aspecting the distributor or located in bound of the distribution, both in the nativity and at the revolution.[170]
- If the partner aspects the distributor[171] (and is not simply in or aspecting the bound), it emphasizes the partner's *effect on* the significations of the distributor, including the native's *state of mind*.[172]

---

[163] III.2.
[164] III.4, III.6.
[165] III.5.
[166] III.2.
[167] III.2, III.7.
[168] III.2. This is the same as above, noting the place of the sign of the profection from the Ascendant of the year.
[169] III.7.
[170] III.2. My sense of this passage is that perhaps one could examine a planet in *any* of that distributor's bounds, and not just the one in the distribution itself. This would be akin to the Hellenistic concept of "neighboring" (Schmidt 2009, pp. 187-191). In fact, Abū Ma'shar might really mean neighboring: if a planet is aspecting the distributor *from any* bound belonging to that distributor.
[171] This is definitely a case of the Hellenistic "neighboring." See footnote above.
[172] III.5, III.6.

- Beware malefic distributors which also aspect the place of the distribution itself by transit in the revolution.[173]
- The meaning of a Lot will manifest more when its Lord is a distributor or partner;[174] likewise any planet will tend to manifest its natal meaning more when it is a distributor or partner.[175]
- If a fixed star shows prosperity in the nativity, then it will manifest prosperity when the Ascendant or any other *hīlāj* is directed to it; but if it did not already show prosperity in the nativity, it will at least show some prosperity according to its stellar complexion; violent stars will show some of their misfortune.[176]
- If a benefic partner or the Sun is involved with a bad distributor, the partner can still show the source of the problem *even if* it rescues the situation from becoming very bad.[177]
- Pay attention to the benefic-malefic patterns when one distributor yields to the next one, or one partner yields to another. Malefics yielding to malefics will have a different effect than malefics yielding to benefics, for example.[178]

3. Intensification. In III.7, Abū Ma'shar identifies several situations in which the effects of a distributor-partner pairing become more intense or certain:

- If the transiting distributor and partner have an aspect which is concordant with their natal relationship.
- If the distributor and partner aspect the place of the distribution and its dispositor.[179]
- If they aspect the natal Ascendant and its Lord.[180]
- If the distributor and the Lord of the Year are the same planet.
- If the profection reached the distributor's natal position, or it were transiting in the sign of the profection at the revolution.

---

[173] III.8.
[174] III.8.
[175] III.1, III.2.
[176] III.2. For a list of the stars, see *Persian Nativities I*, Appendix D. For their delineations and how to identify their role in eminence and prosperity, see *BA* III.2.1, *JN* Ch. 6, and Abū Bakr II.1.0, II.1.3, II.1.7, II.2.0, II.2.1, II.3.7, II.3.11, II.9.11.
[177] III.2.
[178] See the long list of combinations in III.2.
[179] This is probably in the revolution, not in the nativity.
[180] This is probably in the revolution, not in the nativity.

- If the ascensional time of the distributor's natal sign matched the year of life when it has the distribution.

§9: The Moon

Both Māshā'allāh and Abū Ma'shar specifically instruct us to examine the Moon in a revolution,[181] even setting her apart as a separate object of study, though they make few explicit comments about her in the texts we have. Of the twelve or so passages I have isolated from both works, six illustrate her role as a general significator of the year, and six provide some specific things to look for. I cannot say whether this dearth of information is due to the fact that we are missing texts, or because the Moon's role as a general significator in all charts is so common as to make a lengthy treatment unnecessary. Probably one should borrow from horary practice and make her a co-significator in all revolutions just as in questions. On the other hand, this advice almost seems useless, given that the Persian suite of techniques has already got a profection, a Lord of the Year, a distribution and its partner, an Ascendant of the year and its Lord, transits, pairs of *firdāriyyah* Lords, and ninth-parts. How does the Moon fit in here?

1. The importance of the Moon. Several comments, then, address the value of the Moon in evaluating the year as a whole:

(*a*) In a revolution, look at the sign in which the Moon is transiting: it has an equal role to the Ascendant of the year.[182]

(*b*) Continuing the previous thought: the good or bad condition of the Moon and her domicile Lord in the revolution especially affect one's overall bearing, health, and prosperity.[183]

(*c*) The twelfth-part of the Moon should also be examined for its good or bad position in the revolution.[184]

(*d*) The year as a whole will be harmed if transiting malefics aspect the Moon[185] without the aspect of a benefic; but the harm will be described by the Lord of the Year or the distributor.[186]

---

[181] *BA* IV.1, *On Rev. Nat.* II.1.
[182] II.22.
[183] V.10. If this and the previous statement are to be taken at face value, then we should treat the Moon and her sign just as we do the Ascendant of the year, and her domicile Lord as we do the Lord of the Ascendant of the year.
[184] V.10.

(*e*) If a transiting malefic is on the natal Moon at the revolution, and the benefics do not aspect her, it will have a worse effect, especially if the malefic is also the Lord of the Year and has a bad place in the revolution; likewise if the transiting Moon were on a natal malefic.[187]

(*f*) If the Moon is unaspected at the revolution, nor does she aspect the Ascendant,[188] the native will strive for something but will not acquire it.[189]

2. Specific things to examine.

- At the revolution,[190] see if the Moon will have reached the natal place (i.e., the sign) of some planet: transiting her own natal sign or that of the benefics or the Sun, the native will rejoice and be happy;[191] if a malefic, beware of diseases and disasters; Venus can bring disgrace and unhappiness due to pleasures and wastefulness; if Mercury, he will be engaged in Mercurial work.[192]

- See also[193] the kind of natal house the Moon has reached in the revolution: if in the angles, the native will be engaged in those types of activities: in the Ascendant, it elevates thoughts,[194] in the Midheaven, actions and reputation according to the type of planet aspecting her; in the 4th, it is good for hidden things and secret things; in the 7th, the native is successful against enemies.

- Benefics transiting with the Moon at the revolution can liberate.[195]

---

[185] I take this to be the transiting Moon at the revolution. This comment makes me think that the Moon does act in an entirely general way, as a general informant on the tone of the year as a whole, but without many specific details.
[186] III.8.
[187] V.8. Cf. also *BA* IV.14.
[188] Probably the Ascendant of the year.
[189] V.10. This sounds like a maxim from horary transferred to revolutions.
[190] For this paragraph, compare V.10 with *Carmen* IV.1.197-205, and the alternative Dorotheus in Schmidt 1995 (p. 5).
[191] According to *Carmen* IV.1.197. But the parallel text in Schmidt makes thoughts come to the surface in the native's mind, which Schmidt says has a negative connotation in the Greek (i.e., mental turbulence)
[192] The parallel text also says that her ingress upon the natal Mercury will be good if he is in a good condition, but difficult if he is in a bad one.
[193] For this paragraph, compare V.10 with *Carmen* IV.1.206-09, and the alternative Dorotheus in Schmidt 1995 (p. 5).
[194] See the previous paragraph. Just as with the Greek, the Latin *cogitationes* can also mean worries. But *Carmen* makes things turn out badly if the Moon is in the natal Ascendant. The fact that Abū Ma'shar has a reading not found in 'Umar's *Carmen* is evidence that he had an alternative copy.
[195] III.8.

- Jupiter as one of the time-lords,[196] transiting on the natal Moon, and even favorably configured to the Moon in the revolution, brings manifold goods.[197]
- If using the monthly, weekly, or daily rulers, look at the position of the Moon on the days of those smaller units of time.[198]

§10: Lots

As with the Moon, there is not much we can say about Lots based on either *BA* or *On Rev. Nat.* This could be in part because some rules for Lots are described in their own place of the natal material: for example, the Lot of Marriage-Union is used along with a profection and a Jupiter (or possibly a Saturn) transit, but it has its own special rules that do not fall under the very general prescriptions for revolutions. One thing we can say is that Abū Ma'shar does recommend that we recalculate the Lots in the chart of the revolution:[199] thus, just as the revolutionary chart reduplicates the natal houses but in different places, so does it duplicate the Lots by recalculation.

There are so few explicit comments about Lots in the text as we have it, that I feel it is best to simply list them rather than to organize them in some fashion:

- As with other areas of the nativity, the meaning of a Lot will manifest more when its Lord is a distributor or partner[200] (and, one guesses, the Lord of the Year).
- A Lot will also be activated if the Lord of the Year is transiting on it at the revolution.[201]
- A Lot will also be activated if it is on the sign of the profection, and a transiting benefic is with it[202] at the revolution.[203]
- The meaning of the Lot will affect matters more strongly in that year, if it or its domicile Lord were aspecting or with either the Lord of the Year or a planet aspecting the Lord of the Year.[204]

---

[196] I.e., as the Lord of the Year or the distributor.
[197] *BA* IV.14.
[198] *BA* IV.16.
[199] III.8.
[200] III.8.
[201] *BA* IV.14.
[202] I take this to mean "in the same sign with it."
[203] *BA* IV.14.

- If the Lord of the Year (or the planet it aspects) signifies a topic, and they were with some Lot or its Lord, then it will accentuate the effect on those things;[205] likewise if some planet which generally signifies some topic is connected to the Lord of the Year, and the associated Lot and its dispositor are in a good condition, the effect will be good. For example, Mercury signifies children, slaves, and intellectual work: so if he is in a good condition and aspecting the Lord of the Year, while the Lots of Slaves, Children, and Work and their dispositors are also in a good condition, then matters for slaves, children and work will go well.[206]
- Track the transits of the dispositor of a Lot,[207] and what kinds of signs it traverses: this will help show how the matters of the Lot develop.[208]
- Look at the Lots which fall with the Lord of the Year and the distributor.[209]

§11: The firdārīyyāt

Firdārīyyah (pl. firdārīyyāt) is a Persian transliteration of the Gr. *periodos*, which simply means "period." Hellenistic astrologers devised numerous predictive techniques based on planetary periods: the longevity technique of the *kadukhudāh*, triplicity Lords, zodiacal releasing from the Lot of Spirit, and so on. But the *firdārīyyāt* seem to have been devised during the Sassanian period, and were definitely passed on to Māshā'allāh,[210] Abū Ma'shar, and others by writers such as al-Andarzaghar. In fact, there were several systems of *firdārīyyāt* in use by the Persians, including planetary periods in mundane astrology.[211]

---

[204] II.5.
[205] II.5.
[206] II.4.
[207] This might be only if the dispositor also happens to be the Lord of the Year, but perhaps it is intended for the dispositors of any Lot at any time.
[208] *BA* IV.14.
[209] *BA* IV.14. I take this to mean either that the Lord of the Year or the distributor are transiting on the Lot, or else perhaps they rule the Lot. This must mean that the Lot's affairs will become more active in that year and will develop in accordance with the Lord's/distributor's condition.
[210] *BA* IV.17-25.
[211] See for instance Pingree's edition of Abū Ma'shar's *Thousands* (1968).

The natal *firdārīyyāt* are reported in a straightforward way.[212] Each planet (and the Nodes of the Moon) is allotted a different number of years in life. At birth, the sect light[213] is in charge of the first period, then the next one in descending Chaldean order (after the Moon's period, the *firdārīyyāt* cycle back to Saturn, then Jupiter, and so on). Authorities later disagreed on exactly where the Nodes fell in the sequence. But the periods, which are of unequal lengths, were subdivided equally into smaller periods of time, each one again ruling 1/7 of the current period, starting with the Lord of the period itself. So in Jupiter's period (12 years), Jupiter also rules the first 1/7 of that period, then Mars the next 1/7, and so on. The Lord of the whole period and that of the sub-period were examined in their natal contexts and by ongoing transits to determine the exact details of the period, in order to go beyond the cookbook-style delineations found in the texts.[214]

But there are a number of puzzling things about the natal *firdārīyyāt* which make me uncertain about their role and use: (a) What is the source of the period lengths, especially Mercury's? (b) Why are the sub-periods of equal length, when a period system like that of the Lot of Spirit has unequal sub-periods? (c) Where do the periods of the Nodes fall, and why are they given years at all? (d) How do the *firdārīyyāt* relate to the other Hellenistic methods, if they are not an independent system? (e) Why do the texts predict certain events during unusual subdivisions of the sub-periods?[215] (f) Why does Abū Ma'shar keep saying that the periods are constructed from the exaltations of the planets, when it seems clear they are not?[216]

I believe I know the answers to some of these questions, but currently I only feel comfortable mentioning some of them. As for the source of the period lengths, they are clearly related to sacred geometry and numerology, probably some form of Pythagoreanism; and their assignment to the planets is clearly related both to planetary sect and to the 19-year eclipse cycle. Let's

---

[212] A table of *firdārīyyāt* may be found at www.bendykes.com.

[213] The luminary ruling the sect of the chart: in a diurnal chart, the Sun; in a nocturnal one, the Moon.

[214] We must remember that all of these delineation texts can only be archetypal, and cannot simply be taken word-for-word. Otherwise, anyone living the full 75 years of the *firdārīyyāt* would marry and see the death of about a dozen spouses, and probably more children than that.

[215] For example, the Mars-Sun period predicts harm from an associate for 11 (IV.7) or 15 (*BA* IV.23) days.

[216] See for instance I.8 below. Pingree used to echo Abū Ma'shar and state this as though it were an obvious fact, but I have never seen an explanation and do not see how it can be done.

note first that the years associated with the Moon (9) and the Sun (10) are evidently related to their greater planetary years, since the number of months in each period equals the number of planetary years: 9 years in the lunar *firdārīyyah* is 108 months, the same number as the Moon's greater years;[217] 10 years in the solar *firdārīyyah* is 120 months, the same number as the Sun's greater years. So perhaps it is natural to assign such numbers to the Sun and Moon. But what about the rest? If we line up the planets and their years in an arc, we get the scheme in Figure 1 below.

The arc goes from Mars in the lower left, clockwise around to Jupiter, and then down to Mercury. Can you see any patterns? First of all, all of the planets on the lunar (left) side are nocturnal; those on the solar (right) side are diurnal; in himself Mercury is of indeterminate sect status, so he is on neither side. Also, the four non-luminaries on each side are paired as benefics and malefics: Venus-Saturn, Mars-Jupiter. The years in each row also equal 19 years: Venus (8) plus Saturn (11) equals 19, as does Mars (7) plus Jupiter (12). Thus the years of the Sun and Moon provide a sect and eclipse-based rationale for the ordering of most of the planets and their periods, which also incorporates benefic and malefic themes. On the other hand, why does Mercury get 13 years, placed at the end of the series, instead of getting 6 and forming the beginning of the series? It could be that he had to get 13, so that with the Nodes (which get five years between them) the total years would equal 75.

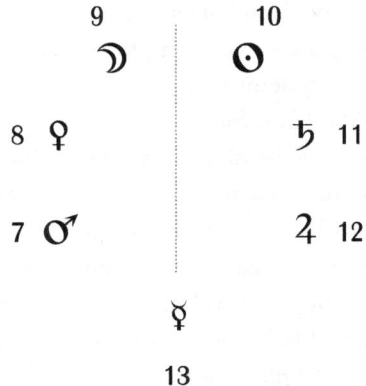

Figure 1: Planetary *firdārīyyāt*

---

[217] 108 is a classic lunar number and is very important in Hinduism. The 9-10 ratio of the Moon to the Sun is also equivalent to the respective heights of the Moon and Sun towers in the architecture of some medieval churches.

But there is still the question as to why the Nodes get years at all, and why those particular years. Two things come to mind. First, the use of the Nodes recalls the Indian emphasis on the Nodes along with the seven traditional planets, so perhaps the natal *firdārīyyah* have an Indian background. Second, there is probably a sacred geometrical reason for their years, whose meaning escapes me right now. On the other hand, Abū Ma'shar's text is absolutely clear on where the Nodes fall: at the end of the sequence of the seven planets, no matter the sect of the chart. Thus in a diurnal chart they will come after the Mars period, and in a diurnal chart after the Mercury period, in each case after 70 years of age.

I do have some ideas as to the unusual spans of days or ways of allotting certain events into different parts of a sub-period, not to mention the nature of the events themselves, but I do not feel ready to state them at this time. I do however think it would be worthwhile to experiment with dividing the sub-periods unevenly, in relation to their years in the *firdārīyāt*. For instance, if the Sun rules 10 years, why shouldn't he also rule the first 10 months, before Venus rules the next sub-period for 8 months, and so on? The equal subdivision of the sub-periods has always seemed odd to me, given the unequal length of the periods themselves.

Finally, there is the question of how the *firdārīyyāt* are related to the usual predictive methods. My sense is that they were not originally part of them at all. In other words, my sense is that they were meant to be an independent Perso-Indian system—and combining them with profected Lords and distributors is really only a case of trying to reinforce as many meanings as possible across predictive systems in order to hedge one's bets.

At any rate, Abū Ma'shar's formal approach to the *firdārīyyāt* is rather straightforward. As with the distributor-partner method, the primary Lord of the *firdārīyyah* sets the fundamental tone and significations for the period, including in terms of its basic good or bad qualities; the sub-Lord presents particular events according to its natural signification and sect status.[218] So for instance, a malefic sub-Lord will show problematic events of the type particular to that planet.[219] Following is a list of items of special importance to note about the Lords of a *firdārīyyah*:

---

[218] IV.2.
[219] IV.1.

- Their natal conditions as a whole, including their angularity and sect status.[220]
- Their natal bounds, especially the benefic/malefic nature of the bound Lord.[221]
- Their natal relation to the Lord of the Ascendant.[222]
- The intrinsic relation between the two Lords in themselves (for instance, Saturn and Venus are not usually a good combination).[223]
- The condition of the sub-Lord in particular,[224] to show whether its effects will be helpful or harmful in relation to the primary Lord.[225]
- The transits of *both* Lords throughout the period.[226]

§12: Transits

Transits are among the first predictive techniques taught in modern astrology, and claim a central role. But modern texts provide little theory on how transits relate to other techniques, nor how to distinguish different types of transits. The three most important types of transits for modern astrologers—in terms of their alleged effectiveness and how frequently they are mentioned—seem to be the following: (1) Saturn returns; (2) retrogradations of Mercury; (3) outer planet transits. This is a somewhat unusual set of transits, with problems surrounding each. The meaning of Saturn returns depends largely upon a psychodynamic understanding of astrology, since they indicate periods of individual crisis and psychological maturation. Mercury retrogradations are applied indiscriminately to all people at a given time, usually without reference to nativities, solely because of Mercury's general way of signifying the mind, and often in the most trivial ways, such as explaining missed phone calls. Finally, outer planet transits claim to explain virtually any event at all: their slow movement allows them to be used at almost any time, and their general meanings are comprised of contraries to cover virtually any context, such as Neptune's signification for both pure spiritual insight on the one hand, or psychosis and delusion on the other.

---

[220] IV.1, IV.8.
[221] IV.1.
[222] IV.1.
[223] IV.1.
[224] Perhaps also by transit at the revolution, and not just in the nativity.
[225] IV.1.
[226] IV.2.

In traditional astrology, transits are subordinated to other techniques, act as triggers for indications already present, and not all planets' transits are important at any given time. Abū Ma'shar's text gives helpful hints for transits which echo other predictive rules, although he gives (to my mind) controversial interpretations of particular transits which ought to be considered separately from the formal rules. Let us consider Abū Ma'shar's transits in the following way, against the background of traditional lore: which transits and transited places are more important, when transits are more intensified or effective, and Abū Ma'shar's interpretive theory.

Hellenistic and late antique Greek texts on transits are scattered across many different authors. Although they do not all contain clear or extensive delineations, they share interpretive approaches. Following is a partial list of texts,[227] all of most of which were available to the first few generations of Perso-Arabic astrologers in the 8th-9th Centuries.

Dorotheus: Carmen IV.1.185-233.[228]
Ptolemy: *Tet.* IV.10.[229]
Paul of Alexandria: Ch. 34, pp. 70-73.
Valens: *Anth.* VI.5.
Pseudo-Valens: see Schmidt 1995, pp. 48-50.[230]

A brief survey of these texts shows that traditional astrologers did not use transits indiscriminately or as applied to everyone, nor were they all equally powerful. Rather, they identified (a) whose transits were more notable at a given time, (b) what transited places to focus on, (c) what types of events or places make an effect more intense or reliable for timing, and (d) a number of planet-place-event combinations to highlight. In the following list, underlined items are explicitly agreed upon by ancient authors and Abū

---

[227] Many of these are contained in Schmidt (1995).
[228] See also Schmidt 1995, pp. 1-6 for a Greek version of the same material from *CCAG* 2:195-98. Also, *Carmen* II.20 credits Hermes either with the transit doctrine, or with delineations which are serviceable for transits at the revolution (II.21-33, which probably refers to natal positions). This is potentially significant because al-Andarzaghar (a source for Abū Ma'shar) also drew on work attributed to Hermes.
[229] See also Schmidt's summary on p. 68.
[230] Based on CCAG 1:163-71.

Ma'shar;[231] normal font items are only in the ancient sources above; italicized items are added by Abū Ma'shar.[232]

Whose transits to note, based on the solar revolution:[233]
- The Lord of the Year.[234]
- The distributors and their partners.[235]
- Any planet making a return to its natal position (certainly by degree, also by sign).[236] *Abū Ma'shar adds: this can include a return to its natal bound.*[237]
- Planets natally in the sign of the profection (whether by annual or monthly profections).[238]
- Planets attuned to the type of time-period.[239]
- *Planets having similar significations in both times.*[240]
- *The Lord of the Ascendant of the year.*[241]

What transited places to note:
- The current sign of the profection.[242]
- The places where directions are taking place.[243]
- The natal Ascendant.[244]

---

[231] At least, according to the Abū Ma'shar of the present translation. We will only know about more points of agreement and elaboration after the Arabic is completely translated.

[232] Remember that Abū Ma'shar did rely on sources such as al-Andarzaghar, so he might not have invented these extra items himself.

[233] Valens (*Anth.* VI.5) indicates the time-lords but does not specify any in particular. Note that Abū Ma'shar does not explicitly draw on the two Ptolemaic points in this list.

[234] The epitomizer of Dorotheus (Schmidt p. 6); *Tet.* IV.10. See throughout Abū Ma'shar's Book V. Based on hints in Abū Ma'shar, I would say that the transiting Lord of the Year represents the native, and the transited places/planets are who and what he will encounter in that year (V.6).

[235] Schmidt p. 6. This is throughout Abū Ma'shar Book III.

[236] This is implied or mentioned in most texts, and includes a return to the sign, not simply to the degree.

[237] V.1.

[238] *Tet.* IV.10.

[239] *Tet.* IV.10: Saturn when using the Ages of Man; Jupiter to the sign of the annual profection; Mars, the Sun, Venus, and Mercury to the sign of the monthly profection; the Moon to the sign of the daily profection.

[240] V.9.

[241] V.3.

[242] See *Tet.* IV.10; pseudo-Valens (Schmidt p. 17); Paul (Scholion 92, pp. 72-73). See Abū Ma'shar V.5. I would also include whole-sign angles to the profected sign of the year.

[243] Schmidt p. 6. See Abū Ma'shar V.9.

- The whole-sign angles of any natal position, especially the superior square.[245]
- A planet transiting the whole-sign angles of its own natal position.[246]
- *The natal place of the Lord of the Year.*[247]
- *The natal position of the current distributor and its partner.*[248]
- *The Ascendant of the revolution.*[249]

Intensification and timing:
- Stations, especially those of contrary-to-sect malefics.[250] *Abū Ma'shar adds: when a planet retrogrades (or stations) in its return.*[251]
- When time-lords ingress the whole-sign angles of key places.[252]
- When other planets ingress upon the (natal place of) the time-lords. But a transiting planet cannot fully reverse or change what the underlying time-lord signifies.[253]
- *The effects will be more manifest when the transiting planet rules the month or day.*[254]
- *The effects will also be more certain if the two planets are also configured natally.*[255]

These lists may seem very complicated, but they boil down to just a few archetypal situations: for example, the Lord of the Year transiting through the whole-sign angles of the sign of the profection, especially if it stations in one of them.

---

[244] Pseudo-Valens (Schmidt pp. 16-23 *passim*). Hand comments (pp. 52-53) that this might also refer to the natal Moon. See Abū Ma'shar V.9.

[245] *Carmen* IV.1.191; Schmidt p. 2.

[246] *Carmen*/Schmidt (*passim*).

[247] See throughout Book V. Based on Abū Ma'shar's use of these transits, I would say that the transiting planet indicates what the native will encounter or how he will be affected at that time (V.6).

[248] V.9.

[249] V.9.

[250] *Carmen*/Schmidt (p. 3).

[251] V.1.

[252] *Anth.* VI.5. Or perhaps, their transits through the angles and succeedents (see Schmidt's note to this chapter).

[253] *Anth.* VI.5.

[254] V.1.

[255] V.1.

Notable planet-place-event combinations:
- <u>Malefics transiting on natal positions of benefics will spoil the good; benefics transiting malefics will remove corruption.</u>[256]
- A malefic transiting a natal luminary, particularly if the malefic is contrary to the luminary's sect (Mars transiting the Sun, Saturn the Moon).[257]
- A malefic transiting the four pivots (angles) of the nativity.[258]
- A contrary-to-sect malefic.[259]
- A malefic transiting a natal malefic.[260]
- Transiting planets in the triplicity of their natal position will be especially good (benefics) or bad (malefics).[261]
- Also watch to see if planets make stations in these key signs.[262]
- Planets returning to themselves or their own opposition is bad.[263]
- Saturn transiting Mars is bad, but Mars transiting Saturn is good.[264]
- If malefics are favorably aspecting the luminaries or benefics in the nativity, then later ingresses by those malefics will not be that bad.[265]
- *The significations of both planets when aspecting each other.*[266]
- *Treat the transited sign as derived from the sign of the profection.*[267]
- *Note the transiting position of the Lord of the Year from the sign of the profection, to identify relevant topics.*[268]
- *If the transiting and transited planets were already configured in the nativity, there is a past cause; but if only in the revolution, a temporary cause; and if an ingressing planet is configured to none in either chart, the outcome is from some unexpected or random cause.*[269]

---

[256] *Carmen*/Schmidt (*passim*), Abū Ma'shar V.1 (references the usual benefic-malefic combinations already described above).
[257] *Carmen*/Schmidt (*passim*).
[258] *Carmen*/Schmidt (pp. 3-5).
[259] *Carmen*/Schmidt (*passim*).
[260] *Carmen*/Schmidt (*passim*).
[261] *Carmen*/Schmidt (*passim*). Note that Dorotheus does not include the sextiles.
[262] *Carmen*/Schmidt (*passim*).
[263] *Carmen*/Schmidt (p. 3).
[264] *Carmen*/Schmidt (*passim*); Anubio in Schmidt p. 13.
[265] Schmidt p. 4. Again, the nativity sets the tone and is more powerful than transits alone.
[266] V.1.
[267] V.1.
[268] V.1.
[269] V.9.

The items above should serve as a handy checklist for students, and help one focus on what really matters in a transit. But as I mentioned above, in V.1 Abū Ma'shar seems to use a delineation template not recognized by ancient authors—and to my present knowledge, not even by his own Persian predecessors. The principle is very simple: for any planetary pair involved in a transit, take the domiciles of each planet as though they are derived houses from the domiciles of the other. Surely Abū Ma'shar cannot be asking us to ignore the rulerships and natal locations of these planets, but the general rule is not really based on the natures of the planets or their places or rulerships at all. Let me give two examples, and show the domicile relations on a zodiacal wheel (*Figure 2*).

Example 1: Moon-Mercury. If we take Cancer (the Moon's domicile) as an Ascendant, then Mercury's domiciles are in a relation of the 12th (enemies) and 3rd (siblings) to it. Likewise, if we take Mercury's domiciles as Ascendants, then Cancer is in the position of the 2nd (money, resources) and 11th (friends) from them. So, the Mercury-Moon transit in V.7 lists the fear of enemies and the multiplication of friends, while the Moon-Mercury transit in V.8 mentions enemies, praise (i.e., 11th house), and resources. The only other notable item in the texts is travel: this could be because Taurus (the exaltation of the Moon) is in the 9th from Virgo.

Example 2: Venus-Jupiter. If we take Venus's domiciles (Taurus and Libra) as Ascendants, then Jupiter's domiciles are in the relation of the 3rd (siblings), 6th (illness), 8th (death, inheritance), and the 11th (friends). If we start from Jupiter's domiciles and derive Venus's from his, we get the same topics. Now, turning to V.3, the Jupiter-Venus transit lists illness and friends. In V.6, the Venus-Jupiter transit lists illness and friends. However, these texts also list glory (10th house) and faith and travel (9th, perhaps 3rd). To my mind, glory could be because Cancer (the exaltation of Jupiter) is in the 10th from Libra, or Sagittarius is in the 10th from Pisces (the exaltation of Venus); and faith and travel could be because Pisces (the exaltation of Venus) is in the 9th from Cancer (the exaltation of Jupiter)—but note that the 3rd, mentioned above, is also a house of travel and religion.

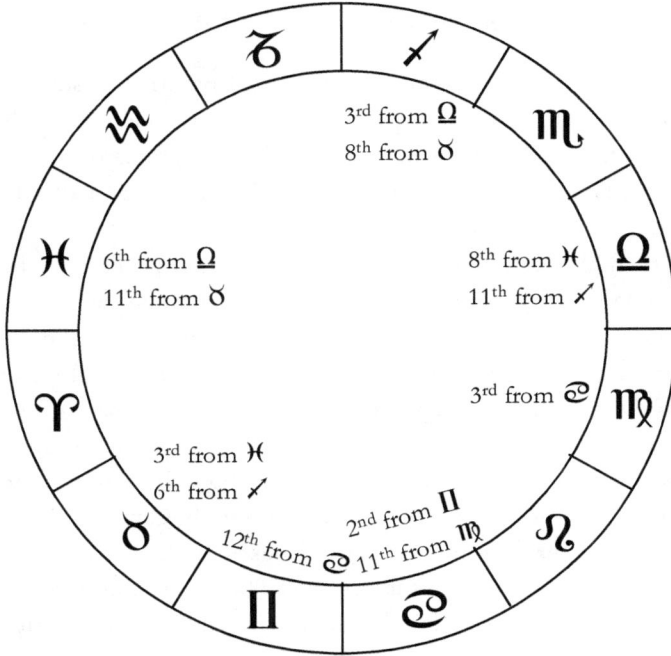

Figure 2: Transit template

Given that this approach to transit delineation is not shared by other traditional authors (so far as I know), it should be viewed with caution if not skepticism.

§13: Ninth-parts

I have my doubts about the "Indian" ninth-parts, for three reasons: first, since Abū Ma'shar treats them as a substitute for distributions through the bounds, they seem unnecessary. Second, the instructions for their directions and profections are somewhat unclear to me, due to the way Abū Ma'shar describes their subdivisions. Third, if the rules are correct as presented, then there can only ever be four Lords of the Year: Mars, the Moon, Venus, and Saturn. That seems like an unlikely system. Interested readers may consult the instructions and my diagrams in III.9-III.10 below.

§14: Monthly, weekly, daily, and hourly rulers and periods

Again, I have little to say on this matter. I have tried to summarize the procedures for determining these rulers as best as I could in IX.7, but I am not sure of their value. I would however like to summarize some related points from Hephaistio II.28, in which Hephaistio claims to be following Dorotheus.

First, monthly profections (and undoubtedly their Lords) may be gained by profecting one sign per month in succession from the sign of the annual profection. So for example, if the sign of the annual profection is Cancer, then Cancer will not only stand for the year as a whole, but also as the first month of the year; Leo will be the second month; and so on.

Second, find smaller profections by advancing from the sign of the month, at a rate of one sign for every 2 ½ days. So if the annual profection is on Cancer, and Cancer is also the entire first month, Cancer will also be the first 2 ½ days of that first month; Leo the next 2 ½ days of the first month; Virgo the next; and so on. Thus the circle can be broken into months for the year, and sets of 2 ½ days for the months—and presumably into smaller units of time as well.

Third, look at the sign of the annual profection, and note the presence of any malefics[270] in it or in its whole-sign squares or opposition, as well as if any New or Full Moons occur there. I take this to mean something like the following. Suppose that a malefic is in a square to the sign of the annual profection: the harm it indicates will manifest either (a) on or just after a New or Full Moon which falls on that sign during the year; or (b) when the monthly profection falls on it (or perhaps even the profection of 2 ½ days).

§15: Superior squares, overcoming, decimation

One important feature of Book II is its constant mention of the superior square: in Hellenistic astrology this is called "overcoming,"[271] and many Latin texts (including *On Rev. Nat.*) call it "elevation." It refers to one planet being in the tenth sign relative to another, and in Greek the planet in that tenth sign is also said to "decimate" the other planet.[272] Thus, suppose that Venus

---

[270] I take these to be natal malefics, but I cannot be sure.
[271] See Schmidt 2009 (pp. 178-86).
[272] Occasionally planets in a superior trine are said to overcome as well, though not to decimate.

is in Gemini and Mars is in Pisces. Regardless of their house positions in a chart, Mars is in the tenth sign relative to Venus: thus Mars is in an overcoming position, and he decimates Venus.

Unfortunately, the texts which define and explain overcoming are few, and those which mention or describe decimation are even rarer. However, Māshā'allāh[273] and Abū Ma'shar refer to both.[274] Still, the meaning of overcoming and decimation is unclear, except that the overcoming planet is always supposed to be more "powerful" or "stronger," whatever that means. In my own opinion, one defect of traditional astrological texts is the abuse of terms like "strength" and "weakness," since wildly different configurations and conditions are usually glossed with these terms, without explaining the differences between them.

At any rate, Robert Schmidt points out that "decimation" in Greek is linked to "extracting a tithe," and he suggests that the overcoming planet possibly extracts some power from the overcome planet, and uses it for itself. This is an interesting suggestion, and could be in the background of some of Abū Ma'shar's delineations. Throughout Book II, the Lord of the Year is delineated in combination with other planets, including when they are in overcoming positions relative to each other.[275] This allows us a rare look into how an important medieval astrologer treated the superior square. I believe I can perceive certain general principles in Abū Ma'shar's work:

- Identify how the planets tend to combine in themselves: are they naturally a good combination, a harmful combination, or ambiguous? For example, Venus-Moon would tend to be good, Saturn-Venus bad, and Jupiter-Mars ambiguous.
- Identify the types of events and people that these configurations usually signify: Jupiter-Mars combinations usually show rulership and conquest, while Venus-Moon combinations accentuate dealings with women.

---

[273] See for instance *BA* II.11 and III.12.3.
[274] The Greek edition of *On Rev. Nat.* treats all or most instances of overcoming as decimation, but the Latin translator used "elevation" (overcoming). This is perhaps understandable since both terms are astrologically linked, but it does muddy the waters somewhat.
[275] The short paragraph at the end of II.22 is an exception: Abū Ma'shar presents it as a more general definition of how the planets operate, but his statements are contrary to his presentation of the delineations in the other chapters.

- Their conditions and house positions diminish or accentuate how these combinations are expressed. So, Jupiter-Mars in a good condition will show positive and constructive rulership and conquest; but there is an incongruity lurking in this combination, since Jupiter likes to accumulate and consolidate, whereas Mars likes to divide and disperse. Therefore, if they were in a poor condition, it would draw out issues like spending and carelessness and harm to the types of people they signify.
- Once the basic relation of good and bad is determined, the overcoming planet will determine the *source* or *cause* of the good or bad, and *with whom* or *on account of whom* the good or bad is experienced. In this sense the overcoming planet takes charge of the relationship by determining why it happens and what is affected.

Let me offer some examples from Book II and *BA*. Most of these identify problems in the year because of how Abū Ma'shar has structured his text, but the same principles should work for showing benefit from planets in a sound condition.

In Saturn-Moon squares (a difficult combination), Saturn overcoming the Moon makes the native unprosperous and negligent, and spending riches. In this case, Saturn's tendency to poverty and laziness drives the delineation and explains whence the problems arise. But the Moon overcoming Saturn brings corruption, quarrels, and makes the native's wife inimical: thus the Moon's signification of the wife is specifically marked as a cause of problems.

Likewise, take the Jupiter-Mars square (an ambiguous combination). With Jupiter overcoming Mars, it shows a firm position, and rule over cities, and a gain of dignities—all of this is especially consistent with these two planets in a good condition, but especially if Jupiter is understood as showing the source of the matter. However, it also indicates sorrow due to children and riches—both of which Jupiter naturally signifies. With Mars overcoming Jupiter, the problems are drawn out: attacks by magistrates, sorrow due to those dealing with metals or the loss of riches and a child, and labor is multiplied due to fraud and accusations. Again, we are still dealing with Jupiter-Mars significations, but loss, metal-working, attacks, fraud, and accusations are the operative sources or causes of the problems.

To take another example from Māshā'allāh:[276] in cases of friendship, if Mars overcomes Mercury, then the friendship suffers *losses* (Mars); but if Mercury overcomes Mars, it harms their *resources* and *household* (i.e., finances, Mercury).

Finally, Venus overcoming the Moon (with both in a bad condition) shows sorrow because of resources and marriage, and the native will have sex with low-class women—these are generally Venusian significations. But the Moon overcoming Venus (with both in a bad condition) shows harm because of women, and sorrow due to riches. This example is more ambiguous because both Venus and the Moon signify women anyway, and each could signify riches in its own way.

Some other combinations in Book II seem to run contrary to these principles, either because there are other considerations I am not sure how to include here, or perhaps even due to mistakes in the Greek translation of the Arabic.

§16: Vocabulary and terms

For the most part, there is no new technical vocabulary in *On Rev. Nat.* Readers uncertain about the few instances of Arabic or Pahlavi terms should consult §9 of my Introduction to *Persian Nativities I* (pp. *xxxix-xlii*), or my "Arabic and Pahlavi Astrological Vocabulary," which is available as a free PDF on my website, www.bendykes.com/reviews/study.php. However, there are a few items to point out.

- "Necessities." *On Rev. Nat.* occasionally speaks about the native encountering or undergoing necessities during the year. This word (Lat. *necessitas*) simply refers to events done from or exhibiting constraints, force, necessity, or compulsion. An example might be acting out of a dire need for money, or because an authority figure issues a command one does not want to follow.
- "Steering." Although I cannot vouch for the Arabic, the Greek and Latin translations of *On Rev. Nat.* do not speak of planets "ruling" the year, but "steering" it. An alternative translation could be "governing," but our word "governor" is really borrowed from the navigation model of steering—thus a governor steers the "ship of

---

[276] *BA* III.12.3.

state." The point is that planets are understood as steering the native's life in a certain direction: sometimes this will involve smooth sailing and success; sometimes one winds up upon rocks or a sandbar. Coupled with Hugo's use of the notion of planets "taking turns" ruling the years in *BA*, not to mention that the revolution is sometimes called the "handing-over" of the nativity, we get the idea that the planets cooperate together in managing and steering the native's life, as though in cooperation with a cosmic plan.

- Signs that "hate" each other, or signs "hateful" to a particular planet. Abū Ma'shar nowhere defines this term in *On Rev. Nat.*, but in *Gr. Intr.* VI.4 he defines signs *hating* each other as those which are in a square: note that such signs differ by both gender and sect. Signs which are *enemies* to each other are those which are in opposition: this could relate to their Lords having oppositional meanings (such as Mars-Venus for Aries-Libra). But this does not really answer the question as to how planets are affected by such a relationship, so I simply suggest that a sign hateful to a *planet* is one forming a square to its own sign—though whether this is the sign in which it is, or the sign which it rules, I am not sure.

ON THE REVOLUTIONS OF THE YEARS OF NATIVITIES

The short compilation of the philosopher Hermes[1] begins:

THE FIRST BOOK
Translated from Greek into Latin:

Chapter I.1: On the revolutions of nativities

With the Sun appearing in some place at the time of the nativity by [his] motion in the zodiac, and passing through 360°, and being restored in that same place [after] 365 days and a portion, it becomes one year for the native. And the second year begins in the second restoration [of the Sun to that place]. The third year begins in the third one, and likewise thereafter. Therefore, in a revolution of the year it is good to establish the horoscope[2] according to what is denoted below, and to form the twelve places, and to write up the degrees of the planets: for horoscopes and the directions of the stars are changed in the revolutions of years. And the [natal] horoscope signifies the first year, and the stars do so in accordance with [how] they are found in the figure of the nativity. Then the second place signifies the second year, but the third [one] the third, the fourth the fourth, and likewise for subsequent [places]. And since the signs of the profections and the horoscope of the revolution and the places of the planets change, on account of this the accidents concerning men come to be diverse.

Chapter I.2: On the usefulness of the revolution

Certain men wondered at the discussion of the ancients (namely concerning the solar year), saying: why did they assign a year to the motion of the Sun's restoration, and not to that of his opposite or of some other place? But

---

[1] I am not sure where the attribution of this work to Hermes stems from.
[2] That is, the calculated Ascendant of the revolution (the calculated "east of the year" in *BA* IV).

others said: since the year consists of twelve months, why did they take only the Sun in the revolutions of years, and not the restoration of the Moon into her own proper place which was at the inception of the nativity, through the twelve periods?[3]

And to the first [group] it must be said that the year is divided into four seasons: spring, summer, autumn and winter. These seasons being completed, the year is restored to its first disposition; and if some of this time was lacking, the year will be defective: indeed the seasons are perfected through the crossing of the Sun in the twelve signs. Indeed, he being restored into [his] original place, the seasons are restored. And the same thing happens in the second restoration. But in the restoration of the Moon or some [other] star, such a thing does not happen, nor is the season restored. And for that reason they indicated the time through the motion of the Sun and his restoration. And the four seasons were made into the parts of the year, and the twelve months are distributed according to the twelve signs. But what is more, because the year is divided into four seasons, each season has a beginning, middle, and end, and three signs are heaped into every season (which, multiplied by four, come to be twelve). What is more, since in every year the Sun cuts 360° (which, divided by twelve, make thirty [degrees per sign]), therefore the solar month will have 30°. We even say that when the Sun begins to be moved from some place, [and] he will have walked through 2' 30", it makes an hour. But when he will complete a degree, it makes a day. But when [he will complete] 30°, it makes a month. But 360° makes a year. Still, certain ones of the hours and days and months are changed into other hours and days and months on account of the diversity of the Sun's motions.[4]

Chapter I.3: Against those who would not accept revolutions

Certain ones of those speaking against astrology have said that one does not need a revolution of years, trying to prove it through two proofs of this kind: by one, that the horoscope and figure according to the nativity [alone] signify accidents for men: therefore a revolution of years is pointless. But

---

[3] Reading partly with Schmidt. That is, the monthly lunar returns, which will happen about 12 times in a solar year.
[4] That is, the Sun's actual motion every day is not exactly equal, so the relation between time and longitude traveled will vary.

through the other [proof] they say that the signification of the nativity is stronger than the signification of the revolution: if therefore some star according to the nativity signified that a certain man will undergo danger in a certain year, [but] after that the year is revolved and that star will not signify danger, will the danger cease, or not? And if you said that it will stop, they destroy the signification of the nativity, claiming that the signification of the revolution of years is stronger. But if you said it would not, they say that the revolution of years is superfluous. But we refute these people in three ways:

Indeed by one [way], that we do not deduce a future thing by that one disposition of the planet, but from two or more. When, therefore, someone will indicate a planet in the nativity, [saying] that in some year something is going to come out [of that], it is proper for us to know the disposition of that star in that year, in order that we might come to know the substance of that matter accurately.

But another reason proceeds thusly: that when a planet will signify something good or bad in a nativity, neither its quantity nor quality is understood accurately from the nativity. For there is a certain great good, and a mediocre good, and a minimal good (likewise for the bad). For the greatness and smallness of each is known when the disposition of the star is considered according to the time of the revolution. If therefore the disposition of the star were good, both through the beginning [of the nativity] and through the revolution, that good will be the greatest; but if its transit is discordant from [what it was at] the beginning, it will be a minimal good. But if the planet will signify according to the nativity that there is going to be a certain good thing for the native, but in the year of the revolution it will not signify [that] there is some good, it will not wholly stop the good but it will be something minimal: the signification of the nativity does not become inactive on account of a revolution, but the operation of that star will appear. For, were it not [for the fact that] the planets have different dispositions at individual times, we would have no need for a revolution of years.

But the third reason is such: that a planet indicates things past, present, and future. And indeed it indicates present things [in the revolution], and signifies future things through the commingling of the present with the past or future. And when we make a comparison to one or the other times, we are considering the matter more accurately: for which reason a revolution of years is not superfluous.

But certain people oppose the revolutions of years thusly, saying that in nativities we make directions to the bodies of the good ones and bad ones for the reason that we may know the years in which the significations of the planets (even the places of them) are being conjoined both to the benevolents and the malevolents:[5] and on account of this, a revolution of years is not useful. But these people have deceived themselves regarding revolutions of this kind, for those who are tired of making comminglings or comparisons of the effects of the planets of the nativity with the effects of the stars of revolutions, invent accusations of this sort. When therefore a direction of planets comes to be according to the nativity, which comes to a certain signification in some year, it is proper to know both that year (what kind it is) and to harmonize its figures to the figures of the nativity. For if you knew dispositions of the [planets] which are at the beginning, and you did not know those which are in the revolution, you would not be able to distinguish their significations accurately. Therefore, of necessity it is good to know the dispositions of the planets according to the time of the revolution, and to compare them to the figure of the nativity, distinguishing them more securely afterwards.

And they state a certain argument [of] such [a sort]: that in the revolutions of years, the sign of the profection is considered, namely the sign which the year has reached. But it is not possible to distinguish the revolutions of it from the horoscope of the year.[6] For when someone's nativity is computed by certain canons, and afterwards the revolution of the year is sought by other canons, much diversity comes to be with respect to the degree of the horoscope, and many times surrounding the horoscope and the day itself; and because the canons differ with respect to [matters] of this sort, the revolution is not certain, [and] especially that the revolution of years is incomprehensible.[7] To which we say: anyone who destroys the horoscope of a revolution is ignorant of both the end and beginning of the year—which,

---

[5] Omitting a redundant *secundum nativitatem*.

[6] That is, distinguishing the profected sign of the year from the calculated east or Ascendant of the year at the revolution. In fact we will see below that Abū Ma'shar makes predictions from the position of the profected sign relative to the calculated Ascendant.

[7] This is not a particularly good argument, because the problem disappears if one simply uses the same calculation tables (and an accurate one) for both the nativity and the revolution. The objection would be more interesting if the reason for not distinguishing the annual profection from the Ascendant of the year was that they give too much or conflicting information: i.e., that the revolution becomes a mess of incoherent information.

BOOK I: DEFENSE & DEFINITIONS

not being known, the year itself is necessarily [left] unknown, and that is the most absurd of all. Indeed, the end of the preceding year and the beginning of the following one is announced by the restoration of the Sun [which is] made to his own proper [natal] place: this being understood, the horoscope of the revolution is understood. For the canons are discordant for the reason that the flowing year of the Sun is taken in one way [here] and another way [there];[8] but the universal canons are discordant from the canons of Ptolemy,[9] and others [differ] from others—and for this reason there is diversity surrounding the average courses and places of the planets. Therefore it is right to compute the Ascendants of the years by the average courses, and the unwavering courses[10] through which the beginning of the nativity was computed, and thus there will be no discord. Indeed the accurate horoscope of the year is the one taken from the annual motion of the Sun observed by a philosopher, through instruments about which [Ptolemy] makes mention in the *Almagest* (which the Greeks call the *Great Construction*), the restoration of the Sun being found through 365 ¼ days (less one-hundredth of a day).[11]

Chapter I.4: How much the ancients used revolutions

Indeed, the usefulness of knowing matters and [their] effects among men from a revolution of years is plain. For everyone of Babylon and Persia and India and Egypt, both kings and private individuals, did not attempt to handle anything in any year unless they first inspected their revolution of the year of the nativity; and if they had found that the year was good, they carried out the work. But if the contrary, they declined. Indeed, kings used to inspect the nativities of those put in charge of armies, and they observed their revolutions of years: and if they found that the revolution of one of them signified power and victory against enemies, they sent them forth. But if the contrary, they passed them over. And they did not observe the nativities of those people alone, but even those of legates, [to see] if the revolution of their year indicated a prosperous end: which if it signified

---

[8] Perhaps in the sense that the Sun's daily motion is not uniform, as stated above.
[9] Reading *Ptolemei* with the Greek for *philosophi*.
[10] That is, the uniform motions.
[11] 365.25 days - .01 = 365.24 days, which is extremely close to the more exact 365.2425 days.

prosperity, they sent them; but lacking this, instead of them they promoted others whose revolutions of the years indicated advancement. And likewise kings, when they saw an impediment to some action in some year of their nativity, they in no way carried it out. In a like manner, both kings themselves and private individuals observed medicines useful for themselves from the revolution of years, even food and drink, sales and purchases, and all beginnings[12] of them, and they used them, passing over things which would be harmful in that year. For they used to make conclusions about matters both from their own nativities and from those of others. Even men wanting to beget sons observed not only their own year, but even that of the woman: and if each of the figures signified procreation, they would lie down with them—otherwise, they sought other women whose nativities signified the birth of children. Wherefore, a revolution of years is very practical and useful.

Chapter I.5: On the arrangement of the figure of the revolution

If you wished to make a figure of a revolution of the year, along with these things which are noted in it, you should make a circular or square figure and divide it into twelve sections, in the way astrologers of our time now make figures. Then you should know the horoscope of the year and its degree and minute, and you should write out the twelve houses in order, with their degrees and minutes, working on them by the parts of hours and the ascensions of the right sphere.[13] And in a figure of this kind you will note the degrees of the planets according to the time of the revolution, and their exaltations and descensions, and also the retrogradations and sending of rays,[14] and their particular twelfth-parts,[15] and likewise the particular twelfth-parts of the degrees of the houses and the Lots (which are also called "Parts"), and the descending and ascending [Nodes], namely the Head and Tail [of the Dragon]. [Then] you will note all of these things in the way it comes to be in the nativity.

---

[12] That is, undertaking or commencing actions.
[13] So far Abū Ma'shar is unequivocally endorsing (a) a separate solar revolution chart, and (b) the use of quadrant houses. In *BA* Māshā'allāh suggested neither of these.
[14] *Radiationes*. The Greek translation uses the technical term *aktinobolia* or the "hurling of rays," but apparently only to mean aspects generally.
[15] *Duodenas*. I am not sure why the Latin translator everywhere speaks about "particular" twelfth-parts.

BOOK I: DEFENSE & DEFINITIONS 59

Afterwards, you will note the place of the horoscope of the nativity, and the planets of the nativity itself, and their disposition and sending of rays and particular twelfth-parts (both of the stars and of the houses), and the Lots and the ascending and descending [Nodes]: you will note all, and individually, in whatever house they were found according to the nativity.

Likewise [you will write down] the place in which the given year has arrived from the horoscope (that is, the sign of the profection), and the place in which the year has arrived from the Lot of Fortune of the nativity, and also the place in which the profection from the principal places of the figure has applied. Then you will note in it, in what place the distribution and distributor and co-distributor or partner has arrived, and the Lord of the *firdārīyyah*, and its co-partner, and the Lord of the orb—you will note especially the individual [stars], in which signs they are.[16] And you will note if there were a fixed star in the degree of the Midheaven or with one of the luminaries or the planets appearing in the angles.[17]

If however you did this, in a figure of this kind you will have 14 planets and two ascending [Nodes], that is Heads, and two descending Tails of the Dragon, and a sending of rays both of the nativity and of the revolution in 98 places,[18] and the particular twelfth-parts of the signs and of the planets in 38 places.[19] But the Lots [will be] more or fewer, as you wished. However, if you wished to note the planets in certain houses, and one house had more [planets in it], it is good for you first to note the one having few[er] degrees in the sign, and lastly to put in the one which had more degrees. It is good for you to do the same thing for both the rays and Lots and individual twelfth-parts. And once you have done this, you have put together a complete figure of the revolution of the year.

---

[16] This was discussed in Tr. VI of the Arabic, but was not translated into Greek or Latin. According to al-Qabīsī IV.19, we are to combine the planetary lord of the hour and the 1st house for the first year of life and the body, the next lord and the 2nd house for the second year of life and the native's wealth, *etc.* The conditions of each lord are assessed at the revolution to which they correspond. Al-Qabīsī also mentions another method, in which the Lord of the Ascendant is studied for the first year, and the next planet in zodiacal order for the second year, and so on—presumably assessing the Lord's condition at the corresponding revolution.
[17] For such traditional indicators of eminence, see *BA* III.2.1, *JN* Ch. 6, and Abū Bakr II.2.0-1.
[18] Reading *xcviii* for *xcvi*. 7 planets multiplied by 7 rays, multiplied by 2 charts = 98.
[19] The twelfth parts of 12 houses and 7 planets (19), multiplied by 2 charts = 38.

Chapter I.6: On the horoscope of the year and the dispositions of the planets in the revolution

Once you have made the figure of the revolution of the year, look at the horoscope to see what it is with respect to the places of the nativity, whether it is of the [natal] angles, or of the succeedents, or of the cadents; and what planet was in it according to the time of the nativity, and whose rays, and what Lots, and the particular twelfth-part of what [planets], and who aspects it in the two times, and what are the *epikratētor*s[20] (that is, the rulers) of [the Ascendant of the revolution],[21] and in what places they were from it,[22] and if in their own place or in an alien one, and if that star itself has one domicile or two (and if it has one, whether it aspects it or not), and if it is retrograde or direct, and if it is strong or weak, and if it is ascending in its *awj* or is descending, and what latitude it has, and if it is in its own exaltation or descension. Consider even if they aspect each other or receded from each other, and their rays from the seventh day, and their conjunctions and receptions with one another, and the co-helpers or harmers of each other, those hating or esteeming, and the comminglings or complexions which they have to one another, and the planets which are in their own sect or likeness (which in Arabic is called *ḥayyiz*),[23] and which are in the contrary one, and the particular twelfth-parts [of the planets], and to what place each of them applied in the revolution of years according to the direction [through] the twelve houses, and with which one of the stars of the revolution it applied, and in the same way where it is being applied in the [revolutions of] months.

However, it is good to consider the aspects of the planets to the Sun, [that is,] I say, oriental and occidental, and if it were in the heart of the Sun or [under] the rays or outside the rays, and the rest of the qualities of the stars.

---

[20] Gr. "predominator."
[21] Following Schmidt.
[22] Reading in the singular to match my addition in brackets.
[23] Lat. *haiz*. Schmidt reads "of the sect or contrary to the sect," which would indicate only the sect membership. But *ḥayyiz* ("domain") in the Perso-Arabic literature is a sect-related rejoicing condition combining gender, the horizon, and sect. According to *Gr. Intr.* VII.6, "this is like if a masculine planet is in a masculine sign and masculine degrees in the day above the earth, and in the night below the earth, and a feminine one in a feminine sign and feminine degrees in the day below the earth and in the night above the earth." Al-Qabīsī distinguishes *ḥayyiz* from a lesser condition called *ḥalb*: *ḥalb* is when (a) a diurnal planet is above the earth by day but below it by night, while a nocturnal planet is below the earth by day but above it by night, and *ḥayyiz* is when a planet in *ḥalb* is also in a sign of the same gender as itself.

But it is right to consider [these] both according to the nativity and according to the revolution. For often a certain planet in the nativity is aspecting some place or planet (of its friends or enemies), but in the revolution it seems otherwise. And on account of this it is right to attend to its position and configurations in both times, as its signification may appear different.

Chapter I.7: On the fact that an astrologer should know beforehand the age of him whose revolution it is

In the revolutions of years it is good to know first the native's age, whether he is a boy or young man, whether of middle age or an old man, or decrepit: for each of the seven planets has signification in each age, and for this reason a planet is always taken in a different way in a revolution of years.

For a boy, on account of the weakness and infirmity of his own nature, and [on account of his] ignorance, even though some planet may have signified a marriage-union for him, or the procreation of children, or the assembling of money, or the acquisition of immovable [property],[24] or a foreign journey or handling of difficult matters, or things impossible for him, still, because he does not have the possibility [for things] of this kind which young men have, nor the patience or prudence, or management [duties], he cannot receive the operations of the stars. The same thing happens for a decrepit and worn-out person when some planet will signify the procreation of offspring or certain other things which he can by no means do. On account of this therefore, it is necessary to know beforehand the native's age, so that the effects of the outcomes are suitable to it.

Certain people have spoken against[25] reasoning of this kind, saying: "for we even see [some] infant and boy who takes [someone] in a marriage-union, but other [boys] are promoted to dignities, and powers are acquired for them, [and] even slaves and oftentimes beasts of burden, and they are taken on journeys; they even acquire real estate,[26] immense riches and immovable possessions." But we say that a boy of this kind does not handle [these things] through himself, but through some caretakers or providers of his, whether[27] parents or others. But these things come out for him when some

---

[24] *Stabilitatis*.
[25] Reading *contradixerunt* with the Gr. for *praedixerunt*.
[26] Reading *haereditatem* for *haereditatum*.
[27] Reading *seu* for *sed*.

planet signifies them, with him wanting[28] nothing, nor knowing [anything], nor discerning [anything], and according to that same means he is [not] said to do something [of this kind], for he does not have sexual intercourse, he does not beget offspring, nor does he handle difficult matters through himself: for his age directs itself impossibly toward such things. But when at some time of his life he arrives to that age which pertains to that planet, he will have a fitness for its signification.

But the stars rule over the ages of men according to the order of their circles, beginning from the lower circle, and some steer a time of years equal to their lesser period, but others [equal to] a half or one-tenth of the least or middle period.[29] And indeed the Moon steers the first four-year period (for she is closer to us than the rest of the stars are), for the infirmity of a child's nature, and moisture, weakness, and a scarcity of food,[30] and wickedness of manners, and ignorance of things, and being removed from doing things, and uncertainty about things to be understood, and easiness of growing and susceptibility to change, signify that the Moon is his steersman, through whom he is steered from the time of the nativity up to four years. But the four years were put here according to the four elements on which our bodies are based, with one year being given to each element: and for this reason the Moon signifies four years, since a boy completing an age of this kind is changed from the aforesaid dispositions to another disposition. But others have said that since the Moon [generally] signifies the years of nourishing, but her middle years are 39 ½, one-tenth of them is taken, which is near four [years]. However, they took four as being one-tenth of 40, and as the middle[31] proportion for observing that same number. For if they had taken one-tenth of her lesser years, they would have been 2 ½ years, but we do not see a boy being changed from one disposition to another in that time. Had they taken one-tenth of her greater years, they would have been nearly 11 years. But plainly we see a boy be transferred and changed [into a new condition] before a time of this length.

Then Mercury takes up the second age and steers it through 10 years, namely one-half the years of his lesser period: for a half of it is particularly

---

[28] Reading *volente* for *valente*.
[29] For this material, cf. *Tet.* IV.10.
[30] Or, "taking of little nourishment" (Gr.).
[31] Reading *medium* for *minorem*, following Schmidt.

the relation of lesser and greater [numbers].[32] Therefore it is plain because a man passes through so many years from some disposition to another. But one must note [that] Mercury steers an age of this kind on account of the nearness of the Moon which is put next to him, and for that which appears in that same time: sharpness of the mind,[33] and an intellect of a human nature, even discernment between things, and the beginning of teaching and learning; but his [period] is the end of the childlike age.

But Venus takes the third [period] and steers it through 8 years according to her lesser period, and this age is the beginning of adolescence. But, it being taken up, she is for steering the [next] age for the reason that the circle of Venus is higher than Mercury and is next to him, and on account of this the appetite is moved from that point and [the native's] rush to sexual intercourse is intolerable.

But the Sun disposes the fourth age through 19 years according to his lesser period, for his circle is set over the circle of Venus (whom he is next to): for then we see a man value exaltation and glory and pass over to a better disposition, and from games to worries, and to suppress venereal pleasures, and just in the way that he is a middle between the superior and inferior planets, in a like way this age is the middle between old age and the childlike one, and its end is the end of the youthful age.

Then Mars takes up the fifth age and steers it through 15 years according to the period of his lesser years, and the beginning of this age is the beginning of a stable age. For Mars is placed next above the solar circle, and on account of [that] men in an age of this kind come to be worked up and they fight it out in the world, and they are wrapped up in cares and worries and labors, reflections, pains, and are afflicted by distasteful things; they even leave behind many pleasures and delights.

Then Jupiter takes up the sixth age and disposes it through 12 years according to the period of his lesser years, being placed next to Mars: and his age is old age, and for this reason men give up many labors and fatigues and contests and deceits, having worry about goods and honest actions and reflecting on the world, and they make use of privileges[34] in an age of this kind.

---

[32] Reading with Schmidt for *habitudo*. The idea seems to be that we take one-half of Mercury's years because his years partake both of childhood and the adult activities of the mind: see the following sentence.

[33] *Ingenii*.

[34] Schmidt reads, "indulge in beneficence."

Afterwards, Saturn takes the seventh age and disposes it until the last day of life, being put next to Jupiter: and on account of this, men run out [of strength] in this age and are weakened, and are dried out in their bodies, they are even lazy, complaining, small-souled, with their nature relinquishing and turning against them in a certain way. And so they abandon hope, are deprived of their desires, and pressed down by illnesses.

Chapter I.8: On the disposition of the planets in the nativity and in the revolution

In the seven ages therefore, each planet shows its own operation according to the disposition which it has at the beginning of the nativity and according to that which it received in the steering of the age. If therefore it were well-disposed in the two times, it signifies very much usefulness. If however [it were] impeded [in both], it indicates much detriment. But if the two times of (of their steering and the nativity are discordant, the advantage and the loss will be [only] moderate.[35] But if someone had not yet reached old age, so that he would pass through the years of the planets, he will certainly die at the age of the steering of that planet to whose age he pertained.

But certain people said that Saturn would steer the seventh age through 30 years, [so that] if the native passed through [them] he is then steered again by the Moon: for he would be weak and moist, and not eating enough, and having nothing to do, and being immovable.[36] Then he is steered by Mercury, and in order by the other planets just as we said. Therefore it must be known that even though the steering or disposition is restored to the Moon, still the native will not have the same things which he had in the first age. For he will not suckle nor be nourished by milk. Indeed in the first period of the ages he used to receive the operations of the stars according to what was suitable to each age. But in the last restoration [to the beginning it is] not so, but the operations of planets descend infirm and weak.[37]

But others used to consider the ages in another way, namely dividing the individual planetary ages just as we do in the *firdārīyyāt*. But we say that it is

---

[35] This advice also applies to comparing the nativity with the solar revolution.
[36] Or, "unable to be motivated."
[37] Schmidt reads this as though the stars' effects pass over him because *he* is infirm and weak.

not good to handle [them] in that manner, for the reason that the years of the *firdārīyyāt* were taken up in a manner [by] which the planets unite between themselves. For the years of the *firdārīyyāt* were ordered according to the order of the exaltations of the planets which they have in the signs.[38] But *these* years [were ordered] apart from[39] the reception of each planet to each age of a planet. And for this reason, when the native reaches some age, he is steered by one star alone, to which the nature of that age is suitable.

Chapter I.9: On those things which an astrologer should know beforehand

Before he determines something about the effects of the outcomes of a revolution of years, it is good for the astrologer to know beforehand these four things:

First, at what age (of the planets' ages) is he whose revolution it is.

Secondly, of what rank or grade of men he is.

Thirdly, his habits and qualities.

Fourthly, some of his matters or his capacities.

And firstly it is good to know how old the native is: for, this being known, both his age and by what star he is steered is known. So we say that for this reason it is good for the astrologer to know the native's years beforehand: because all inexperienced people, if they were worn out and remiss in the comprehension of some science, intend to annihilate and detract from that science, so that they appear to be deprived of [its knowledge] not on account of the unsoundness of their own nature, but because the science itself is fallible and unuseful: and on account of this they try in all ways to impose sophistical words and deprive those present of that very science. For certain

---

[38] This is not true for nativities, at least according to how Abū Ma'shar describes them below (and how Māshā'allāh got them from al-Andarzaghar in *BA* IV.17-25). But Pingree (1968 pp. 60ff) claims it was so.

[39] Reading somewhat with Schmidt. The idea seems to be that the Ptolemaic ages do not have subperiods as the *firdārīyyāt* do. See the next sentence.

ones of them offer the figures of a revolution of years for an infant or decrepit old men, and they present them to astrologers and ask them about some operations of the stars which ages of this kind cannot take up, so that they could detract from [this] science. And for this reason it is necessary to know the year beforehand.

It is even good for us to know those things which are of the second heading [above], since there are four ranks of men: the first of kings, the second of nobles, the third of middling people, and the fourth of paupers. For the many who rail against [this] knowledge mislead the eloquent, showing them a revolution of the year of a king, and they do not say that the revolution belongs to a king. But [the astrologers], being ignorant of what rank of men [the native] is, do not distinguish [their predictions] as for a king, but in the way they would regarding some common person, [in response] to which the aforesaid detractors take the opportunity to detract from a science of this kind. For the revolution of a king, when it is good, signifies [he is] successful against the rest of the enemy kings, even [signifying] plundering and the ravaging of fortresses and cities, and of climes, and the accumulation of treasures. But when it is a revolution of someone of the common people, it indicates success against enemies, and the king's caution towards him, and prominence over those who are of a like [social] level to him.

The third heading is to know the operations which he (whose revolution it is) is able to take up. For this reason however, it is useful for the astrologer to know [him] beforehand, lest perhaps, finding the revolution of a eunuch [which] shows the procreation of children, he should predict such a thing, and appear ridiculous (and not undeservedly so): for the beginning[40] of the nativity signifies him to be a eunuch and without children. Therefore in what way could he become a father at some time, who at once is deprived of them through the figure of the nativity? Likewise if at some time we happened to find someone's revolution signifying the procreation of many children, we do not [necessarily] say he generates [them], on account of two reasons: one, when the star which steers his age does not signify the power of procreating; but the other, that his nature is not capable of bearing the significations of the stars. For if someone made the revolution of a dead man, and he found some significations through the figures, nothing would come out for him because he is powerless to take them up. However, it is good to distinguish

---

[40] *Initium.* In most Latin works this would be *radix* or "root," referring to the nativity itself. It should be understood as such throughout the rest of this work.

the determination of the outcomes, and to write down what the stars signify, and to pronounce that such-and-such a thing will come forth if he persists in an age susceptible of those outcomes. Which if it were not susceptible, we say that the stars generally indicate such-and-such; and if the nature of this man were susceptible of such things, it would be able to bring it forth for him in any case.

The fourth heading is to know the substance and condition of him whose revolution it is, so that the judgment is appropriate to his person. We do not say about one having no riches that he will acquire [them], but about one having [them], that his riches will be increased. And what is more, if he has brothers, with the figures signifying the birth of a brother, we say he is added to in brothers; and if he does not have [them], we say that brothers will come to be for him. And likewise about lands[41] and dignities and the like. For it should not be determined about one not having possessions, that his possessions will be destroyed, or, about one not having revenues that his revenues will have decrease. But certain people say that if the figures signify for someone the death of the parents, and he does not have [any], some old men in his household will die. For at the beginning of the nativity, if the figures signified that someone would not be able to beget children, and at the time of the revolution a figure of begetting will come about, certainly he will not procreate, but sometimes it will make an adopted child. And if he does not have good buildings, and the figures signified the building or repairing of built things, this will [happen] to [the native] through his own hands. Again, if a figure signified a marriage-union for someone, with the beginning of the nativity denying it, and if the figure of the revolution will show the contrary, he will have it without nuptials—that is, a concubine. And if the figure of the revolution signified familiarity for someone with kings, the beginning of the nativity not showing such a thing, he will have exchanges with magnates. It is even good for the astrologer to know whether the revolution belongs to a man or women, so that he might make a determination according to the nature of each; and not only this, but even their condition and qualities: for many times, women rule in cities.[42]

And for this reason it is good to know beforehand the accidents of men at the time of the revolution. For even though [accidents] of this kind could be known from nativities, still the understanding of them in individual years is

---

[41] Reading with Schmidt for an unclear word.
[42] This is an interesting claim; I wonder to what cities Abū Ma'shar is referring.

most difficult. However, the outcome of children may be known from the revolution of a dead man, for after the death of the father it comes to be as though as a second report to the son, just as the accidents of the father are understood from the nativity of the child, even if he is dead.

BOOK II: [PROFECTIONS]

Chapter II.1: On the number of the significators of the year

It must be known that the year is divided into months, days, and hours, and for each of these there are many significators and planets. [And] through the diversity of their dispositions it signifies diverse effects for individual times; and indeed in a revolution of the year they generally signify the quality, but these have their own certain greater signification at a particular time of the year through their ingresses into the signs which indicate intensifications and slackenings of goods or evils.[1] But others signify the revolution of months and days, and that signification is particular. But there are 19 significators of the whole year:

And the first is the sign of the profection and its Lord.[2]

Second, the status of the distribution and the distributor.[3]

Third, the one which cooperates with [the distribution and distributor].[4]

Fourth, the star with which the *firdārīyyah* cooperates, and [the one] which partners with it.[5]

Fifth, the Lord of the orb.[6]

Sixth, the horoscope of the revolution of the year, and its Lord.[7]

---

[1] For example, the whole-sign angles from the profected sign of the year.
[2] See esp. II.3-22; also *BA* IV.2-7.
[3] See esp. Book III below; also *BA* IV.8-13.
[4] That is, the partner. See esp. Book III below; also *BA* IV.8-13.
[5] See esp. Book IV below; also *BA* IV.17-25.
[6] Omitting *defectus vel*. The "orb" (Gr. *periodos*) could also be related to the method of the orb found in al-Qabīsī IV.19 and *BOA* pp. 1408-10. Schmidt believes it may relate to the application of planetary periods and ascensional times, which is certainly possible.
[7] See esp. I.6, II.23, and VI.3 (missing); also *BA* IV.14.

Seventh, the Moon and the planets which are being conjoined with her, [when] appearing in the sign in which she is.[8]

Eighth, the entrance or arrival of the planets into their places according to the nativity, and their entrance upon each other.[9]

Ninth, the Lord of the Year, according to the signification of the place in which it is [at the revolution].[10]

Tenth, the places of the planets from their own domiciles, and[11] the places of their domiciles from them.[12]

Eleventh, the period or orb of the stars and of the twelve houses.[13]

Twelfth, when the sign of the profection and the horoscope of his revolution touch in some place of [the same] planet according to the nativity.[14]

Thirteenth, the sign of the profection, or the Ascendant of the revolution falling in the places of the planets [in] the nativity.[15]

---

[8] That is, not by aspect. This is different from Māshā'allāh, who explicitly allows aspects (*BA* IV.1). But Māshā'allāh does make special note of planets in the Moon's sign (both in the nativity and the revolution): *BA* IV.14, p. 206. The Greek text also says that if she is void in course, one should examine her dispositor. See also *Carmen* IV.197-209, and the Dorotheus excerpt translated by Schmidt (1995, p. 5).

[9] I.e., both returns and normal ingresses/transits. See esp. Book V.

[10] Reading with Schmidt. See Book II throughout, and III.8.

[11] Omitting *in alio rotatus*, which does emphasize their derived positions.

[12] See for example V.1 below.

[13] Reading with Schmidt for *annorum* ("years"). See possibly Book VI.2 (missing). Again, it may refer to planetary years and ascensional times.

[14] I have followed Schmidt in specifying *both* the profected and revolutionary Ascendants, so as to distinguish this from the following point (#13). I take this to mean either that both Ascendants fall on the same sign, or else that the same planet appears natally in the profection, and in the revolutionary Ascendant by transit. See possibly VI.4 (missing), but also II.24. But note: if we consult *BA* IV.1, items [2] and [5], these two indicators could refer to planets *in* (#12) *or aspecting* (#13) the profected sign and the Ascendant of the year, in both the nativity and the revolution.

[15] Following Schmidt, this might mean a comparison between natal planets in the sign of the profection, and those in the Ascendant of the revolution.

Fourteenth, that a planet would be in some place in the nativity, and in another in the revolution.

Fifteenth, the conjunctions of the planets with each other.

Sixteenth, the significations of a planet crossing over from place to place throughout the whole year.[16]

Seventeenth, the significations of planets touching upon some one of the signs of the year.[17]

Eighteenth, [the significations of a star when in its own domicile or bound, or in that of another.][18]

Nineteenth, the significations of the ascending and descending [Node], namely of the Head and Tail of the Dragon.[19]

These are the significations of the revolution of the nativity, and indeed the first is stronger than the second, and the second [stronger than] the third. For it was good to arrange their accounting in order, but for the sake of eminent instruction and the natural sequence of statements, sometimes the last things are put first, and the first ones put last. Therefore [each] individual [member] of the aforesaid has its own proper signification, but frequently [it has] certain other significations, and sometimes they have the same signification as do the Lords of the months.

But certain astrologers,[20] wanting to scrutinize the revolution of years, make a [primary] direction of all of these, and they resolve [them] into days, months, and hours. But these [astrologers] used to handle it in a mistaken way, for the reason that those significations [at the annual revolution] do not persist. But it is good to establish the horoscope of the month, and to sketch out the planets and their casting of rays, and the particular twelfth-parts, and

---

[16] See probably Book VII (missing).
[17] Schmidt takes this to mean planets transiting through the profected sign of the year. See probably Book VII (missing).
[18] Adding with Schmidt. See possibly Book VII (missing), but also II.4 for general ideas about the Lord of the Year being in its own or in another's sign; see also Māshā'allāh's *On Sig. Planet.*
[19] See possibly Book VII.2-9 (missing).
[20] Possibly a critical reference to 'Umar al-Tabarī in *TBN* II. See my Introduction.

the Lots, and to determine the significations of the outcomes according to them, with the planets of both the nativity and the revolution being taken up. If [just] one planet had indicated the accidents of men for him in [only] one way, his every condition and disposition and movement would have existed in any case, according to the nature of that star. But since there are many [things] which signify what affects men, for this reason diverse things which are undergone will come out for them.

Chapter II.2: On the significations of the soul and body, from revolutions

We take some [of] the aforesaid significations over the passions of the soul, others over the state of the body, and others over the dispositions and movements[21] and works of men throughout the whole time. And firstly in revolutions it is good to consider the disposition of the mind and body, and their particular co-tempering and harmonization,[22] then the rest of his dispositions throughout the whole year of the revolution.

For there are five significators of the body's condition:

First, the sign of the profection.

Second, the bound in which the direction of the horoscope has arrived.

Third, the bound in which the direction of the *apheta* (which the Persians call the *hīlāj*) has arrived.

Fourth, the Moon.

Fifth, the horoscope of the revolution of the year.

But those which signify the condition of the soul are eight:

First, the Lord of the Year.

---

[21] Or even, "motives" (*motibus*).
[22] I note that the translator, if not Abū Ma'shar, has drawn on a Pythagorean notion (*consonantia*) rather than the usual *commixtio* or *convenientia*.

Second, the Lord of the bound in which the direction from the horoscope has arrived.

Third, the Lord of the bound in which the direction of the *apheta* has arrived.[23]

Fourth, the one which unites and co-partners with them by body or aspect.[24]

Fifth, the lord of the *firdārīyyah*.

Sixth, the Lord of the period.

Seventh, the planet which receives the conjunction of the Moon, or the planet which receives the conjunction of the Lord of her domicile.

Eighth, the Lord of the horoscope of the revolution of the year.

When therefore the aforesaid significators (all or many of them) appear in good places according to the heavenly disposition, and they are unobstructed by the bad ones, they signify the concord of the body and soul, and their good bearing and durability.

But the remaining significative [parts] of the figure signify movements and operations, which if at some time they will signal concerning the condition of the soul or body, that signification will not be a principal one, but according to an accident.[25] But the aforesaid figures only signify those things which are according to the body and soul and their harmonization with each other, and even all of the rest of the dispositions and movements with them. Still, nevertheless, their principal and proper signification is regarding the soul and

---

[23] The Lord of this bound is the *jārbakḫtār*. 'Umar and Abū Bakr prefer to call the bound Lord of the directed Ascendant the *jārbakḫtār*.

[24] That is, any planet in or aspecting that bound in the nativity. Abū Bakr (I.17) also takes planets aspecting the bound Lord as modifying its signification.

[25] In the Aristotelian sense of a quality or event that accompanies something else, without primary being on its own. However, I am doubtful about Abū Ma'shar's statements here. First, how will we know which is primary? If Mercury were both the Lord of the Ascendant of the year and also made various ingresses, is his role as the Lord (and thus the soul) primary, or as a transiting planet? Second, Abū Ma'shar frequently describes the Lord of the Year in terms of bodily health, state of mind, *and* actions.

also the body, and the significations which they themselves signify are not to be found in any of the other ones making significations.

Chapter II.3: On the sign of the revolution and its Lord

In a revolution of years it is good to look at the horoscope of the nativity, and to compute one sign for every year, and where it applied, that one will be the sign of the profection, whose Lord will be the Lord of the Year (which in Persian is called the *sālkḥudāy*); then [it is good to] look at the sign, which place it possessed at the beginning of the nativity, to see whether it was of the four angles, or of the succeedents or the cadents, and indeed whose domicile it is, or whose exaltation, but [also] whose triplicity, and whether good or bad, and if some planet was in it at the beginning of the nativity, or a particular Lot or twelfth-part, and if one of them was aspecting the sign itself or was projecting rays from the seven fires,[26] and from what sign or degree it was inspecting it, whether from the signs harmonious with it or discordant, from those which are of many ascensions or few, ascending directly or of those which are [ascending crookedly, or of equal ascensions or equal in the journey],[27] and whether the aspect is from the bright degrees or from the shadowy and dark ones, from fortunate ones or unfortunate ones, or in what bound the ray applied, and in what decan and in what particular ninth-part, and in what degree (whether lucid, shadowy, or dark). Then it is right to look at the sign of the profection to see whether it was cadent from an angle at the beginning of the nativity and was not being inspected by the rays of the stars.

Then consider if there is a planet in that same sign in the revolution, or the ray of a planet, or a particular twelfth-part, and if it is being looked at by someone, or none[28] is aspecting, and if it is being looked at by some or by all, and from what directions: where the aspecting stars were at the beginning of the nativity, and where they were by transit, and how they were at the beginning [of the nativity], but how they are established in the transit of the

---

[26] *Focis*, referring to the notion of aspects as casting fiery rays of light.
[27] Reading and adding partly with Schmidt, for "of one angle." Equally-ascending signs are Pisces-Aries, Aquarius-Taurus, Capricorn-Gemini, and so on. Signs agreeing in the journey are pairs of signs with the same domicile Lord, such as Capricorn-Aquarius, Sagittarius-Pisces, and so on. See Abū Ma'shar's *Abbr.* I.90-97.
[28] Reading *nullus* for *nullum*.

revolution. One must also know the disposition of each, and especially the disposition of the Lord of the Year, just as we have said before.

If therefore the sign of the profection, both in the nativity and in the revolution, were unencumbered, and its Lord will be direct in each figure, and in its own sect[29] (whether it would be diurnal or nocturnal), and in a place in which it would have some dignities, even appearing strong through itself, and likewise that the stars are aspecting it, it also being placed in a good place both from the horoscope of the nativity and from the sign of the profection, and even from the horoscope of the revolution: then it signifies for him (whose revolution it was) the health of the body, pleasantness and goodness, namely in matters of which the Lord of the Year is the significator (and the stars co-helping it), both at the beginning of the nativity and in the revolution, namely in riches, dignities, glory, the acquisition of real estate, the acquisition of children, the acquisition of slaves, and the delight of women, according to the complexions of the stars and of the houses in which they are.

But if the Lord of the Year is unencumbered with respect to the horoscope [at the beginning][30] of the nativity, and good, but impeded or bad in the revolution, again if it is retrograde, or under the rays, or that it would touch[31] an alien place, or that it would be occidental, or that it will be conjoined to the malevolents by body or aspect, or that it appears outside of its own sect, and the like, it signifies that [the native's] operations in that year will be obscure, weak and infirm, according to the proportion of the misfortune touching it by the above-stated dispositions.

Moreover, if the Lord of the Year were impeded in the nativity, but well disposed in the revolution, it signifies a moderated good for him whose revolution it is, and joyfulness will be renewed for him, for the power of the Lord of the Year is greater for annual outcomes.

But if the Lord of the Year were impeded in both the beginning of the nativity and in the revolution of the year, it indicates the intensity of a harm according to its own proper signification.

---

[29] *Conditione.*
[30] Adding with Schmidt.
[31] That is, "be in."

[General template for examining the Lord of the Year]

With these, you should even look at the Lord of the Year to see in what place it is, both in the figure of the beginning [of the nativity] and in the figure of the revolution, to see whether it is unencumbered or impeded. But if it were unencumbered [and] in good places at the two times, it signifies the possession and usefulness of goods. If however it were well disposed in each figure, but was not configured to benevolents, it signifies that he will indeed obtain goods, but they will be made smaller and reduced gradually.

Moreover, if it were impeded and cadent from the angle in each figure, but is configured to certain benevolents, it signifies the discovery of goods and slight usefulness, in small matters and low-quality ones.

Moreover, if the Lord of the Year were impeded by bad ones in the two times, and appearing in an angle in the revolution,[32] [and] were impeded by some malevolent planet from a square or opposite, it signifies adversities, dangers, and manifest offenses in that year. But if that malevolent itself is going under the rays of the Sun or goes retrograde, it signifies that [some] irrational necessity will rush in upon him from some matter. And if it were impeded in the angles[33] in the two times, it signifies adversities even more so. But if the Lord of the Year will not be in an angle in the two times, but it is impeded and aspects the horoscope, the evil will be diminished, and it will not be well-known and public, but known to his kin by blood or his household intimates. But if it were in one of the four places which do not aspect the horoscope (namely in the 2nd, 6th, 8th or 12th), the offense of [the year] will be clandestine and hidden and unknown to all. And if, as was said, it were removed from the horoscope,[34] but it is being viewed by some planet appearing in an angle, the offense will appear after some hidden time. But if it is being conjoined to a star appearing in an angle, the one whose revolution it is will make his offense public.

On must also consider the conjunctions and rays of the Lord of the Year to the stars, and the particular twelfth-parts [and the Lots], and thus after that one would be able to make a determination more securely.

---

[32] Reading with Pingree for "nativity."
[33] Omitting *maiores*, "greater."
[34] That is, in one of the four places cadent from it (not aspecting it).

Chapter II.4: On Saturn, when he is the Lord of the Year and is made fortunate

For instance, Saturn is a malevolent and a corruptor by nature. But Jupiter [is] a benevolent by nature and a significator of good things. But it often happens that a malevolent signifies prosperity but a benevolent adversity, and [this is according to] their diverse dispositions. And specifically, a badly-disposed malevolent indicates detriments and losses[35] on the one hand on account of his nature, but on the other hand even on account of the contrary disposition. And if he were configured to another planet, and to one badly disposed, his harm will be extended even more so. But if that [other] planet were well disposed, aspecting through a trine or sextile aspect, it will not harm, but will signify good.[36] And a benevolent, when it is badly disposed and is weak, its significations are weakened. But if a malevolent aspected [while the benefic were] bearing itself thusly, it will receive the operation of evils from that same malevolent, and the benevolent will perform the operation of the malevolent [because of their commingling].[37]

So when Saturn is badly disposed and Jupiter (or any of the benevolents) is being configured to him, his malice is diminished. Therefore if Saturn were the Lord of the Year, and appearing oriental according to the nativity and according to the revolution, and direct in his own domicile, sect, or exaltation, in places in which he had dignity, and in some place of friends and his own cooperators, and in a good place of the distribution of the houses, and in his own sect, it makes [the man] whose revolution it is to be a manager of advantageous matters, and prosperity in them, strong and lasting, and especially busy in the care of lands and villas and in buildings and their acquisition, not to mention in the erecting of houses and in the diverting of waters and the planting of trees.

And if he is of [the lineage of] kings or princes, and Saturn were so disposed, aspecting Jupiter by a trine at the beginning of the nativity, it signifies that he will build cities in that year, and he will construct palaces and blockade them, and he will raise walls and renovate gardens, and he will make aqueducts, and dig brooks and restore corrupted and old things. But if at the beginning [of the nativity] he is not aspecting Jupiter by a trine, but by a sextile, things of this kind will be lesser. And if Jupiter aspected Saturn

---

[35] *Iacturas*. This can also mean "sacrifices."
[36] Switching *bene* and *bonum* with its instance earlier in the sentence.
[37] Reading with Schmidt.

from a trine or sextile through the revolution, [and] he was even aspecting him thusly at the beginning [of the nativity], it signifies in addition to the aforesaid that he will be respectable and cheerful and that he will acquire many riches and will rule, and he will have advantage in all of his works, he will even beget a child and he will be abounding in happiness with his child. Moreover, if Saturn were aspecting Jupiter both at the beginning of the nativity and in the revolution, in royal signs, he whose revolution it is will handle royal works in that same year; it signifies the same if he is being conjoined to Jupiter.[38]

However, in addition to these it is good to observe the rays and Lots and particular twelfth-parts in each figure, and [to see] in which of these Saturn is established, and which of these he aspects in the two times, for they have significations of this kind. For if Saturn has some dignity in the place in which he is, or he would rule over the house in which the Lot of Fortune fell, or he will be aspecting a Lot from a sign in which he has dignity, advantage will come about for him from some known direction, or from a certain friend of his. But if it happened in an alien place, the usefulness will come to be from an alien direction.[39]

Likewise, if Saturn were the Lord of the Year, and both he and Mars were made fortunate both according to the nativity and according to the revolution, but Mars aspected [Saturn] from a trine or sextile aspect, and they received each other, he whose revolution it is, is going to handle advantageous matters, and his riches and glory will be increased, and he will have an acquaintance with kings, and he will rejoice [in] his brothers, and progress will follow him prosperously. But if Mars were conjoined to him in the two times and both were made fortunate, he whose revolution it is will bear himself well in that year, [being] even fit in counsels, and inserting himself into matters with shrewdness, and business matters will be easy for him, and so he will be generous and will make many expenditures.

Moreover if Saturn were the Lord of the Year, and both he and the Sun were made fortunate in the two times, with the Sun aspecting Saturn from a sextile aspect, it signifies the increase of honor in that year, and the advantage of the father, and an opportunity from kings. But if the Sun aspected him from a trine, with Saturn beginning to go retrograde, the advantage will be

---

[38] Reading *Iovi* with Schmidt for *Iam*.
[39] That is, from a stranger.

less. It will be the same if the Sun aspected him in [only] one of the two times.

Likewise,[40] if Saturn were the Lord of the Year and both he and Venus were unencumbered in the two times, and Venus were configured to him in the two times from a trine or sextile aspect, and[41] the Lot of Marriage-Union is being made fortunate, he will delight in women in that year, and he will have a care for decoration and purity, and his riches will be copious; he will even love paintings and beauty in houses. But if they were so disposed in only one time, not very immoderate goods will touch him. Certain people will even despise and contradict him, and he will be made sad because of women and effeminate men, and he will handle venereal things with difficulty, and one of his wives will be saddened, and something of his own movable substance or his ointments[42] will be corrupted, and he will be saddened in the middle of [some] enjoyment, and he will be humiliated in the middle of a game.

Moreover, if Saturn were the Lord of the Year and both he and Mercury were unencumbered in the two times, and Mercury is being configured to him by a trine or sextile aspect, and each receives the other, but the Lot of Slaves and Lot of Children and the Lot of Work are well disposed at the same time with their Lords, he will be respectable and steady, and he will study at the reading of writings, and computations and teachings, and he will rejoice over children and slaves. But if Mercury is being conjoined to him in the two times, he will be of a most elegant mind in that year. But if they bore themselves thusly in [only] one of the times, all of the above-stated things are diminished.

Likewise, if Saturn were the Lord of the Year and both he and the Moon were unencumbered in the two times, and he aspected her by a trine or sextile in the two times, and the Moon happened to be increased in light and number,[43] his riches and glory will be increased in that year, and he will be attached to kings and be praised by men, and he will be glad with respect to mothers and women. But if he aspected in [only] one of the two times, or they were impeded, everything which we said before will be diminished.

---

[40] For this paragraph, cf. *BA* IV.2 p. 189.
[41] Omitting a redundant *et*.
[42] Or, "perfumes" (*unguentis*).
[43] Reading *lumine et numero* for *luminibus et numeris* (pl.).

Chapter II.5: On the significations of Saturn when he is the Lord of the Year and would be of a bad condition

When Saturn is the Lord of the Year and impeded both in the nativity and in the revolution, and he is cadent from an angle and in a bad place and in an alien sign and under the rays or retrograde, and especially if he were in his own descension, not helped by Jupiter whether by commingling or a figure[44] by means of signs of equal power, and if the revolution is nocturnal and he were above the earth in the seventh[45] place or in the Midheaven, or if the revolution is diurnal and he will be found below the earth and especially in the angle of the earth, it signifies detriment in that year from the older people in the household, and in parents and in grandparents. And if the sign is masculine there will be danger to men, but if a feminine one, women. And if he is in a double-bodied sign in each, in addition to these it indicates that he whose revolution it is will endure great dangers and lengthy illnesses from moisture and coldness and fevers, and a tremor of the body, and painful urination[46] and melancholic diseases and consumptive fevers[47] and the like. It even signifies detriment in immovable things and in riches, and in fields and waters and in every movable and immovable substance, and being unconcerned about handling matters, and difficulty in obtaining things, and he will even have familiarity with greedy men, and pains, and especially if [Saturn] is retrograding.

But if Saturn, bearing himself thusly, were in an alien sign, he will suffer this in a foreign land; and if Saturn were in a friendly place, he will endure this from friends; and if the Lord of his domicile aspected him in the nativity, he will suffer this from an old enemy. If however it aspected him both in the nativity and in the revolution, he will be harmed by each, and in the three ways we stated it will be an enemy already known to him.

But if Saturn were under the solar rays in the two times, it signifies contentions and fears from the commanders of dignities in that year, [and] even a disease in a hidden place, and detriment from parents and grandparents and old men, according to the natural property of Saturn; and if the Sun were stronger the detriments will admit of intensification; but if weaker, they will be diminished.

---

[44] Reading this phrase with Pingree for "aspect."
[45] Following Pingree, omitting "in a trine."
[46] *Dysuria*.
[47] Reading with Pingree for *trecticis*.

And if he is badly disposed in such a way, in the conjunction of a certain star or ray or Lot or particular twelfth-part, or he aspects them by a contrary aspect (whether in the nativity or in the revolution), it signifies the corruption and abandoning of that type [of thing]. In fact Saturn sometimes will signify the contrary if it is a diurnal revolution, for the reason that he is in his own sect: evils will come about more quickly, but they will be dissolved and there will be [only] a moderate harm.

Likewise if Saturn were the Lord of the Year and both he and Jupiter were impeded in the two times, but he aspected him by a sextile or trine aspect [while] appearing in a bad place, it signifies the destruction of a certain house or possession of his in that year, and the loss of part of his riches, and obscurity and negligence with respect to accomplishments. But if he aspected him by the square in the two times, and both were impeded, it signifies the diminution of riches in that year, and difficulty in handling all matters; his parents will even be in danger. Likewise if Jupiter aspected Saturn in the two times through an opposite [aspect] and both were impeded, he will have difficulty in all of his business matters in that year, and he will have sorrow because of children. And if he is being conjoined in the two times, it signifies the loss of riches, and contentions and detriment. But if there were a conjunction or aspect in [only] one time, evils of this kind will be easier.

Moreover, if Saturn were the Lord of the Year, and both he and Mars were impeded in the two times, and configured to each other by any aspect, and both would be in signs of the likeness of men, it signifies that dangers will develop in that year for him whose revolution it is, and being detained by enemies, or by some leader of an army, and he will be saddened with regard to his brothers. But on the other hand, were Mars to aspect Saturn from a trine or sextile in the two times, and both impeded, it indicates idleness[48] in that year, and the death of brothers, and sufferings and great danger for him whose revolution it is, at the same time as for his brothers.[49] But if Mars aspected him by a square in the two times, and Saturn were elevated above him, he will be sick from fever and cold, and the substance of his father will be corrupted, and one of his own brothers will die. But if Mars were elevated over Saturn, he will envy his blood-relatives, and he will labor with a great illness, and his goods will be badly disposed. But if Mars aspected Saturn in the two times through an opposite [aspect], and both were

---

[48] Omitting *desiderium vel* ("desire or").
[49] Reading with Pingree for *sitis*.

impeded, his riches will be diminished in that year, and he will endure great losses, and he will be sick, and he will suffer necessities on account of envy and false accusations, and he will have controversies with his own blood-relatives. And if it were in a watery sign, there will be danger from water and moist things. But if in a four-footed sign, the danger will be from a blow or bite or poison. And if Mars is being conjoined to him in the two times and both are made unfortunate, he will be very sad in that year, and of wicked morals and not well manageable, having difficult efforts, [and] even his older brothers will be harmed. But if they were well disposed in the two times, evils of this kind will be moderate.

Likewise, if Saturn were the Lord of the Year and both he and the Sun were impeded in the two times, and configured to each other from whatever kind of figure, it signifies sorrows in that year, and injuries and false accusations and attacks on fathers, and the diminution of riches. But if it were with the Lot of the Father or with its Lord, or they are impeded by others, it indicates harm for the parents and maternal uncles, or he whose revolution it is [will be] harmed by them or because of them. But if the Sun aspected him from a trine or sextile aspect in the two times, and both were impeded, and especially with it being a nocturnal revolution, both he and his father suffer diverse harms in that year. Also, he will be occupied in diverse ways with riches and dignity. But if the Sun aspected Saturn through a square in the two times, and both were impeded, and the Sun was elevated [over Saturn], some things will vanish in that year, he will inherit from the parents, and he will be sick with cold illnesses, and perhaps he will suffer the sacred illness, and he will be oppressed in pains and labors. If however Saturn were elevated over the Sun, he will suffer sorrows in which his strength will fail, and he will fall into prison and be captured, and he will be idle in all useful matters. And if the Sun aspected him through the opposite in the two times, and both were impeded, chronic suffering will happen to him and his father. If however Saturn will be under the rays in the two times, he will squander his father's riches in that year, and there will be a contrary outcome in his matters. And it will be worse if the revolution were nocturnal, for both he and his father and brothers will suffer many adversities. If however the Sun were in fewer degrees it will be worse in all things, [for] it will rush in [because of] his dignity, and he will be ready for every quarrel, contention, and fight. But if either the conjunction or the aspect would be in only one time, and they were not impeded, lesser evils will touch him.

Moreover, if Saturn were the Lord of the Year and both he and Venus together were impeded in the two times, but Venus would be configured to him, and the Lot of Marriage and its Lord is being impeded by a conjunction or aspect of the bad ones, his women will suffer many evils, or there will be loss on the occasion of them, and there will be loss in his ointments and clothing and money. But if at the two times she aspected him through a trine or sextile aspect and they were impeded, he will linger in unclean places in that year, and his monies will be corrupted, and he will be disturbed in life, and he will make friends with low-class men and women, and he will suffer harms through noble men and women. But if Venus aspected him in the two times through a square, and both were impeded, with Saturn being elevated over Venus, he whose revolution it is will not rejoice with his women in that year, but certain ones of them will have harms, or he will have a quarrel with them, and divorce and separation. If however Venus were elevated over Saturn, his women will obey him and esteem him and be esteemed by him. But if Venus aspected him from the opposite in the two times and both were impeded, he will be sad in that year and moderately glad, and he will suffer harm by women or will be sick, or some one of his women will die; and if Venus is being conjoined to him in the two times, and both were impeded, he will lie down with women or prostitutes in that year, or he will take a sterile wife, or he will cross over from one to the other, and he will never esteem them, nor will he be esteemed by them. If however Venus is being conjoined to him in [only] one of the two times, or she will be configured to him, [the evils] of this kind will be lesser.

Likewise, if Saturn were the Lord of the Year and both he and Mercury were impeded in the two times, it indicates detriment in that year for the one whose revolution it is, [and] corruption, sorrows, anxieties, regrets, and worries about slaves, children, associates, and about things which he will have before his hands, or he will suffer it from an action of this type and on account of hostile and stupid rule. But if Mercury aspected him from a trine or sextile aspect in the two times, and both were impeded, he will suffer on account of computation and letters and teaching and riches, and he will be sluggish and negligent and not well manageable, and lazy in these things which are not impeded for him. But if he aspected him through the square in the two times, and both were impeded, and Saturn[50] is being raised up [over Mercury], he will endure griefs and dangers in his life, and in riches, and he

---

[50] Reading *et* for *autem*.

will lose the rule which he exercises, and he will serve certain people out of necessity, and he will endure necessities on account of talk, and it will pain his mouth or ear. But if Mercury is being elevated, the evils will be less. If however he aspected by the opposite, and both were impeded in the two times, pain will come to be in his mouth and tongue, and he will have detriment on account of words, and he will be impeded in his own acts, and so he will have a cold complexion, and his mind and intellect will be corrupted, he will be sick from windiness, and will be made sad on account of some thievery, and he will endure troubles from all of those with whom he will contend, and his hope will be dashed,[51] for he will embrace life and be made sad on account of riches, and on account of some aforesaid matters. But if Mercury is being conjoined to him and they were both impeded in the two times, he will endure diverse griefs, and he will be lazy and timid in words and matters, and wicked thoughts will rule over him, and he will have a disturbed mind, and when speaking he will not be believed by many and will be sick, and his boys and slaves will suffer harm, and he will endure every kind of evil in that year. In addition to all of this, if Mercury is being conjoined or configured to him in [only] one of the two times, if they were not impeded, all of the above-stated things will be less.

Moreover, if Saturn were the Lord of the Year and both he and the Moon were impeded in the two times, and they are being configured to one another by any figure in the two times, especially with her being minimal in light and number in the two times, it signifies bodily sufferings in that year, and sorrows because of mothers, and on account of sinister rumors. But if the Moon aspected him from a trine or sextile aspect, and both were impeded but Saturn is elevated above her, he will be unprosperous and negligent in doing his [business], and he will disperse the riches of his own parents. But if the Moon were elevated [over him], he will have corruptions, hatred, quarrels with certain [people], he will even disperse the riches of the parents, and be made sad because of children; and if the Moon were in a feminine sign at the time of the revolution, his wife will be inimical to him, and she will seek his harm. If however the Moon aspected him through the opposite [aspect] and both were impeded, illness will befall the parents in a hidden place, and his substance will be used up, he will even have bad habits,[52] and be sad, and he will be harmed in his riches and resources. But if both were in signs of the

---

[51] Omitting *et solita*. Role unclear.
[52] *Consuetudinis*, referring generally to one's habit, customs, and social ties.

likeness of men or wild animals, you should make a determination in that same way: if they were in signs of quadrupeds, he will suffer evils with respect to quadrupeds. But if the Moon is being conjoined to him in the two times [and] both were impeded, it signifies the disease and infirmity of the mother. And if the Moon is being conjoined or configured to him in one of the two times, and both were unencumbered, the above-mentioned things will be less.

And these are the significations of Saturn when he is the Lord of the Year, and he is impeded in the two times and benevolent or malevolent stars are configured to him.

[General comments on delineating the Lord of the Year]

If[53] however the Lord of the Year were also unencumbered in the two times, and an impeded planet aspected him, the signification of good things is diminished (but they will come forth for him with labor). But if the aspect were from the opposite or the square, it signifies much evil with sorrow and labor. And if the aspect were from a trine or sextile, then the harm signified is lessened. Moreover, if the same Lord of the Year were impeded in the two times, but configured to a benevolent planet, [then] he is nevertheless made fortunate. If however the star aspecting him were impeded in one time but unencumbered in the other, it takes away from its own proper signification (whether it were good or bad), but moderately.

Moreover, if some planet aspected the Lord of the Year from the opposite or the square in the nativity, but at the time of the revolution from a sextile or trine, it is good to blend the judgments together. For the square aspect has greater power for harming than the trine does, since the trine is weaker for enmities than the square is. Likewise if diverse stars aspected the Lord of the Year, it is good to make a determination concerning the individ-

---

[53] I have rewritten parts of this paragraph because I believe both the Greek and Latin texts have mixed up some of the conditions (at any rate, the Latin version seems a little more mixed up than the Greek). The Greek version puts it this way: (1) If the Lord of the Year is unharmed in both times, and is being looked upon by an impeded planet, then the good things signified will be lessened. (2) If the aspect is from a square or opposition, then the harm is lessened. (3) If the aspect is from a trine or sextile, then the harm is not lessened. (4) If the Lord of the Year (Saturn) is harmed in both times, but aspecting a benevolent planet, then he becomes (more like) a good planet. It does not make sense to me that (2) squares and oppositions from a planet in a bad condition should be better than (3) trines and sextiles.

ual ones according to [their] own proper disposition and signification and place, just as we said before. But the conjunction of the Lord with the planets, and the conjunction of the planets to each other, if they were concordant, signify goods and luckiness. But if discordant, they indicate unluckiness. The quantity and quality of the outcome is known from the Lord of the Year through himself, and from the planets configured or conjoined to him in their places.

Indeed Saturn, if he were of a bad condition in both the nativity and in the revolution, just as we said before, he will make many troubles in that year, and it will spread affliction. If however Saturn were of a bad condition in the revolution, but he would bear himself well in the nativity, it reduces the wickedness; but in addition if the benevolents will be configured to him, [then] likewise he who had the revolution will be rescued from dangers, and especially with that nativity appearing diurnal and with Saturn going out above the earth. But if he were made unfortunate in the nativity and fortunate at the time of the revolution, he will have mediocre evils. But if a planet will signify some good or evil according to the nativity, and will signify the same course in the revolution, this will be perfected and great, and perhaps will be inevitable and unchangeable.

Moreover, if [a planet] signifies something is coming to be according to the nativity, [but] according to the revolution it signifies that same thing will not come to be (or the other way around), it signifies something will be according to the revolution, but it will not be according to the nativity: you should[54] make an examination of the two significations, and make a determination according to the stronger one. But if they were equal, the determination will be in the middle. Therefore, if the signification of the nativity is stronger, it will surmount one-half of the judgment. But if the signification of the revolution is stronger, [the signification of the nativity] goes down. But if the revolution alone signified something with weakness, it will be middling, and its outcome weak, or the movement[55] will be only imperfect.

In addition to all of this, the significations of revolutions are determined up to one year or whenever the significator was strong. But if the planet which is configured to the Lord of the Year signifies some good or evil, then it shows its own signification when it will steer some part of the time of the

---

[54] Reading *facias* for *faciat*.
[55] Or, "motive."

year, and especially if it were associated to the Lord of the Year by a figure at that time, or to the sign in which the Lord of the Year is, whether according to the nativity or according to the revolution, or it will be configured to the sign of the revolution or to the horoscope or to its Lord, or to the Lord of the disposition of the day.

And these are the significations of Saturn by himself, and of the planets which are configured or conjoined with him. However, there are 8 ways: [1] one, when that planet is of a good condition by itself; [2] second, when it is of a bad condition; third and fourth, when it [3] is being made fortunate by some planets but [4] being made unfortunate by other planets; [5] fifth, [whenever a planet is good by itself, but on the other hand being made fortunate by others];[56] [6] sixth, when it is made unfortunate by itself, but is being configured to a benevolent planet; [7] seventh, when it is being conjoined to that same planet; [8] eighth, the significations of the place, concerning which we must speak immediately.

Chapter II.6: On the signification of Saturn when he is the Lord of the Year, concerning the places in which he is

When Saturn is the Lord of the Year and he happens to be of a good condition in the two times, in his own domicile or exaltation or triplicity, and he were in an angle either in the figure of the profection or in the figure of the revolution: if that angle happened to be that of the Midheaven, it signifies that in that year he acquires possessions and will build buildings and will dig aqueducts; and if it were in an alien sign, these things will be committed to him by an alien person: for instance,[57] he will be applauded as a trustworthy commander and administrator, and he will be praised, [and] will find profit. But if he [were] in an alien sign and in addition were impeded, but the impediment was moderate, he will have disgraces on account of [things] of this kind. If however [it were] immoderate, the loss will be such.

Likewise, if the Lord of the Year were Saturn and he were in the eleventh or fifth place in both times,[58] [and] in a good condition, and in his own

---

[56] Adding from Pingree.
[57] Reading the rest of this sentence primarily with Pingree.
[58] This probably means transiting in a certain house in the nativity, and in that house *derived from* the Ascendant of the year at the revolution. But I can imagine Abū Ma'shar would also allow the planet to transit through the same *natal* house at the revolution.

domicile, he will be happy in that year regarding with respect to his friends, and he will contract with some people about certain matters, and he will build and procure vessels or furniture. But if he were in an alien sign, he will be saddened on account of children and friends, and he will suffer faults[59] and difficulty in his substance. But if in addition he were retrograde, his little abode will be destroyed, and his riches and revenue will be diminished. And if Mars aspected him by a contrary aspect, his riches will suffer loss, and his enemies will rejoice, and he will be saddened with regard to children.

Likewise if Saturn were the Lord of the Year and he happened to be in the 3rd or 9th, in his own domicile and unencumbered by bad ones, in that year he will perform an act about which he will hope to have favor from God, and with respect to a bestowal by some man in the future, and he will construct workshops for himself or for someone of those for whom he has concern; and he will go to some region known to him, and he will labor on account of hoped-for advantage, and he will have concern for his blood-relatives and brothers and foreigners. And if he were in these two places, and they were alien, it signifies things of this kind at a time when he will travel abroad on a long foreign trip, and he will have advantage in it. And if he were moderately impeded, contrary reports about him will be stated on account of faith and [his] sect, and he will fall into worries, and he will suffer evils on the foreign journey, and he will have discords towards blood-relatives and those nearby. If therefore he were retrograde, his intellect will be thrown into confusion, and he will have doubt about his own [religious] sect, and he will perform his work on account of which certain people will be suspicious about him, because he is impious.[60] If, however, with Saturn appearing in such a status, Mars aspected him from the opposite figure,[61] he will suffer loss from thievery or fire.

Moreover, if Saturn were the Lord of the Year, appearing in the second in the two times, free from the bad ones, and in his own domicile, his riches will be increased in that year, and his condition will be prosperous. But if he were in an alien [sign], of a bad condition, his riches will be corrupted by the harm of waters. Likewise, if Saturn were the Lord of the Year, appearing in the 8th in the two times [and of a good condition], he will have advantage on

---

[59] Reading with Pingree (ψόγον) for *imperium*.
[60] Reading with Pingree for the misspellings in the Latin.
[61] Reading *figura opposita* with Pingree for *figura propria*.

the occasion of the dead in that year. But if he were of a bad condition, his riches will be destroyed and he will be saddened because of the dead.

Moreover, if the same planet were the Lord of the Year, appearing in the 6th in the two times, free of the bad ones, he will suffer moderate illnesses from cold and moisture. But if he were impeded it indicates delirium[62] and long diseases; and if a benevolent aspected him, he will be healed and helped by medicines. If however the Lord of the sixth were impeded in addition, his beasts of burden and his slaves will be given up. But if the Lord of the sixth place were unencumbered, they will indeed be sick but they will be healed. Likewise if Saturn were the Lord of the Year, appearing in the twelfth place in the two times, in his own proper domicile, free from the bad ones, he will have success against his enemies, and he will be made friendly to them, and they will praise him, but he will not care about the useful things of life. And if he were in an alien place, or retrograde, he will fall into prison or custody, and will suffer compulsion from his enemies. If however he were of a bad condition or is configured with Mars by a contrary figure, he will endure the greatest torture and wounding.

Moreover if Saturn were the Lord of the Year, in one of the four places which do not aspect the horoscope (namely in the 2nd, in the 6th, in the 8th, and the 12th), and he were impeded, it signifies indifference and idleness and losing hope over things hoped for and the useful things of life. But if in addition he were in an alien place, he will have a bad intention and endure necessities, and some will speak bad things about him, and they will accuse him, and he will be sick with a fever from coldness and moisture or coldness and dryness. If however, appearing in places of this kind, he were oriental or in his own proper place, he will be involved in goodness, while at that time he will be a wanderer and idle.

Moreover if Saturn were in some place in the nativity, and in [that same] place in the revolution (whether from the sign of the profection or from the figure of the revolution of the year), he will have a more ample and more certain signification, and it will show the more desirable nature of the place, and especially if he aspects the rooted place.[63] But if he were in some place in the nativity, but in another one according to the revolution, you should make a commingling through the system of the places which I showed you, so that the judgment would be certain for you. In the same way, consider the

---

[62] Reading with Pingree (φρενίτιδας) for *desipientiam*.
[63] This probably means "his natal place."

significations of the remaining planets from the disposition of the places in which they are. We, however, will make mention of the remaining planets just as we brought it up concerning Saturn and his own proper signification and the configuration or conjunction of the planets to him, and the disposition of the places.

Chapter II.7: On the signification of Jupiter, if he were the Lord of the Year and he were of a good condition

If Jupiter were the Lord of the Year, and he were of a good condition in both the nativity and in the revolution, in that year he will become friendly to kings and princes, and he will be managing their matters, and speedy in [his] accomplishments, having a good outcome, remaining in peace on account of the friendship he will have, he will even be increased, and he will be commended by many, and he will manage a dignity[64] in his fatherland; and if the nativity signified the procreation of children, he will have a child in that year, not to mention he will have opportunity and joy from diverse [people], and he will often acquire riches from the gifts of others or will inherit his father's [goods]. But if he whose revolution it is, is in a dignity in that year, he will rule over many and will acquire that much more. But if [his] fortune were mediocre, he will rule over his equals in that year, and will rejoice in diverse matters and profits and prosperity, and especially if Jupiter were in his own proper domicile or triplicity or bound.

You should also look at both the rays and the Lots and the particular twelfth-parts with which Jupiter is conjoined, or [which] he aspects in the two times: for if he is configured to them by a praiseworthy aspect, it indicates advantages according to their nature.

Moreover, if Jupiter were the Lord of the Year and both he and Mars, both in the nativity and in the revolution, were in a good condition, and [each] is configured to the other by a trine or sextile aspect, he whose revolution it is will be an ruler in that year, experienced in doing things and diligent in works; but he will hold onto honor and an excellent dignity, and advantage from some dignity, and the common people will praise him. But if Mars is being conjoined to him in the two times, and both were of a good

---

[64] *Exercebit*. Medievally, a dignity was a social position and function which one fulfilled and carried out; it should not be considered in terms of a personal sense of dignity.

condition, in that year he will take on a grade and dignity in his own fatherland, and he will be glad. If however either of them were in the domicile of the other, free from the bad ones, he will be powerful in that year, and will gain a dignity. But if Mars is being conjoined or configured to him in [only] one or two [of the] times, the aforesaid will be less.

Likewise, if Jupiter were the Lord of the Year and both he and the Sun were of a good condition in the two times, and they are configured to each other by a trine or sextile aspect, prosperity will be widespread in that year for him whose revolution it is, and he will be involved in the enlargement of life, and he will gain a good marriage-union and a good child. If however the Sun aspected him from a trine[65] aspect [while Jupiter is] retrograding, the aforesaid will be less. But if the Sun were conjoined to him in the two times so that Jupiter happened to be oriental, he will obtain a dignity and diverse advantages, and his parents will rejoice in them, and they will have advantage from him. If however he is conjoined to him in [only] one of the times, with [Jupiter] appearing oriental, the aforesaid will be less. And if the Sun is being conjoined to him in the two times, and he will be under the rays, he will suffer necessities in that year according to the significations of Jupiter. But if the Sun were stronger and he were of a bad condition, the impediment will be greater, and one must fear for him lest perhaps he dies. If however the Sun were not impeded, the impediments will be less; and if Jupiter were stronger, the corruption will be less.

Moreover, if Jupiter were the Lord of the Year and both he and Venus were of a good condition in the two times, and Venus aspected him by any aspect, it signifies an increase of riches in that year from women and noble and well-considered men who mediate, and he will delight in women, and will have advantage from them. And if Venus aspected him by a trine or sextile aspect in the two times, and both were of a good condition, his glory and dignity will be increased in that year, and riches and clothing and grace and well-wishing and exaltation, and these will be because of a woman. But it frequently happens that a child is born to him, and he will rejoice in his child, or he will be glad on account of the children of kings. And if Venus had dignity in the sign in which she is, there will be advantage from some noted people and friends, and especially women. But if she were in an alien sign, the advantage will be from foreigners or enemies, [both] men and women. If however Venus is being conjoined to him in the two times, and both were of

---

[65] Reading with Pingree for "sextile."

a good condition in that year, the one whose revolution it is will acquire glory from people put in charge and administrators, and he will be honorable among men, and will acquire many friends, and will be praised by many superior men,[66] and he will have goodness and advantage on the occasion of miracles and prodigies, and the places of favorably-disposed churchmen, and he will rejoice in women and a marriage-union and children. But if they aspected each other by the opposite, or the aforesaid configurations were in [only] one of the two times, all of the aforesaid will be less.

Likewise, if Jupiter were the Lord of the Year and both he and Mercury were of a good condition in the two times, and Mercury aspected him by a trine or sextile aspect, he whose revolution it was will acquire some good in that year on account of practical knowledge and business and selling and buying, and through writings, and being a treasurer,[67] and estate management; however, he will be a preserver of secrets and a custodian of riches, prudent and sufficiently understanding in matters of this [type of] knowledge; he will overcome those equal to him in dignity and glory and resources and mandates and knowledge; the administrations of some magnates will even be committed to him, and he will be praised by all men, and he will please them and will remain steady and persevere in orations and what is like these, [and he will] sow the seed of his sect. And if he whose revolution it is were of a lesser fortune, and of the common laborers, he will have advantage from his profession and the work of his own hands. And if Mercury is being conjoined to him in the two times, and both were of a good condition, he will have advantage in that year, and his condition will be increased, and his faithfulness toward the Lord [God], and modesty and prudence of the mind, and eloquence in discussions, and he will have advantage on account of things of this kind, and on account of other diverse matters, and he will have familiarity with magnificent men, secretaries, and the administration of those goods will be committed to him. But if Mercury were conjoined [to him] in one of the times, or configured in another figure, it will be taken away from all of the above-stated things.

Moreover, if Jupiter were the Lord of the Year, and both he and the Moon were unencumbered in the two times, and they are being configured to each other from a trine or sextile aspect, it indicates that his glory and

---

[66] Or, "elder" (*prioribus*).

[67] *Dispensationem.* This can also refer to weighing things (as one weighs produce or coins); it refers essentially to managing money.

dignity will be increased in that year, and he will acquire a good reputation and praise from men, and that he will perfect quickly whatever work and whatever kind of act he undertook; he will even seek to generate children, and children will be born to him in that year, or his women will conceive; and he will inherit the paternal substances; and if he whose revolution it is, is of royal birth and the Moon were increased in light, he will obtain renowned glory. If however he were of mediocre fortune, they will commit to him some dominion over the multitude of the people, and he will practice justice with them, and he will embrace a blameless life of good presumption. But if he were of the lowest fortune, he will be elevated over those equal to him in fortune, and he will have a position of first place in those things which we said.

But, concerning the aspect of the planets to Jupiter, namely by their square and opposite, we have not dealt with it [here] on account of a reason of this kind: because in this section[68] we are comprehending it with respect to the friendship of Jupiter and of the planets with him. But the squares and oppositions of the planets to him often signify some contrariety about which we have[69] proposed to speak in what follows, but we will lay it out plainly.

Chapter II.8: On the significations of Jupiter if he were the Lord of the Year, and were of a bad condition

If Jupiter were the Lord of the Year and in both the nativity and the revolution appearing retrograde or under the rays, or in an alien place, or occidental or in the domicile of a malevolent, or cadent from the angles and in contrary places, it takes away the renown of him whose revolution it is, and decreases his luckiness, and puts down his glory. It even signifies a multitude of expenses and a troublesome pouring out of riches, and he will do these things with a voluntary and spontaneous will, for the reason that he craves praise from many people; he will even be saddened on account of parents and children, and certain noble persons, and diverse matters, and on account of the violence of his life, and especially if Jupiter were in the 6th. But if the malevolents were conjoined or configured to him from the opposite or the square, and they were elevated over him while he was

---

[68] Reading *divisione* for *derisione*.
[69] Omitting *non*.

impeded, and especially in the place of fathers or in the place of children, or if he had dignities in these places, [and] it even happened that the Lot of the Father or the Lot of the Mother or the Lot of Children or their Lords were of a bad condition, it signifies that he whose revolution it is will be saddened on account of the death of the children or the father or mother, according to the nature of the sign in which Jupiter is, or the nature of the Lot and its Lord. And if he would be conjoined to some one of the Lots or to one of the rays or the twelfth-parts in the two times, or he aspected them by a contrary figure, it signifies griefs and instabilities for those things whose aforesaid signifiers are present.

One must even inspect both the aspects and conjunctions of the planets toward [Jupiter]. For if the malevolents aspected him from a trine or sextile [while he is] disposed in such a manner, they do not signify great danger on account of the suitability of the figure and the friendship of the complexion; nevertheless, on account of [Jupiter's] own impotence and the impediment, he is not able to attain to the perfection of luckiness. If the planet were even of a bad condition, it adds its own misfortune, namely in those things of which it is the signifier: for he whose revolution it is will be saddened over things of this kind, and he will endure labor or fatigue. [This] also [pertains to] the square and its opposite, about which we will speak in what follows.

Therefore, if Jupiter were the Lord of the Year and Mars were of a good condition in the nativity, and they aspected each other by a square, but Jupiter were elevated over Mars, they signify that his degree will be made firm, and he will rule over his city; frequently he will even obtain dignities and advantages from kings or the leaders of armies. However, he will be saddened on account of children and riches, and some portion of his parents' riches will be harmed. But if they aspected each other by an aspect of this kind in the two times, and they were both of a bad condition, it takes away the prosperities which we stated before, and he whose revolution it is will suffer expenses and intolerable adversities. And if Mars were elevated above Jupiter, in whatever [quality] it was, he whose revolution it is will be harmed by magistrates and those having power, and he will even be made sad by those who have a position of rulership in metals, and on account of the removal of advantages and riches, also of close associations with people and a child; and his labor will be multiplied on account of some trick and fraud and envy and false accusations and contention. Likewise, if they were configured in an aspect of this kind, [and] they were good in both times, the evils [will be] less. Again, if Mars aspected him from the opposite in the two times, and both were impeded, he will endure anxieties in that year because of glory and women and children, and he will see the death of someone of those who are protected by him, and perhaps he will be conjoined to a wife, and a child will be born to him, and his quarrels[70] will multiply and his affairs will be confused, he will corrupt his own riches and acquire others; in that year he will even have disturbances until the middle of [the year]. But if they were unencumbered, little of the aforesaid will come about, or on the occasion of such he will suffer many tumults and movements, and he will believe he is going to suffer the greatest adversities, but he will not suffer [them].

Likewise if Jupiter were the Lord of the Year and the Sun with him, of a good condition in both the nativity and the revolution, and they aspected each other by a square, and the Sun were elevated, his glory will be increased in that year, and the glory of his own father, and he will have advantage in diverse matters. But if he were of a bad condition, both he and his parents will suffer need and difficulty in their riches, and he will be removed and they will travel abroad on a joyless[71] foreign journey, and they will have discords with superior persons—but the persons of this kind will be people known [to him] or [his] neighbors, or blood-relatives who envy them. But if Jupiter were elevated over the Sun and both were of a good condition in the two times, he whose revolution it is, and his parents, will find advantages and glory and dignities and a superior honor in that year. But if they were of a bad condition, they will be made sad on the occasions of such things. And if the Sun aspected [Jupiter] from the opposite in the two times, and they were both of a good condition, there will be joy in all of his things in that year, and his glory will be increased, and secret business matters will be committed to him by those having power, and by some noble men, and kings will consult him in their business, and they will listen to his advice. But if they aspected each other by the aforesaid aspect and they were impeded, not only will all of the aforesaid be diminished, but they will even have detriment on the occasion of [things] of this kind.

Moreover, if Jupiter were the Lord of the Year and both he and Venus were of a good condition in the two times, and they aspected each other,

---

[70] Reading much of the rest of the sentence with Pingree; the Latin has missed a few words.
[71] Reading with Pingree for "delightful."

with [Jupiter] being elevated [over Venus], in that year his glory will be increased, and he will have advantage on account of women, and he will have a splendid life, and will practice purity, and he will prove [the truth of] his own sect and of its secrets, and he will perform works of sanctity and justice. But if he were of a bad condition, he will suffer trials on the occasion of the aforesaid. And if Venus were elevated over Jupiter, and both were impeded in the two times, in that year he whose revolution it is will compete with respect to games and with respect to the close association of women, through which he will be saddened; he will even acquire riches from other women, but he will harm some [women], and he will be angry at some one of his friends, and certain of his monies will be destroyed, and likewise with banquets. But if they were of a good condition, he will have advantage and joy in all of the above-stated things. And if Venus aspected him from the opposite in the two times, and both were of a good condition, his glory will grow, for many will yield to him and they will praise and esteem [him], and he will rule over his own family and acquire riches, and he will preserve them. If however both[72] were of a bad condition, all of the above-stated things will be diminished, and he will be saddened on the occasion of them.

Likewise if Jupiter were the Lord of the Year and both he and Mercury were of a good condition in the two times, and they aspected each other by the square, with Jupiter being elevated over Mercury, he whose revolution it is will be given to the teaching of letters, and he will assist many people, and he will attain goods and advantages on account of his assistance. And if they were of a bad condition, all of the above-stated things will be diminished, and he will be saddened on the occasion of them. But if, with Mercury being elevated [over Jupiter] in the two times, both were impeded, [he will be] anxious, he will rejoice in the acquisition of riches, and with respect to worthless profit and mediocre advantages, and he will be without thanks among men, and he will be angry in spending time with them, and he will harm some and will be an enemy to them. And if they were of a good condition, he will have joy and advantage with respect to all the above-stated things. And if Mercury aspected him by the opposite in the two times, and both were of a good condition, his teaching and knowledge will be added to in that year, he will even know secret counsels, and will handle sales and purchases, and will be praised by many, esteemed by his family. But if both[73]

---

[72] Reading with Pingree for "it."
[73] Reading with Pingree for "it."

were of a bad condition, all of the above-stated things will be diminished, and he will be saddened on account of these.

Moreover, if Jupiter were the Lord of the Year and both he and the Moon were of a good condition in the two times, and they are configured to each other by a square, and Jupiter was elevated [over the Moon] (whether it was a nocturnal or diurnal revolution), he whose revolution it is ([and] even his parents) will be in a good condition in that year, and they will be commended by all. They will also have advantage through blood-relatives and they will take up an increase of glory. But if they were of a bad condition, the aforesaid will have diminution, and they will be saddened on the occasion of them. But if the Moon were elevated [over Jupiter] and they were of a good condition, they will be praised by many, and honored by those having power as well as by private individuals. And if they were of a bad condition, the above-stated things will fail, he will even suffer contention[74] [and] the diminution of glory and riches, and he will be deceived with respect to his own estate management. And if the Moon aspected him by the opposite in the two times, and both were of a good condition, [and] were the Moon even in fewer degrees, his glory will be increased in that year and he will acquire riches, and he will be glad with his blood-relatives and children, and he will have familiarity with kings and princes, and he will be in a good condition, and he will bestow much upon himself, and his own intention will be good enough for himself, nor will he follow the counsels of others, and if he set out to go abroad he will return. But if they were impeded in the two times, and the Moon were in more degrees, he will suffer the diminution of riches and will be saddened on account of diverse reasons, and especially at the beginning of the year.

[Remember that] we [already] spoke before about the configuration of Saturn to [Jupiter], in which we dealt with the disposition of Saturn; and indeed these significations belong to Jupiter when he is of a good condition and benevolent planets are conjoined or configured to him, or if he were of a bad condition and malevolent stars are being conjoined or configured to him. But if Jupiter were of a good condition, and a malevolent planet aspected him, or he were of a bad condition and a benevolent star is configured to him, it signifies the same things as we said before with respect to Saturn.[75]

---

[74] Reading *contentionem* for *contentionis*.
[75] Not the same content, but the significations will be formally mixed or improved or made worse in the way they were for Saturn.

Chapter II.9: On the signification of Jupiter if he were the Lord of the Year, from the places in which he is

If Jupiter were the Lord of the Year and he were of a good condition in both the nativity and in the revolution, and in his own proper place or one in which he has dignity, and he were in one of the four angles (whether they were of the angles according to the inception or of the angles according to the revolution, or the Ascendant of the revolution),[76] he will be famous in that year, and his glory will be augmented, [and] even [his] dignity and riches. And if he were in the Midheaven, there will be [things] of this kind on the occasion of magnates. But if the Ascendant, from his own motive and his own struggle and labor. But if in the west, this will be because of women and adversaries. And if in the angle of the house of fathers, because of fathers and blood-relatives and immovable things and little abodes. And if he were of a bad condition in these places, or retrograde, it signifies the diminution of glory, and the corruption of riches, and his negligence in acquiring [them]. Indeed he will be saddened according to the signification of the angle in which he is.

Likewise, if Jupiter were the Lord of the Year and of a good condition in the two times, and he happened to be in the eleventh place, he will have a praiseworthy life in that year, and be involved in every [form] of rest, and he will be praised by many, and his friends will have advantage through him. And if he were of a bad condition, he will be very inquisitive, and have a bad high-handedness, doing no work; he will even be saddened because of friends and things hoped for.[77] Moreover if Jupiter were the Lord of the Year and he were unencumbered in the fifth in the two times, he will be made fortunate in generating children (if the nativity indicated the generation of children), and he will rejoice in children, if he had children. And if he were of a bad condition, he will be saddened on account of children and certain legations and foreign travels.

Likewise, if Jupiter were the Lord of the Year, appearing in the ninth or third in the two times, of a good condition, he will be praised in that year because of piety, and he will go on a pilgrimage for the sake of divine worship, and he will be praised by many and will be glad regarding his

---

[76] Reading with Pingree. The angles of the revolution and the angles of the Ascendant of the revolution are redundant; my guess is that the original included the angles of the profected sign of the year, as well.

[77] Reading with Pingree for *per annos…species*.

brothers and about certain rumors. But if he were of a bad condition, he will have empty glory in that year, and he will learn sinister rumors, even [suffer] harms and griefs because of brothers, and he will disdain his own faith, and have doubt about it. And if set out to go abroad, he will encounter things appearing against his wishes.

Moreover, if Jupiter were the Lord of the Year and in the second or eighth place in the two times, of a good condition, it signifies leisure and staying [in one place]. However, he will obtain some advantages without seeking [them], and without a struggle, or on the occasion of the dead. But if he were of a bad condition, it signifies that he will make many expenses with reluctance; even griefs and contentions because of the acquisition of riches.

Likewise if Jupiter were in the sixth or twelfth in the two times, of a good condition, he will be praised by a certain low-class man and the ignoble vulgar [people], and he will have advantage from captives, and he will be reconciled with his enemies. But if he were of a bad condition in the two places, he will suffer illnesses from windiness and certain other ones, and griefs through enemies and prisons. But if Jupiter were in one [of them] at the time of the nativity, but he happened to be in [the other] in the revolution (whether he has the same disposition in it as he had in the nativity, or another), it is good for you to make a commingling of his dispositions from the two times (as we stated before in the treatment of Saturn); and make a determination according to a commingling of this kind.

Moreover, if Jupiter were the Lord of the Year and at the time of the revolution he was in one of the four places which do not aspect the Ascendant, [then] he whose revolution it is will be inconspicuous in that year, nor will advantage reach him, and many of his friends and those known to him will despise him; he will even handle certain unuseful matters, but he will have [only] a middling or no concern for useful things. And if he were of a bad condition in these places, he will suffer anxieties on the occasion of them.

Chapter II.10: On the significations of Mars if he were the Lord of the Year and of a good condition

If Mars were the Lord of the Year and in both the nativity and in the revolution he was in his own light,[78] direct and quick in course and in good places, and in his own proper sect, and in a sign in which he has dignity, it makes him whose revolution it is, strong of mind and throwing out every laziness and idleness and sorrow, and he will be skilled and prudent, and ready for works and the handling of diverse matters, and eager for works, and proficient in acquiring [things], and he will obtain what he sought from powerful men, and he will be glorious in his own parts [of the land], and he will have great advantages from his works; and the end of his matters will be the best. But if Mars were in an alien sign, of a good condition, there will be advantage from pilgrims and foreigners; and if he were in his own proper sign there will be advantage from friends and noted[79] people; and if he were in signs of the likeness of men, he will acquire friendships from men, and he will have gladness and advantage and praise from them. And if he were in a watery sign, there will be usefulness on the occasion of waters and moist things.

In the same way, and in the rest of the signs, consider[80] even the projections of rays and the Lots and the particular twelfth-parts to which Mars is being conjoined or configured in the two times, in harmonious and friendly figures: because even their Lords have significations, and you should make a determination according to that declaration of advantage.

Moreover, if Mars were the Lord of the Year and both he and Jupiter were of a good condition in the two times, but he is being conjoined or configured with him from a trine or sextile aspect, he whose revolution it is will have good fortune from older people;[81] his prosperity and glory will be increased, even his subordinates and household intimates will be subject to him and [be his] followers, and the militia and the people and the army, and he will rule over many, and his enemies will be subject to him. And if Mars were in Aries or Capricorn, he will rule over his enemies, and his power in battles will be increased, and also his beasts of burden and arms, and

---

[78] This probably means he is of the sect of the chart (see Sahl's *Introduct.* §7), but it could also mean that he is outside the Sun's rays.
[79] Or, people "known to" him (*notis*).
[80] Omitting an extra *considera*.
[81] Reading with Pingree for "kings having long-lasting prosperity."

everything which Mars signifies. But if he whose revolution it was, were of middling fortune, and his nativity does not indicate great luckiness, he will befriend glorious and illustrious men, and leaders and soldiers of armies (namely, great persons), and he will have advantage from them. And if he were conjoined to a fortune, in the end he will acquire advantage from militant persons, and from those who handle Martial arts. Consider even the sign in which Mars was, both in the nativity and in the revolution, whether [it was] of royal signs, or [those] of middling fortune or the lowest [kind], and you should make a commingling of it and the nature of the sign.[82]

Likewise, if the Sun aspected him in the two times from a trine or sextile aspect, and both were of a good condition, his glory and prosperity and riches will be increased, he will be conjoined to a wife, he will even have children, and he will obtain an increase of glory from powerful men and magnates, also soldiers and the leaders of armies, and he will be praised by many.

Moreover, if Venus aspected him in the two times from a trine or sextile aspect, and both were of a good condition, and he were the Lord of the Lot of Marriage-Union in the seventh, in the aspect of fortunes, his riches and advantages will be increased, and he will be conjoined in marriage, and he will be delighted in women and in their sexual intercourse, and he will rejoice in them, and he will have advantage through them, and he will go to bed in a hidden way with some [people], and his children will have increase and clothing, and he will have friendship with princes and powerful men and humbler ones. And if Mars and Venus were in signs in which they have dignities, he will have [the aforesaid] because of a woman or someone noted.[83] But if they were in an alien sign, these things will happen in a foreign land and through alien persons.

Likewise, if Mercury aspected him from a trine or sextile aspect and they were both of a good condition, the advantage and shrewdness of him whose revolution it was will be increased, and he will be experienced in doing things, and he will be nimble and praiseworthy in matters, and his eloquence and teaching and knowledge, too, and intellect.

---

[82] There may be a mix-up by Abū Ma'shar between two notions: the native being of a given status, and the type of sign showing the source of the benefit/harm. *BA* IV.2-3 (pp. 188, 190) is helpful here. If the Lord of the Year is in a royal (i.e., fiery) sign, it indicates kings; if in the domicile of a friend, from friends; if in a royal but alien sign, from alien kings, *etc.* But whether the native is of a high, middle, or low status is a different matter.

[83] Or perhaps, those "known to" him (*notis*).

Moreover, if the Moon aspected him in the two times from a trine or sextile aspect and both were of a good condition, and the revolution is nocturnal, but with the Moon appearing in minimal light, it signifies the acquisition of goods and advantage, and prosperity in handling business matters through him, and enjoyments.

But we have not made mention of the conjunction of the planets with him by the other aspects, because they signify adverse things—[but] the present intention is [to speak] concerning good aspects.

Chapter II.11: On the signification of Mars, if he were the Lord of the Year and was of a bad condition

If Mars were the Lord of the Year, and both in the nativity and in the revolution he was retrograde or under the rays, or in the heart of the Sun,[84] or occidental, or in an alien place, or cadent from the angle in bad places, it signifies (for him whose revolution it is) wrath and disturbance of the mind, and the storminess and foolishness of the intellect, and unsettledness of thoughts, and being troubled and inexperienced in doing things; he will even be attacked by wild animals and horses, and fire, and heat, and blood, and diverse illnesses, and not-unencumbered journeys, and useless foreign travels, and the detriment of brothers and sisters. But all of these [are] according to the signification of Mars and of the sign in which he is; and if he were under the rays, it indicates detriment from fire, and burning and thievery, and hidden matters, and deceptions, frauds and illnesses. But if Mars is impeded in the other ways which we said before, it is good to make a commingling of him and of the sign in which he is—both him and the malevolent who impedes him—and to make a determination according to this. For if he were in signs of the likeness of men, there will be harm from certain works and his discussions, even from a fight, the false accusations of enemies, and thievery and robbery. But if in addition Mars were in his station, and slow in course, it will spread the evils, it even signifies harms, chains, also confinement and anger, and especially if he were in a sign hateful to him. But if he were in a feral sign, in a sign of reptiles, there will be an attack by wild animals or by reptiles; but if he were in another[85] sign, it indicates a flowing of blood, also

---

[84] This probably indicates combustion, not the good condition of *kasmīmī*.
[85] I am unsure what this means—perhaps that any other type of sign will indicate normal Martial things.

wounds and sores,[86] and brandings[87] from fire, and illnesses from heat, and useless foreign travels. But if in addition to these he were in the domicile of a friend of his, the impediment will be moderate and from some known cause. But if he were in an alien sign, or in the domicile of an enemy, the evils will be stronger and more durable. And if he were in his own sect, the harm will be middling. If however he were impeded in an angle, the adversity will be greater.

Consider also the rays and the [Lots and the][88] particular twelfth-parts to which Mars is being conjoined, and to which he is configured in the two times, by a contrary figure. For these signify some misfortunes. But when Mars will signify some misfortune in nocturnal revolutions, it will be dissolved quickly. Moreover, if Mars were the Lord of the Year and some unfortunate planet aspected him in the two times from a trine or sextile aspect, it will introduce to him (whose revolution it is) detriment according to its own proper nature.

Likewise, if Mars were the Lord of the Year and both he and the Sun were of a bad condition in the two times, and they aspected each other by a square, and Mars were elevated over the Sun, he whose revolution it is will be rash and irrational, and litigious and sad, curious about diverse things, and about riches and expenses, and wicked misfortune will happen to him regarding his children, or one of them will be destroyed, and especially if the revolution were diurnal and both [of them] were above the earth. But if the Sun were elevated [over Mars], he will fall into illnesses and diverse dangers, and he will entreat some one of the rulers on his knees, and he will endure harms from him. But if the Sun aspected him in the day by the opposite in the two times, and both were of a bad condition, he will suffer griefs and diverse harms in that year, and he will fall from on high, even his father will endure a contrary danger or will be killed in a violent death. But if the revolution were nocturnal, he will be negligent, succeeding in nothing, [and] even if he undertook some work he will not perfect it; he will use up [his] riches, and he will suffer affliction in his business matters. Moreover, if the Sun were conjoined to him in the two times and both were impeded, he will be very fickle in that year, not persevering in any matter, and he will be denounced and blamed by many, and he will endure diverse sorrows, and

---

[86] Or, "ulcers" (*ulcera*).
[87] This could also include cauterizing (*cauteria*).
[88] Reading *partes et* for *per*.

perhaps iron or fire, or experience the royal wrath; he will even disperse his paternal riches, and he will have pain in the eyes, or a misfortune will come to be with respect to them, and his father will endure great misfortune or he will be destroyed, and especially if it were in an angle or in one succeeding the angle. But if the Sun were conjoined to him, or configured [to him] in one of the two times, the aforesaid will be less.

Moreover, if Mars were the Lord of the Year and both he and Venus were impeded in the two times, and they aspected each other through a square, with Mars being elevated over Venus, he whose revolution it is will be saddened on the occasion of women and enemies, and enmities [towards] him will be renewed, and he will have detriment through them. He will even go to bed with slave girls, or he will practice foul things on account of a marriage-union and sexual intercourse. But if Venus were elevated [over Mars], appearing in the same disposition, each of the aforesaid will be more moderated and respectable. And if Venus aspected him by the opposite in the two times, and both were of a bad condition, there will be excessively changeable things in that year, and he will be saddened on the occasion of a child, [and] even of enemies and women, and certain of them will be ill or die. Moreover if Venus were conjoined in the same [way] in the two times, with both appearing in a bad condition, she signifies just as we said about the square. But if she were conjoined in one of the two times, or they were not both of a bad condition, the evils will be less.

Moreover, if Mars were the Lord of the Year and both he and Mercury were impeded in the two times, and they aspected each other by a square, with Mars being elevated over Mercury, in that year he will harm some people with an obvious harm, [but] without a reason, and he will rob certain people, and will accuse, and frequently will have contentions with some people and because of certain estate managements, and he will have the greatest harms on the occasion of them, and on the occasion of speaking, and he will be accused regarding things which he has neither done nor spoken, and especially if the revolution were diurnal (for the reason that Mars is not in his own sect). But if the revolution were nocturnal, whatever things we said before will be diminished. And if Mercury were elevated [over Mars], in that year he will do [something] unjust to some people, and he will have a bad high-handedness, and be quickly sated,[89] and remembering evil

---

[89] That is, fickle.

[done to him],[90] and capable at [stealing] things, and proficient in the assembling of riches. And if Mercury aspected him by the opposite in the two times, and both were impeded, in that year he will be shameless and immodest, loving to lie, and despising the truth, while handling frauds and tricks, and perhaps he will handle poisons in order to harm some people; and his revenue[91] will be constricted, and he will make a pledge[92] in faith [to marry] some [women], and on account of that he will have contentions and judgments, and he will have detriment on the occasion of such things. (And if Saturn had dignity in the place of Mercury, he whose revolution it is will go into exile from his own fatherland.) But if Mercury were conjoined to [Mars] in the two times, and he were of a good condition, his knowledge will increase in that year, and he will love frauds and tricks, [and] even lies and contentions; and if he were of a bad condition, he will suffer detriment on the occasion of [things] of this kind. But if they were of a good condition, he will have advantage from them, he will even be praised and will obtain whatever he desires. If however both were impeded and under the rays, he will have a close association with thieves and he will pursue counterfeit[93] letters. And if they were of a good condition, he will have advantage on the occasion of them. But if Mercury were conjoined to Mars or aspected him in [only] one of the two times, the aforesaid will be less.

Likewise, if Mars were the Lord of the Year and both he and the Moon were impeded [in the two times] and aspected each other by a square, and Mars were elevated [over the Moon], in that year he will suffer the harm of his mother, and his riches will be restricted, and he will see the death of someone esteemed by him; but oftentimes he whose revolution it is, will die, or someone of his own blood-relatives will, or he will have an illness involving the brain or through which his mind will be captured, and especially if Mars were in the bounds of Saturn but the Moon in the bounds of Mars or Mercury. But if the Moon were elevated over Mars, his mother will suffer harm in that year, and he will be distressed with regard to riches. And if the Moon aspected him by an opposition in the two times, and both were of a bad condition, he will suffer a vicious illness, and some limb of his will be amputated by iron, and he will endure sorrows on the occasion of women.

---

[90] Adding with Pingree.
[91] Gr. *eisodos* (missing in Latin). This word can also refer to one's rights of entry and passage into various places. At any rate, his ability to do what he wants will be restricted.
[92] Reading with Pingree for *iubebit* (which might be a misread for a manuscript's *nubebit*).
[93] Reading with Pingree for *adaptabit*.

But if the Moon is being conjoined to him in the two times and both were of a bad condition, he will be full of labor and will grow terribly ill, and a limb of his will be amputated by iron. But if the Moon were conjoined to him in [only] one of the two times, and both were of a good condition, the evils will be less.

Chapter II.12: On the signification of Mars from his places, if he were the Lord of the Year

If Mars were the Lord of the Year and both in the nativity and in the revolution he were of a good condition in one of the angles, in that year he whose revolution it is will obtain what he wanted from powerful men and soldiers, and he will be frightful among those like him,[94] victorious with respect to those turned against him, and praiseworthy in all of his close associations, and he will find dignity and glory. And if he were in the Midheaven, he will obtain what he wanted from kings; which if he were in another place, the signification of the goods will be according to the nature of the angles. But if he were of a bad condition in the two times, either he will endure fire or robbery, or he will be sick from [bad] blood, or from some hot disposition. And if he were retrograde, he will flee from his fatherland and will endure dangers, and it must be feared lest perhaps he suffer by iron. And he will make expenditures on the occasion of journeys and children, and especially if the revolution is nocturnal and Mars is in the Midheaven. But if he were in the west, diseases and cuts from iron and diverse griefs will befall him, though he will prevail against his enemies. But if he were in the fourth, his habitations will be corrupted, and the houses in which he stays, and he will use up [his] riches, and he will suffer misfortunes for diverse reasons, but after that he will be liberated from them.

Moreover, if Mars were the Lord of the Year and were of a good condition in the two times, in the eleventh or fifth, it signifies gladness through blood-kin, and an increase of children, and of glory and dignity on the occasion of friends, and these things will all happen to him from militant persons; he will have advantage from works of fire or blood, and he will often trouble himself with foreign travel, and perhaps he will complete [a journey]. And if Mars were in an angle or in these two places, in a good

---

[94] That is, among people of his own social rank.

condition just as we said before, and he whose revolution it was were a pilgrim,[95] far from his own fatherland, he will return to it. But if Mars were of a bad condition in these two places, it indicates anxieties and worries from blood-relatives and children, and the enmities of enemies.

Likewise, if Mars were the Lord of the Year, appearing in the ninth or in the third in the two times, of a good condition, he whose revolution it is will go on a foreign journey and will discover goods, and he will be praised and strong in his foreign travels. But if he were of a bad condition, he will be accused over some things, of which certain ones will be true and certain ones false; and he will go on a foreign journey and be harmed, and he will incur necessities and will be sick from a hot infirmity, and he will be put in danger from [some] danger and wild animals, especially if Mars were in Leo and Scorpio.

Moreover, if Mars were the Lord of the Year and he were of a good condition in the two times, [and] in the second place, he will obtain good things and advantages from the resources of someone unknown to him; but if he were of a bad condition he will disperse and use up [his] riches. Likewise, if Mars were the Lord of the Year and he were of a good condition in the two times, appearing in the eighth place, he will get advantage from the dead and inheritances; but if he were of a bad condition, he whose revolution it is will have enmities and contentions on the occasion of them, and he will disperse his own riches.

Likewise, if Mars were the Lord of the Year, of a good condition, appearing in the twelfth in the two times, he whose revolution it is will not be eager in the useful affairs of life in that year; and he will have advantage from his parents, and will have security from his enemies. But if he were of a bad condition, he will endure trouble on the occasion of the aforesaid. Moreover, if Mars were the Lord of the Year, of a good condition, appearing in the sixth in the two times, he will have a good disposition in the body [and] will overcome his enemies. But if he were of a bad condition, he will have illnesses from hotness and moisture, and the bubbling up of blood. And if Saturn aspected him, bloody froth and illnesses and black choler will come to be with them.

But if Mars were disposed in some place in the nativity, and in that same place at the time of the revolution, or namely [in that same place] from the

---

[95] Or, a foreigner (*peregrinus*).

Ascendant of the revolution or from the sign[96] of the profection, and he aspected his own place according to the nativity, or he were in it, what he determines will be very strong. But if he were altered, it will be right to make every commingling in the significations of the places, just as we showed [you] before.

Chapter II.13: On the signification of the Sun if he were the Lord of the Year and he were of a good condition

If the Sun happened to be the Lord of the Year, we do not take him principally for determining the condition of that year, but we look at the sign in which the direction of the *hīlājes* has arrived (whether the Sun is the *hīlāj* or another), taking as the [primary] significator (with [the Sun]) a planet of the nativity or a planet of the revolution, and the ones which are configured with the Sun, wherever the Sun was in that sign; then we look to see in what place the Sun was, and we take secondarily the determinations which are from that. And if they were in a good condition in both the nativity and the revolution, in its own proper domicile or exaltation, or in some place in which it had dignity, and it were above the earth in good places, it signifies in that year (for him whose revolution it is) nearness to kings, and the dignities of powerful men, and more illustrious rankings, and an increase of glory and riches and advantages; he will also be praised by many and in councils; he will be experienced in his works and in discussions and knowledge, he will harm certain people but he will help others, and he will be promoted in the service of powerful men, and the condition of his parents will be prosperous, and that of his middle brothers.

However, it is good to consider the projections of the rays, and the Lots and the particular twelfth-parts to which the Sun is conjoined or figured in the two times: for they signify determinations according to their nature.

Likewise, if the Sun were the Lord of the Year and Venus aspected him in the two times by a sextile,[97] and both were of a good condition, he whose revolution it is will be praised by many in that year, and he will be steered well, and his knowledge will be increased, and he will prosper in discussions too, and in works, and he will have manifest and true dreams. And if Venus

---

[96] Reading with Pingree. This paragraph allows him to be in the same place natally, or derived from the profection, or derived from the Ascendant of the year.
[97] Obviously this could only be by a whole-sign sextile configuration.

were conjoined to him in the two times, and they were both unencumbered,[98] and the revolution were nocturnal and Venus occidental (or with the revolution appearing diurnal and she oriental), disposed in each [figure such that she is][99] distant from the solar rays, and appearing [from under them], in that year he will obtain benefits from the children of kings and [from] kings, and he will be praised by many, and he will be fortunate in all of his close associations, and he will be happy about certain works of Venus. But if the sect of the revolution were to the contrary, namely according to day and night, while Venus [is] with the Sun, under[100] the rays, it takes away some of the aforesaid.

Moreover, if the Sun were the Lord of the Year and he were with Mercury [and] of a good condition in both the nativity and in the revolution, and Mercury were distant from the solar rays, whether he was oriental or occidental, in that year some dignity will be committed to [the native], and he will rule over many, and he will be eager in speeches and in things written, and he will be friendly with excellent secretaries, and he will be praised by many, and pronounced fortunate by all, and he will have advantage from slaves and clients.

Likewise, if the Sun were the Lord of the Year and the Moon aspected him from a trine or sextile aspect in the two times, he will acquire immense riches, and his glory will be increased, and he will beget offspring, and he will be involved in good things and handling those things which the Moon signifies. And if she aspected him from the square in the two times, and both were of a good condition, he will arrive at an honor and riches and diverse advantages, and he will be praised by many, and he will be prosperous in administrating.[101] But if she aspected him by the opposite in the two times, and both were of a good condition, his contentions and quarrels will be multiplied, and he will be verbose, and he will overcome his enemies. And if she were conjoined to him in the two times, and both were of a good condition, and the Moon were far from his rays, they signify the same things which we stated about the sextile and trine, but he will be subjected to griefs whose outcome will be for the good; he will even engage in frauds and hidden things. But if the Moon were under the rays in the two times, and

---

[98] Adding this phrase with Pingree.
[99] Reading with Pingree.
[100] Omitting "not."
[101] *Dispensationibus.* This also has banking connotations.

both were of a good condition, he will stick to plotting frauds, defrauding and false accusations, and he will have a provocation of this kind.

In addition, one must know that if the planets were in the heart of the Sun and of a good condition, good things will be signified; but if they were of a bad condition, the contrary.[102]

Chapter II.14: On the signification of the Sun if he were the Lord of the Year and were of a bad condition

If the Sun were the Lord of the Year, we have already said before that the signification belongs to the distributor, and to the Lord of the sign in which the distribution from the *hīlāj* is, with the uniting significators which we stated before. Which if the Sun were impeded, it is signified that he whose revolution it is will incur necessities from these things on the occasions which we stated before, and it will go badly [on account of] the condition of his parents, and dignities, and the glories of him whose revolution it is. But it is good to observe their conjunctions to the Lots, and the rays, and the particular twelfth-parts, and the impediment will be according to the kinds of their significations.

Therefore, if the Sun were the Lord of the Year and Venus aspected him in both the nativity and the revolution from a sextile aspect, and both were of a bad condition, it signifies that he will be saddened on the occasion of officials and women and money, and he will have anxiety and much sorrow, and will handle it badly, and he will be blamed and accused by many.

But if Venus were conjoined to him in the two times, and they were both impeded, and Venus were under the rays, he will suffer from women, and on the occasion of them, and from enemies, and [he will suffer] sorrows on account of riches and children, and his body will suffer from illness, and he will be accused by many, and he will engage in frauds and difficulties and certain hidden things, and he will be harmed on account of Venereal works.

Likewise, if the Sun were the Lord of the Year and Mercury were conjoined to him in the two times, and both were impeded, he whose revolution it is will endure griefs and diverse troubles from political powers and from certain powerful men, and some one of the powerful people will be angry at

---

[102] This is potentially an important point, that being in the heart does not necessarily make a planet's operation good and successful. But it does go against *Gr. Intr.* VII.630-35, which states that planets in the heart will signify (good) fortune.

him. However, he will turn towards writing implements, and business, and writing, and people in authority,[103] and he will be subject to someone, and he will have contentions on account of diverse reasons, and he will be saddened on account of children and slaves and those subject to him.

Moreover, if the Sun were the Lord of the Year and he were configured to the Moon in the two times from a trine or sextile aspect, and both were impeded, on account of the harmony of the figure it will take away from the evils which we said before, but nevertheless he will be in much tumult and handling many works. And if the Moon aspected him by the square in the two times and both were impeded, he will be led to contentions and illnesses, and his resources will be corrupted, and he will be saddened by riches, and he will suffer violence from certain people, and they will envy him; but he would be able to harm those he wanted to. And if the Moon aspected him by the opposite in the two times, and both were impeded, he will fall into contentions and enmities, and he will most often be harmed by some powerful man, and he will be angry at him, and he will be saddened on account of women and blood-relatives, and children and riches. But if the Moon were conjoined to him in the two times, appearing under the rays, he will endure fears and diverse harms, and he will be saddened by some political authority and on the occasion of parents. But if the aforesaid configurations were in [only] one time, the co-significations of the outcomes will be weaker.

Chapter II.15: On the signification of the Sun from the places in which he was, [while] appearing as the Lord of the Year

If the Sun were the Lord of the Year, and were in an angle in both the nativity and in the revolution, he whose revolution it is will be glorious, and will find good things and be praised by many. And if he were in the horoscope or in the Midheaven, his glory will be increased, and he will be more famous than his own companions, and he will obtain goods from the king. And he were in the west, diverse [responsibilities for] steering [matters] will be committed to him, and he will dominate his enemies, and will be in safety, and he will have advantage from women. And if he were in the angle of the earth, he will have opportunity because of the habitation[104] of his parents and

---

[103] Reading with Pingree for "dignities."
[104] Reading *habitaculum* (with Pingree) for *humationem*.

old people. But if the Sun were in these places in the two times [but] of a bad condition, he will be harmed according to the signification of the angle in which he is, and he will endure terrors from the king.

Moreover, if the Sun were the Lord of the Year and were in the eleventh or fifth in the two times, of a good condition, in that year he whose revolution it is will run wild with extravagant dishes and clothing, and he will have advantage from friends, and he will rejoice in his children, or a child will be added to him, and his revenues will become more ample, and he will receive guests and [have] diverse dishes. And if he were of a bad condition in the two times, he will be saddened on the occasion of friends, and certain people having power, some people will treat him badly, and he will be turned against them, and he will be saddened on account of children.

Likewise, if he were the Lord of the Year, appearing in the ninth or in the third in the two times, of a good condition, he will go on a foreign journey by reason of [some] officials, and he will be praised by many, and his brothers and blood-relatives will have faithfulness and advantage through him, likewise he will be helped by them. But if he were of a bad condition in these places, he will be disparaged on account of doctrines, and he will take a useless journey in which he will suffer impediment, and he will be saddened by some pilgrims [and] by his brother and blood-relatives.

Moreover, if the Sun were the Lord of the Year, appearing in the second or the eighth in the two times, of a good condition, it signifies humbleness and rest in that year, and certain successes will come about for him without fatigue and labor. But if he were impeded in these places, it signifies inactivity and middling advantage, and affliction in worldly business, negligence and idleness, and contempt for accomplishments.

Moreover, if the Sun were the Lord of the Year, appearing in the sixth in the two times, of a good condition, it signifies rest and welfare. But if he were of a bad condition, it signifies illness from hotness and dryness, and pains around the upper parts, in the head and in the eyes. Moreover if the Sun were the Lord of the Year, appearing in the twelfth in the two times, of a good condition, it signifies that he will be ridiculed[105] by his enemies; but if he were in a bad condition, it signifies chastisement,[106] anxieties and exile.

---

[105] Reading *illusus* for *illesus*.
[106] Or even, "torture" (*districtionem*).

Moreover, if the Sun were in a like disposition in the nativity and in the revolution, the judgments of the outcomes will be more certain; and if it[107] were [so] in [only] one or the other, they will be weaker.

Chapter II.16: On the signification of Venus if she were the Lady of the Year, and she were of a good condition

If Venus were the Lady of the Year, and she were of a good condition in both the nativity and in the revolution, in her own proper domicile or in a place in which she has dignity, in that year he whose revolution it is will be involved in pleasantness and games or dances, and in singing, and in sexual intercourse, and in the ornamenting of vestments, pleasantness, and the anointing of ointments; he will have familiarity and pleasantness with friends, and he will acquire other friends, and he will take a wife, and will wear decorations. And if she were in her own proper domicile, goods of this kind will come about for him from some known direction. But if in an alien place, they will [come about] for him on a foreign journey through an unknown person.

One must [also] consider the sending of rays, and the Lots, and the particular twelfth-parts to which Venus is being conjoined or configured in the two times: which if it were by an agreeing figure, it indicates preservation and prosperity according to their signification.

Moreover, if Venus were the Lady of the Year, and both she and Mercury were of a good condition in the two times, with Mercury aspecting her by a sextile, in that year he will embrace jokes and delights, and his children and wives will be increased, he will even have familiarity with educated and beautiful women, and he will linger with them in cheerful things and in decorations, he will even associate with experienced and eloquent and liberal and political[108] men, and he will be aware of secret counsels, and sometimes he will be saddened by the things of his which we stated before. Likewise if Mercury aspected her by a square in the two times, with Mercury [elevated] over her, or she [were] elevated over Mercury, in that year he will be esteemed by many, and will stick to teaching and letters and mathematical science and adornments and paintings, and his dignity will be increased, and

---

[107] Reading *fuerit* for *fuerint*.
[108] *Civilibus*.

he will rejoice in good-looking women, he will then be saddened at some times because of certain impediments. But if Mercury were conjoined to her in the two times, and both were unencumbered, in that year he will embrace dancing and pleasant things, and he will be attached to educated women, and will rejoice over them and over children, and he will work with[109] the compositions of speeches, and harmonious affairs, paintings and apparel and good-smelling ointments, and the subtlety of his character will be increased, and he will benefit many, and he will know many things about secret councils, and he will endure labor, and he will jump at the chance to travel.

Moreover, if Venus were the Lady of the Year and the Moon were configured to her in both the nativity and in the revolution from a trine or sextile aspect, he will be in [his] exaltation in that year, and will rejoice in women, both his own and alien ones, and perhaps he will long for boys and will be engaged in dancing. But if she were configured to her by a square, and the Moon were elevated [over Venus], riches will be added to him in that year, and he will be saddened on account of women and pleasures. And if Venus were elevated, in that year he will be esteemed by many, and be well manageable, then he will be saddened on account of [his] marriage-union and women, and he will go to bed with ignoble women, and the condition of his mother will be prosperous. And if the Moon aspected her by the opposite in the two times, he will be saddened on the occasion of women and daughters. And if she were conjoined to her in the two times, he will be cheerful and educated, and he will care for alien women, despising his own, and he will have irritation with them.

Chapter II.17: On the signification of Venus as the Lady of the Year, if she were impeded

If Venus were the Lady of the Year, and she were of a bad condition in the nativity and in the revolution, and even in an alien sign, he will suffer anxieties and great and manifest dangers in all venereal acts, he will be saddened about women in that year, and about children and friends, and on account of decoration, dancing, and clothes, even food and drink. And if she had some dignity in that sign, he will be saddened on account of his own women. But if she did not have [a dignity there], on account of alien ones.

---

[109] *Adaptabit*.

And if she were in a sign hateful to her, he will suffer [something] of this kind from enemies, and on the occasion of them. But if she were in a sign friendly to her, he will suffer [things] of this kind from friends. And if the sign in which she is, is not of the signs of the likenesses of a man, it indicates the infirmity [of his] love, and illness, and sorrow regarding women too, and mothers, and regarding their condition. And if Venus were retrograde or under the rays, it ratifies the aforesaid, and his cheerfulness and delights will be thrown into confusion, and he will be saddened on account of them, and he will incur harms on the occasion of pleasure. But if she were so disposed with the Lot of Marriage-Union, it indicates a breakdown on account of women.

However, it is good to consider the sending of rays and the Lots and the particular twelfth-parts to which Venus is being conjoined or to which she is configured by a contrary aspect. Moreover, if Venus were the Lady of the Year, and she were impeded, it indicates impediment in matters of which she is the significatrix.

Likewise, if Venus were the Lady of the Year and both she and Mercury were of a bad condition, and Mercury aspected her by a sextile, it signifies griefs and disturbances in those matters which the same aspect signifies[110] [above] when these planets appeared to be of a good condition. But if Mercury were configured to Venus by a square, and both were of a bad condition, he will be saddened and harmed, and he will be disgraced on the occasion of women and estate managements and in all of these things which they signify when they are configured to each other in such a way [and] these planets appear in a good condition. And if he were conjoined to her in the two times, and both were impeded, he will be eager about women and dancing and cheerful things, and he will suffer troubles on account of them, and even more so on account of letters, and on account of written things,[111] and in all of these things which they signify when these planets are appearing in a good condition.

Moreover, if Venus were the Lady of the Year and both she and the Moon were of a bad condition in the two times, and they aspected each other by a trine or sextile observation,[112] in that year he will be very inconsistent in sexual intercourse and women, and he will suffer sorrow from mothers on

---

[110] Reading *significat* for *significatur*.
[111] *Notariatum*.
[112] *Conspectum*, an aspect.

account of them, and diverse sinister rumors will reach him, and he will be impeded with regard to his pleasant [pursuits] and delights. And if the Moon aspected her by a square in the two times, and both were of a bad condition, with the Moon being elevated over Venus, he will be harmed thanks to women, and he will be saddened on account of riches. But if Venus were elevated [over the Moon], he will administer his own matters, and he will be saddened on account of resources and a marriage-union, and he will go to bed with low-class women. But if the Moon aspected her by the opposite, he will be saddened on account of a marriage-union, and will be sick, or some one of his children will die. Moreover, if the Moon were conjoined to her in the two times and both were of a bad condition, he will suffer anxieties from certain eloquent men, and he will have a contention with his blood-relatives, and indeed he will be conjoined to alien women, but women [natives] with alien men. But if the aspect were [only] in one of the two times, what the outcome determines will be weaker.

Chapter II.18: On Venus if she were the Lady of the Year, namely from the places in which she were found

If Venus were the Lady of the Year and she were unencumbered in the angles in both the nativity and the revolution, it signifies that he whose revolution it is will be constricted on account of diverse reasons, and he will have favor from those having power, and princes; his glory and riches and his animals will be increased, and he will persist in attendance at the gate of the king, and he will be delighted in diverse clothes, and he will rejoice in women, and his sexual intercourse will be multiplied, and he will obtain his desires; his movable substance will even be increased. And if she were retrograde in these places, he will obtain certain ones of the aforesaid, except that [they will be] ignoble.[113] But if she were of a bad condition, he will be disturbed about his life and will suffer certain losses, and a certain man will rail about him, and he will have contentions with certain people, and sorrows and anxiety according to the nature of the angle in which she is. And if she were impeded by Saturn, he will suffer diverse cold and contrary illnesses, like colds and epileptic [attacks] and insane[114] passions. And if she were

---

[113] Reading with Pingree.
[114] *Phreneticas*.

impeded by Mars, he will be saddened thanks to women and sexual intercourse, he will even suffer fire or robberies, or bubbling up of the blood will come to be in him. And if she were in the fourth, he will see the death of the wife.[115]

And if Venus were the Lady of the Year and she were in the fifth or eleventh in the two times, of a good condition, he will have an increase of women, friends and things, and he will rejoice over children, or he will have a child. But if she were of a bad condition, he will be saddened without cause, or on account of women and a child, and he will make enemies of his friends.

Likewise if she were in the ninth or in the third[116] in the two times, of a good condition, he will jump at the chance to travel in that year, and he will find prosperous things on that journey, and he will be praised by many, and he will have advantage from brothers and kin, and certain ones of his women will go on a foreign journey. And if she were of a bad condition, he will jump at the chance for a journey [which will be] hindered; and certain people will consider him to be unfaithful, and he will contend with his friends, and part of [his] riches will be destroyed.

But if she were in the eighth or in the second in the two times, of a good condition, he will have advantage from low-class persons, or from a bad act, but particularly in the eighth it signifies a multitude of expenditures. And if she were impeded in the second, it signifies his idleness, and his negligence, and a diminution of riches. And if she were in the eighth, it indicates disadvantage and quarrels.

Moreover, if she were in the sixth or twelfth in the two times, of a good condition, he will have advantage from low-class men and because of poisons. And if she were impeded in the sixth, it signifies illness; and if the impediment were by Saturn, the illness will be from black choler; but by Mars, from blood; but by the Sun, from hotness. But if she were impeded in the twelfth he will be saddened by enemies and will suffer detention. And if Venus had a like disposition in both the nativity and in the revolution, appearing in the same place, the judgments will be more certain; but if not, they will be weaker.[117]

---

[115] Or, "of a woman" (*mulieris*).
[116] Omitting *aspectu*.
[117] Inserting this last clause with Pingree.

Likewise, if Venus were cadent from an angle at the time of the revolution, it signifies that the joy of him whose revolution it is will be mixed up, and he will have harm on account of food and drink, and especially if the year leaves off in the place of Saturn,[118] or Saturn were in some angle of the revolution.

Chapter II.19: On the signification of Mercury if he were the Lord of the Year and were of a good condition

If Mercury were the Lord of the Year, and he were of a good condition in both the nativity and in the revolution, it signifies the acquisition of riches in that year, and praise by many, and he will have advantage on the occasion of business matters[119] and intellect and knowledge and teaching and orations and proclamations and managements and contention and certain estate managements, and he will please and be seen by all, and praised by many.

It is also good to look at the sendings of rays and the Lots and the particular twelfth-parts to which Mercury is being conjoined or configured in the two times: for it indicates luckiness in the matters which they signify.

Moreover, if Mercury were the Lord of the Year and both he and the Moon were of a good condition, and were configured to each other from a trine or sextile aspect, he whose revolution it is will attain to diverse teachings. And if the Moon aspected him by a square in the two times, and she were of a good condition, with Mercury being elevated over her, his knowledge and prudence will be added to, and he will be saddened on account of many things. But if the Moon were elevated [over Mercury], in that year he will be unsound and vulgar and fickle in all things. And if she aspected him in the two times by the opposite, and both were of a good condition, he will have enmity against some people and will overcome everyone resisting and contending against him. But if she were conjoined to him in the two times, and both were of a good condition, in that year his teaching and knowledge will be increased, he will give to many from his own knowledge, and he will be praiseworthy and have familiarity with low-class persons; and if he had a mother, her knowledge and prudence and estate management will be added to.

---

[118] This must be by profection.
[119] Reading *negotiationum* for *negociationibus*.

In addition to all of this, if the inspection[120] were in [only] one of the two [times], it will take away the greater part[121] of the signification.

Chapter II.20: On Mercury if he were the Lord of the Year and were of a bad condition

If Mercury were the Lord of the Year and were of a bad condition in both the nativity and the revolution, he will suffer diverse troubles in that year on the occasion of slaves or children, or low-class persons, or teachings, or associates, or writings and letters, and estate managements, and conversations, and contention, and a quarrel, he will lose hope and reject all help.[122] But if he were occidental and both he and the Lot of Children were impeded, his child and slaves will suffer adversities. And if he were conjoined to the Lot of Friends, there will be impediment from friends; but if to the Lot of Work or the Kingdom,[123] the impediment will be from some people having power, and he will endure fetters and leg irons, and he will suffer diverse troubles. But if he were oriental, the aforesaid will be less.

But if he were the Lord of the Year and both he and the Moon were of a bad condition in the two times, and they were configured to each other by a trine or sextile aspect, he will suffer sorrows on the occasion of travel, even friends or teachings, or the loss of certain things. But if it were by a square, he will suffer sorrow on account of many things, he will be obstructed by many on the occasion of letters, and he will be confined or incarcerated. And if the Moon were elevated, he will be timid in that year, and unstable. Moreover, if they aspected each other by the opposite and they were impeded, he will be timid and will have contentions and enmities. And if the Moon were conjoined to him in the two times, he will be easily changeable, and will make up some lies, and he will suffer harm on account of low-class persons.

---

[120] *Inspectus*. That is, the aspect.
[121] *Multam parte*.
[122] Reading the last part of this sentence with Pingree.
[123] See also III.8. Traditionally these are two separate Lots: (1) the Lot of Work is taken by day from Mercury to Mars (and by night the reverse), and projected from the Ascendant; the second one is probably (2) the Lot of Exaltation, taken from the sect light to its exaltation, and projected from the Ascendant.

But we have [already] told you [about] the configurations of Mercury with the rest of the stars; you, however, discern the comminglings of the judgments by your own intellect.

Chapter II.21: On the signification of Mercury if he were the Lord of the Year, from the place in which he was found

However, if Mercury were the Lord of the Year and in an angle both in the nativity and in the revolution, [and] free from the bad ones, it signifies that he whose revolution it is will find dignity and glory from letters and business and serving the ruling people; but his knowledge will be increased, and he will acquire teaching, and will be praised on account of these things, and especially if he were in the Ascendant or in the Midheaven. And if he were impeded in these places, sorrows will happen to him in that year on the occasion of letters or computations, and he will be sick, and whatever business dealing he will handle will create a loss. And appearing in the seventh or in the fourth, it signifies contentions with blood-kin. And if he were retrograde, he will be accused on account of sexual intercourse; he will [also] be sick with an illness according to the nature of the impeding planet.

Likewise if Mercury were in the eleventh or in the fifth in the two times, unencumbered by the bad ones, he will obtain many goods in that year, and he will be friendly to powerful men and officials, and he will be involved in profits and business dealings and sales and purchases; and if he had a child, he will rejoice over him, or a child will be born to him (if the root of his nativity signified the birth of children). But if he were impeded in these places, his children will be inimical to him, and he will be dull at understanding; and if he had a child, it will be sick and perhaps it will die; and if he were retrograde, he whose revolution it is will waver in creating accomplishments.

Moreover, if he were in the ninth or in the third he will go on a foreign journey in that year, and he will discover good things on his foreign journey, namely with [Mercury] appearing in a good condition both in the nativity and in the revolution; he will even have manifested dreams,[124] and he will be praised over doctrines and faith and prudence, and the best estate management, and he will know things accurately, and both his brothers and those known [to him] will have advantage through him. But if he had a bad

---

[124] That is, he dreams things which come true.

condition in these places in both times, he will go on a foreign journey and suffer harm on the foreign journey, and doubt about his faith, and on account of these he will suffer jeering and will have terrible dreams, and he will be harmed[125] in business dealings, and in sales and purchases, and he will hate his sisters and blood-kin.

Likewise, if Mercury were in the second or in the eighth place in the two times, free from the bad ones, he will have advantage from selling and buying, and he will have prosperity in his condition. But if he were of a bad condition, he will be harmed,[126] and he will be false in his actions, and he will have contentions on account of riches.

Moreover, if Mercury were of a good condition in the two times, in the twelfth place or in the sixth, in that year he will be negligent about the acquisition of riches and lazy about business matters and useful things, but he will acquire these things from certain low-class men, and from some middling and low-class action. And if he were impeded in the two times, illnesses will come about for him according to the nature of the planet impeding him. And if Saturn impeded him, he will be sick by windinesses through coldness, he will suffer arthritis and pains of the nerves and veins.[127] But if Mars impeded him, he will be sick from being filled with blood and the like, and he will be arrested for something he did not do, and he will be accused about things which he did not do, and he will suffer dejection and sorrow.

And if Mercury were in some place in the figure of the nativity, and he were in the same place and in a like disposition even in the revolution, the judgments will be more certain. But if the figures were different, it is good to commingle them, and to make a determination according to the complexion of each.

Chapter II.22: On the Moon, if she were the Lady of the Year and were of a good condition

If the Moon were the Lady of the Year, the ends of the outcomes will be according to the disposition of the distributor and of the Lord of the sign in which the distribution from the *hīlāj* is, whatever kind [of planet] the *hīlāj*

---

[125] *Damnificatur.* This work also indicates fines in particular.
[126] See previous footnote.
[127] Reading with Pingree for "fibers."

was; however, we take the partner and [also] a planet which was in Cancer (whether according to the nativity or according to the revolution), even a planet to which the Moon is being conjoined in the sign where she is. By means of the two planets, we divide the year into two. But if there were three, [we divide the year] into three; and if more, into more. And we make a determination according to every planet just as it was disposed.

However, we do take the testimony of the Moon into [our] testimony. For if she were well disposed, it indicates a prosperous condition for him whose revolution it is, namely in those things which the Moon signified. But if [she were] badly [disposed], the contrary and illnesses. And if she were northern [in latitude] and increased in numbers, it indicates good things; but if southern and diminished, contrary things—and especially if [she were] subtracted in light.[128]

However, it is good to observe her conjunctions to the rays and the Lots and the particular twelfth-parts, [and] her significations[129] which they signify when she is configured[130] with the aforesaid planets.

But it is good to look at the sign in which the Moon was at the time of the revolution, for it has an equal role[131] to the horoscope of the year. And if she were in her own proper sign, of a good condition, everything he undertook will come about for him prosperously; and if she were impeded, it indicates impediments according to the nature of the impeding planet. And if she were void in course, and in a sign of Saturn, he will have advantage through lands and wells and plants, if he were of a good condition; but if he were of a bad condition, it signifies afflictions and anxieties and wounds. And if she were in a domicile of Jupiter, if he were of a good condition, he will be commended by many, and will lead whatever he undertook to its end, and he will inherit the paternal riches, and some working will be committed to him. But if he were of a bad condition, it indicates diverse griefs and he will be accused by some. And if she were in a domicile of Mars, with him appearing in the Midheaven, it indicates attacks by those who are subservient, and the cutting of his body by iron, and the flowing of blood.

But it is good not to consider the Moon alone (if she were the Lady of the Year), but even the Lord of the sign in which she is. For if it were in a domicile of Saturn, with him appearing free from impediments, it signifies

---

[128] Reading *lumine* for *Lunae*.
[129] Reading *significationes* for *significationis*.
[130] Reading *configurata* for *affigurata*.
[131] Reading *partem* for *planetam*.

good things; and if he were impeded, the contrary—and it is the same for the rest of the planets.

[Superior squares over the Lord of the Year]

Moreover, if a planet were elevated above the Lord of the Year, it shows its working. For if the Sun were elevated over Jupiter (with [Jupiter] appearing as the Lord of the Year), it shows some authority; but over Mars, a foreign journey.[132] And if the Sun were of a good condition, the foreign journey will be good; but if he were of a bad condition, the contrary. And if Saturn were elevated over the Sun in the twelfth, it signifies contrary and useless foreign travels, and being thrown out from place to place, and prison, and impediments.

Chapter II.23: On the signification of the Ascendant of the revolution

After the Lord of the Year, the distributor has its own signification. But we[133] have made mention of the Ascendant of the year and of its Lord, for the reason that it has a partnership with the sign of the revolution[134] and its Lord. Therefore, it is good for you to know the Ascendant of the year and the sign of the revolution, and the place of its Lord, [and] even the places of the remaining planets. For the virtues of the nativity, of the planets, and of the revolution, are known from the figure of the year and its angles and the rest of the places: therefore every place has its own proper signification.

And indeed the angles signify those things which belong to the body, and honors, even women and parents.[135] But the succeedents signify those things which belong to substance, children also, and the dead, prosperity and friends and a good reputation. But the cadents signify brothers and illnesses and journeys, and enemies and contentions, and bad reputations and impediments and prison. But for those who handle astrology accurately, there is a certain proper [and] manifest signification for each [place]. However, the planet which enters into it shows the signification of each house.

---

[132] Probably because Mars is a significator of travel and moving around.
[133] Omitting a stray parenthetical remark in the Latin.
[134] That is, the sign of the profection.
[135] That is, in order: the Ascendant, Midheaven, 7th, 4th.

Therefore, [if] the Lord of the Ascendant of the year were unencumbered at the revolution, and in the domicile of a luminary, he whose revolution it is will find good things and glory. And if it were in the Ascendant or the Midheaven, he will be sound in body, and he will attain dignity and degree. But if it were in the seventh or in the fourth, his blood-kin and women and subordinates will be increased. And if he were of a bad condition in these places, he will be harmed by persons of this kind.

Then[136] it is right to look at the Lord of the Ascendant of the year, to see in what place of the figure it is, and to which of the planets it is conjoined, or which ones were conjoined to it, and it will have this signification alone; but it will have another signification if it is judged along with the Lord of the profection and with the Ascendant of the nativity and its Lord, and [with] the Moon and the rest of the planets, and the places of the benevolents or malevolents, both in the nativity and the revolution.

If therefore there were a malevolent in the Ascendant of the year, it will be very much impeding, and especially if it impeded the Moon or the Lord of the Year. If therefore it were Mars, it signifies that his enemies will do wrong to him. And if it were Saturn, it indicates illness and harms, and detention, and prison and the like, but it is right to assume with these the nature of the sign in which it is.

And if one of the malevolents were in the squares of the Ascendant of the year, but the Lord of the Ascendant itself in a good place, configured with benevolents, and it aspected the Ascendant, it will take away many of the adversities which the malevolent signified. Moreover, if one of the two malevolents were in the Ascendant of the year, but the other in the Ascendant of the nativity, it indicates the year is contrary, and very difficult; but if one of them were of a good condition, it very much takes away from the wickedness.

Likewise if there were a malevolent in the Ascendant of the nativity, but the year reached it [by profection], but the Ascendant of the year happened to be that sign itself, and the malevolent aspected it according to revolution by a contrary aspect, even if the other planets were in a good condition, still in that year he will suffer troubles and illnesses according to the nature of the malevolent. And if the malevolent bears itself thusly as is said earlier, and in addition the Lord of the Ascendant of the revolution or the Lord of the sign of the profection were of a bad condition, one must fear lest perhaps he die.

---

[136] Reading this paragraph with Pingree.

And if a malevolent in the fourth place were impeding the Lord of the Year, one should fear more. But if there will be a benevolent in that place instead of a malevolent, it signifies safety and welfare and gladness, and even the acquisition of goods according to the nature of the benevolent.

Moreover, if Mars and Saturn were in the Midheaven at the time of the revolution, they make indifference and laziness and idleness, and uselessness[137] through the whole year; and he will use up his riches uselessly, and [things] of this kind. But if some planet in that year signified some certain good for him, the good itself will be easily convertible, and easily destructible.

If however the Sun or the Moon were with Saturn in the revolution, in an angle, in the fourth place, it signifies the death of the father or mother.

But if the year reached a good place [by profection], and the Lord of the Year were in a bad place,[138] or the year reached a bad place and its Lord in a good place, it indicates the mediocrity of both goods and evils.

Moreover[139] if the year reached a malevolent, or a malevolent were in the Ascendant [of the revolution] at the time of the revolution, it signifies harm.

If the year reached the Midheaven of the nativity, and malevolents were there, it harms [the native's] work.[140]

[Chapter II.24: Notable profection-revolution positions][141]

And if the year reached the second place, and there were a malevolent in it in the nativity, it indicates losses and useless expenditures, and especially if there were malevolents in an angle in the revolution of that year, or in the succeedents of the angles. But if they were in cadents from the angles, the evils will be lighter.

Moreover, if the year reached the place of foreign travel and Saturn were in that same place according to the nativity, [and] the same [planet] in the revolution even aspected that [same] place in a disagreeable way, [and he] even [aspected] the Moon by a square, and Mars were slower in course in the

---

[137] Reading *inutilitatem* with Pingree for *utilitatem*.
[138] This must mean by transit in the revolution.
[139] Reading this sentence with Pingree.
[140] Adding this sentence with Pingree.
[141] The following may well be based on actual charts, but seem to play the role of illustrating archetypal *types* of profection-revolution combinations.

Ascendant of the nativity, [and] were Jupiter even in the Ascendant of the year, the presence of Jupiter in the Ascendant signifies exaltation and dignity and power, but his soul will not be calm in action; but Saturn and Mars signify trouble and detentions, and prison, and tortures, and fear of robbers, and enmities, and injuries, and harms and griefs.

Moreover, if the sign of the profection were the sixth sign in the figure of the revolution, and the malevolents aspected it, with no benevolent aspecting it, it signifies a vicious illness.

Likewise if the year arrived in the sixth place or in the twelfth, or in the fourth or in the seventh[142] or in the eighth, it will not be good, and especially if its Lord were either retrograde or stationary or configured to a malevolent at the time of the revolution.

Likewise, if the year reached the second place of the nativity and the Lady of the Year were Venus, appearing together with Saturn in the angle of the earth, and the Ascendant of the revolution will be the eighth place of the nativity, it indicates impediments and perverse detriments.

Moreover, if the year reached the twelfth place of the nativity, and its Lord were Jupiter, and he happened to be together with Saturn in the seventh place, and Mars were in the angle of the earth: it signifies the enmities of harm, and danger of his own death.

Moreover, if the year reached the place of marriage, and at the time of the revolution its Lord and the Moon were in the opposites of their own domiciles[143] or exaltations: he whose revolution it is will hate his own fatherland, and will go on a foreign journey into another region.

Likewise, if the Lord of the Year arrived, impeded, in the western angle, it signifies exile from the fatherland and serious dangers.

Moreover, if the year of the father,[144] [profected] from some place which signifies the condition of the father, reached some [other] place, and its Lord was conjoined with the Lord of the third place from the Ascendant of the nativity, it signifies that the father will have a child, or the child will have a sibling.

Likewise[145] if the sign of the profection and the Ascendant of the revolution were the same as the Ascendant of the nativity, and one of the

---

[142] Omitting an extra *sive in septimo*.
[143] Reading instead of "trigons/triplicities."
[144] This is probably the profection of the 4th, but perhaps even the profection of the Lot of the Father.
[145] Reading this paragraph with Pingree.

luminaries was the Lord of the Year and it is eclipsed or with the Tail of the Dragon, with Saturn aspecting it, it indicates detriments and dissensions by the common people against him.

Moreover,[146] if the place of children [in the nativity] were Sagittarius, and Sagittarius were the Ascendant of the revolution, and Saturn [were] in it by transit, and Jupiter and Mars and Mercury and Venus were in Leo, in the Ascendant of the nativity, and Mars aspected the Moon from the opposite by degree, it indicates fear and prison, and detentions, and harm [for] the children, and afterwards welfare.

Moreover, if the Lord of the fifth place of the nativity were Saturn, and it[147] was the angle of the earth at the revolution, it signifies the death or especially the detriment of the children. But if the year arrived to a fifth place of this kind, and Saturn, the Lord of the Year, were in a good condition, it signifies a middling harm for the child.

Moreover, if the year arrived in a place in which Saturn and Mars were at the time of the revolution, but in the figure of the revolution it was [in] a square to the Ascendant [of the revolution], it indicates harm, and injuries, and impediments with respect to substance.

Likewise, if the Lord of the Year were Saturn or Mars and [that Lord] were in the Ascendant of the revolution, namely in one where it does not have a dignity, and especially if it were in the Ascendant according to the nativity [as well], or in its opposite or square, Saturn signifies infirmities and long illnesses, but Mars signifies fear and prison and detriment in riches.

Likewise, if Saturn were the Lord of the Year and he were under the earth, but Mars arrived to his own place according to the nativity,[148] and he were conjoined to Saturn in that same place, [and] the Lord of the Ascendant of the revolution were even in the seventh place or under the rays, with the benevolents appearing in the cadents from the angles, it indicates detriment and detention through the whole year.

Moreover, if the year arrived in the place of Jupiter, and Jupiter were of a good condition by transit, aspecting his own place which he was possessing at the time of the nativity, but were he [also] the Lord of the Year, not cadent from the angles, it indicates prosperities and abundant goods, *if* Jupiter had much signification for that.

---

[146] These positions are so precise they sound as though they are from a real chart, but I have not been able to find a corresponding date.
[147] Neither the Greek nor the Latin specifies whether this is Saturn or his domicile.
[148] This is probably a Mars return.

If[149] the Ascendant of the revolution reached a sign in which a malevolent had been in the figure of the nativity, or the sign of the year is in a place where there was a malevolent, take that malevolent as the Lord of the Year, especially if the Lord of the sign of the profection or the Lord of the Ascendant of the revolution did not aspect its own Lord.[150]

Moreover, if Mars were the Lord of the Year and Saturn (in the revolution) arrived to the place of Mars according to the nativity, and Mars were in an angle or in the succeedents of the angles in the revolution of the year, and [he were] elevated over Venus, also with the benevolents being cadent, it signifies the roughness of the year, even fear and detentions and prison, and harms from dukes and princes.

Likewise if the Ascendant of the year were the sign in which the Sun and Moon were,[151] it is good to take the Lord of the luminary having signification in the year.[152] But[153] if the Sun and Moon were of a bad condition in the revolution of the year, and they were in the seventh place or in the fourth [place] of the figure of the revolution, and especially if they were with the Head or Tail of the Dragon, it signifies the death of the parents, and especially if they signified [the parents'] condition according to the nativity.

Moreover if Jupiter is in Capricorn in the revolution of the year, and he were impeded by Saturn, and also [by] Mars and the Sun, it signifies harms and destructions.

Moreover if a malevolent were with the Lord of the Year in the Ascendant of the revolution, and it impeded the Moon, it signifies the impediment of the year.

Moreover, if the Lord of some one of the places were retrograde according to the nativity or according to the revolution, or under the rays, or it were impeded by some one of the bad ones, or it were in an unfriendly place, it signifies harm according to the station[154] of that place: whether it were the significator of riches or of immovable [property] or any of the other things.

---

[149] For this paragraph, following Pingree. See a very similar formulation in III.8 below. This sentence seems mainly to reinforce the idea that a natal configuration is more important for the themes of the year than locations and rulerships by transit alone at the revolution.
[150] I believe this should probably read "sign."
[151] Undoubtedly at the nativity.
[152] That is, the luminary will have a special signification, and thus its Lord. But its dispositor would *already* be the Lord of the Year.
[153] For the rest of this paragraph, cf. *BA* IV.14 p. 206.
[154] That is, its position in the chart: the second, the third, and so on.

Likewise, if the Lord of the Year were a malevolent and it were in the sixth place according to the nativity, and it impeded the Moon in the revolution, but the benevolents aspected the Moon from good places according to the revolution, and there were a malevolent in the Ascendant of the year, it indicates the greatest detriments and a long illness.

Moreover,[155] if a benevolent were the Lord of the Year and a malevolent was in the Ascendant of the revolution, but the Moon is being impeded by some one or another of them, it indicates the worst attack by enemies, and the greatest loss, even some limb of his will be amputated, and there will be fear for his soul, and especially if benevolents do not aspect the Ascendant.[156]

Likewise, if the Lord of the Year were a benevolent and retrograde, and Mars aspected it from the opposite by transit, [and if] even the Moon [did so] from a square, and the Ascendant of the year were impeded (whether by the Sun or by any one of the ways), with its Lord not aspecting it, it signifies the greatest harms in the body, and from enemies and robbers, even damages and the loss of riches.

Likewise, if Saturn were the Lord of the Year and he were restored in the place in which he was presented at the time of the nativity, and Mars aspected him at the revolution, it signifies detriment according to the station of the house in which Saturn was. But if in the Ascendant of the revolution, or with the Moon, it signifies harm for the body.

Moreover, if the Lord of the Year, and the Ascendant of the revolution and its Lord, and the Moon, were impeded by some [planet] from the conjunction, or from the square or from the opposite, it signifies his destruction, and the loss of riches. But if Jupiter or Venus were with the Moon or with the Lord of the Year, he will be rescued from these impediments.

Moreover if the Moon were in Cancer according to the revolution, and the Sun in Aries, and there was an impediment by Mars from Capricorn,[157] it signifies detriments and destructions.

Likewise, if the Moon were in a masculine sign according to the revolution and she is being impeded at the same time by Saturn and also Mars, and the Lord of the place were a malevolent, it signifies adversities and harms.

---

[155] For this paragraph, cf. *BA* IV.14 p. 207.
[156] Reading this last clause with Pingree.
[157] Reading with Pingree for "Cancer."

Likewise if the Lord of the Year were impeded by some malevolent, it will be a year of fear and much worry and losses. But if Jupiter were configured with it,[158] it indicates liberation from [things] of this kind.

Likewise,[159] if Mercury were the Lord of the Year and he were impeded by Mars and is in the fourth place of the Ascendant of the revolution, or in the fourth place from the sign of the year, or in the fourth place from the Ascendant of the nativity, it signifies the death of the brothers. Likewise, if Mercury were the Lord of the Year and is impeded by Mars in the western angle, it signifies the death of his siblings.

Moreover, if the Lord of the Year were in the tenth according to the nativity, but likewise in the tenth or in the eleventh at the time of the revolution, inspected by benevolents, it signifies the discovery of riches and power. Moreover, if the Lord of the Year were in the tenth according to the nativity and according to the revolution, it signifies the obtaining of some dignity.

Moreover, if the Lord of the Year were in a cadent from the angle and under the rays according to the nativity, and in the sixth or eighth or under the rays according to the revolution, and configured with Saturn, it signifies the taking over of a duty, and being summoned, and irrigation,[160] but even more so impediments like death.

Moreover, if Jupiter were of a good condition according to the nativity, but in the angles in the revolution, and he aspected the Lord of the Year, it signifies the attainment of a degree and honor from officials and kings too; they will commit useful works to him, and he will have prosperity in his operations and estate management.

Moreover, if the Lord of the Year were occidental, even in the domicile of a [planet] unfriendly to him, or in the sixth or in the twelfth, configured with Saturn or Mars, with Jupiter being cadent from the angle, and not aspecting the Moon nor the Lord of the Year, it signifies suffering breakdowns of the mind, and injuries from enemies.

Likewise, if the year arrived in the angle of the earth or in the angle of the west, and Saturn were in the same place or he aspected that place by a contrary aspect, there is fear lest he whose revolution it is, would die.

---

[158] Probably to the Lord of the Year, referring to the previous sentence.
[159] For this paragraph, following Pingree.
[160] Uncertain translation. The Greek reads: "leisure time and irrigation," while the Latin reads "being summoned and leisure time." Leisure time does not make sense to me in this context.

Let this be a rule for you in the revolutions of years:

If you found a malevolent in the Ascendant of the revolution, and the malevolent impeded the Ascendant of the nativity or the Moon or the angles, know that you will bring in the greatest impediment. But if a bad one of this kind were in the Ascendant by transit, or it impeded one of the places of the figure, and you found that it was not impeding a place of this kind in the nativity, you should know that this makes the impediment moderate. Likewise if a malevolent were oriental, configured to a benevolent, and it had a relationship[161] to the Ascendant or the Moon, it brings in advantage through labors and afflictions.

Moreover, if benevolents were in the Ascendant of the revolution, or they will enter some places of the planets of the nativity, they signify a moderate advantage, if at the beginning of the nativity they were aspecting that place by a corresponding[162] aspect. If however it was retrograde or under the rays, or cadent from the angle, its domination is weaker.

Moreover if the Ascendant of the revolution were a sign in which a malevolent had been according to the nativity, or there were malevolents in each, it signifies changing over from a place, flights and losses.

Moreover if there were a malevolent configured to a benevolent according to the nativity, and it were conjoined to that same benevolent at the time of the revolution, or it were configured from the opposite or the square, it signifies a not-moderate harm.

---

[161] Reading *logon* with Pingree. The Latin makes it seem that this is a relationship of dignity; certainly *logos* can refer to value, which is the root of the word *dignitas* (*dignus*, "worthy").

[162] Or perhaps, "harmonious."

BOOK III: DIRECTIONS IN REVOLUTIONS

Chapter III.1: On undertaking directions in revolutions

In the revolutions of years it is good to direct many places, some according to the nativity but others according to the revolution: for each one has its own proper signification in these things, which another one does not signify. For if some planet or place signified good or evil in the nativity, then the signification will appear when the planet rules over the distribution by some circuit of years, and when it steers by [its] body or by the hurling of rays, or it applied to benevolents or malevolents.

Therefore it is good to make a direction of the five *hīlāj*es separately: for the first *hīlāj*[1] indicates the years of life, illness, even the quality of death; but the remaining *hīlāj*es signify soundness or illness or dangers and the remaining affections, concerning which we will make mention in what follows below.

Likewise it is good to direct all the Lots, and the particular twelfth-parts, and the twelve places, both those of the nativity and of the revolution, and also to put together the figures of the months, and to make their directions, and to take the degrees in the Ascendant of the nativity for years, but in the figure of the revolution for months or days, and indeed in the figure of the months for days or hours.[2]

But for knowing the place of the distribution and the distributor in the revolutions of years, you will make a direction thusly: look at the degree of the Ascendant of the nativity, to see which planet's bound it is and how many degrees remain (of the degrees of the bound[3] of the planet), and turn that bound into degrees of ascensions of the city in which he was born, and you will write down how many they were. Then, look at the following bounds to see how many degrees they are, and turn those into ascensions, and thus you will do it through individual bounds, both from the Ascendant

---

[1] That is, the primary *hīlāj* found in the longevity calculations. Most traditional authors have us direct many or all of the *hīlāj*es for different purposes.
[2] See *TBN* II.5-6.
[3] Reading "bound" as singular in this sentence for clarity's sake. But there is some precedent in Valens for calling each degree of the bound a "bound."

and from the remaining *hīlāj*es, planets and Lots, so that thus a complete direction comes to be. But the bound to which the year arrives is the place of the distribution, and its Lord is the distributor, whether it aspects [the bound] or not.

Now, the direction of the Ascendant and of those which are in it comes to be through the ascensions of the city in which someone was born; but a direction of the Midheaven [and] even of the fourth and of those which are in them, comes to be through the ascensions of the right sphere. But for the other places the direction comes to be just as we have shown before in our treatises.[4] Then, look to see how many degrees [in ascensions] are collected, and you will make each degree into one year, but 5' into a month, and 1' into six days, and 10" into a day, and twenty-five sixtieths[5] [of a second] into an hour.

The Persians used to call the distributor (namely [the bound Lord] who is found from the direction of the Ascendant by ascensions) the *jārbakhtār*,[6] which is translated as [meaning nothing] else than "distributor [of the time]."

But when you have directed the bounds it is good to consider both the places of the planets and the hurling of their rays. Often indeed the body or ray of a planet touches in some place, and when the direction reaches one of these, that planet itself is taken as the partner with the distributor, until another planet occurs [in a later degree], whether by body or by rays, and from this the disposition is changed from the first [partnering] planet to the next; and this [next one] even becomes the partner to the distributor, whether the encounter were by body or by rays.[7]

However, it is good to know both the places of the Lots and of the particular twelfth-parts, and where their direction arrives. For if they arrived to benevolents or malevolents, by rays or by body, their signification appears (whether it were good or wicked).

Therefore, let us make an example to signify the direction and the distribution, [and] even of the disposition of the Lots and the particular twelfth-parts:[8]

---

[4] See for instance al-Qabīsī IV.11-12, and Gansten.
[5] Reading with Schmidt for *tertia*.
[6] Abū Ma'shar may very well be following 'Umar in using "*jārbakhtār*" in a wider sense; Māshā'allāh restricts the *jārbakhtār* to being the bound Lord of the directed *hīlāj* of the nativity.
[7] This is essentially 'Umar's method in *TBN* II.2.
[8] This chart appears to be that of Abū Ma'shar's own nativity, approximately 10:00 p.m. on August 10, 787 AD, near Balkh, Afghanistan. See Pingree (1962 p. 487, 1968 p. *v*).

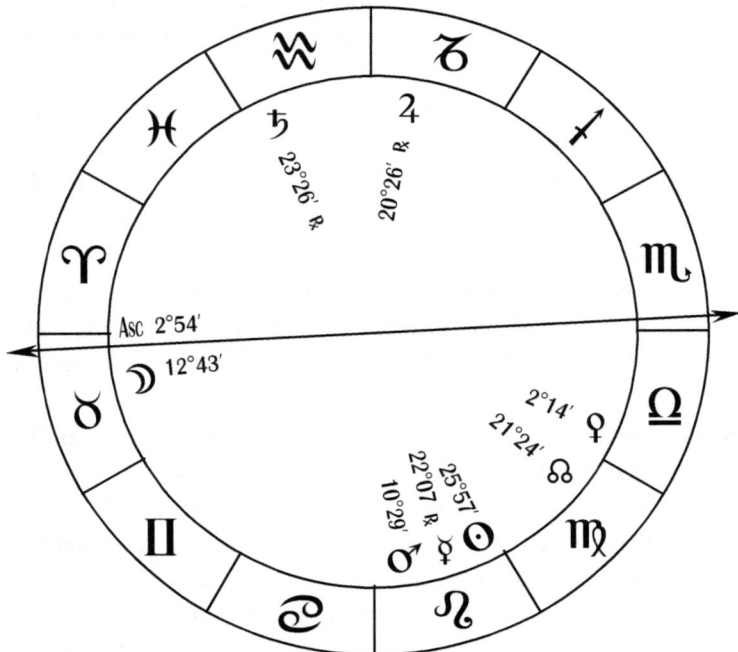

Figure 3: Abū Ma'shar's nativity[9]

A certain man was born in the fourth clime in a certain city, whose latitude is 36°. But Taurus was ascending with 2° 54', and the Moon in it by 12° 43', Mars in Leo by 10° 29', The Sun in Leo [by] 25° 57',[10] Mercury retrograde in Leo [by] 22° 7', Venus in Libra [by] 2° 14', Jupiter retrograde in Capricorn [by] 20° 26', Saturn retrograde in Aquarius [by] 23° 26', the Head of the Dragon in Virgo [by] 21° 24. But we formed the figure, and we put the locations of the planets in order in it, and their sendings of rays, even the Lots falling in them, and the rest, so that the knowledge of them would be easier.

Therefore, wanting to know the place of the distribution and the distributor (which is called the *jārbakhtār*), and to direct the degree of the Ascendant for knowing when it arrives at the bodies of the good ones and bad ones,

---

[9] This is my reconstruction of the Arabic diagram which originally accompanied the text: see Pingree 1968, pp. 127-28.
[10] Reading "25" for "15," against the text, in order to match the calculated value.

and even the rays themselves, and the particular twelfth-parts and the Lots, [I worked as follows.] I found Taurus on the Ascendant, at 2° 54', which is the bound of Venus, nor did I find the body of any planet or [its] ray from the beginning of the sign up to the degree of the Ascendant. And if I had found something of this kind, I would have said that the degree of the Ascendant is disposed by that planet, and I would have received that planet as the partner of the *jārbakhtār* (namely, the distributor). And since I found neither the body of a planet nor a ray from the beginning of the sign up to the degree of the Ascendant, I took Venus as the sole distributor. I even found 4° 20' between the degree of the Ascendant and the Lot of Boldness or Courage,[11] which are 3° 02' by the ascensions of the fourth clime. So, Venus disposed 3 years and 12 days according to her bound, then the degree of the Ascendant adheres to the Lot of Courage and Boldness, with 46' yet remaining to Venus from her degrees, which are 32' 12" by ascensions. And through this we said that in her distribution Venus disposed the Lot of Courage and Boldness for 6 months and 13 days, which are 3 years, 6 months, and 25 days in total.

Next then, the direction comes to the bounds of Mercury, and he receives the distributor, and disposes the Lot of Courage and Boldness for 1 year and about 8 days, and the direction reaches the sextile ray of Saturn after 4 years, 7 months, and about 3 days, and Saturn disposes the Lot of Courage and boldness through his sextile[12] ray in the distribution of Mercury, for 1 year, 10 months, and about 17 days. And then occurs the Lot of Success[13] and Victory, namely after 6 years and about 12 days, and through his sextile[14] ray Saturn will dispose the two Lots (namely that of Courage and Boldness, and of Success and Victory) with the partnership of Mercury for 5 months and 29 days, which are in total 7 years and near 21 days.

---

[11] *Animositatis*. This is the Hermetic Lot of Courage (attributed to Mars) from Paul of Alexandria Ch. 23: from Mars to the Lot of Fortune by day (and the reverse by night), projected from the Ascendant. The Lot of Fortune in this chart is at 16° 08' Leo, which would put the Lot of Courage at 8° 33' Taurus, almost exactly 1° later than the value given above. From this point on I will take Abū Ma'shar's values for granted without correcting them.

[12] This should be a square.

[13] *Profectus*. Schmidt reads "advancement" for the Greek, a valid alternative in the Latin as well. This is the Hermetic Lot of Victory (attributed to Jupiter), by day from the Lot of Spirit to Jupiter (and at night the reverse), projected from the Ascendant. The Lot of Spirit is at 9° 40' Capricorn, making the nocturnal Lot of Victory at 22° 08' Aries. Abū Ma'shar has mistakenly turned it into the diurnal Lot, which should be at 13° 40' Taurus but is a little off here.

[14] This should be a square.

Then the Moon regards the disposition corporally from the sextile[15] raying of Saturn, and she disposes the two Lots by her own body, with Mercury partnering, through 11 months and 16 days. The distribution of Mercury is perfected after 7 years, 11 months, and about 27 days. Then the distribution crosses over to Jupiter, and together with the Moon he disposes the Lot of Courage and Boldness and the Lot of Success and Victory, through 4 months and 24 days, and the direction arrives at the Lot of Prudence and Reason[16] after 8 years, 4 months and about 21 days. Then through the distribution of Jupiter the Moon disposes corporally the Lot of Prudence and Reason, and the aforesaid two Lots (namely the Lot of Courage and Boldness, and the Lot of Success and Victory) through 1 year, 6 months, 8 days.

And the square aspect of Mars receives the corporal disposition of the Moon after 9 years [and] about 11 months, and Mars disposes the said three Lots through his own square ray and the distribution of Jupiter up to 14 years, 2 months and about 3 days.

Then the distribution is changed to Saturn, and Mars disposes the said three Lots through his square ray and the distribution of Saturn through 2 years, 6 months, [and] about 6 days, and he hands over the disposition to the trine ray of Jupiter for 8 months and about 8 days; then Jupiter disposes the said three Lots by his own trine ray and in the distribution of Saturn, until he hands the disposition over to the square ray of the Sun.

And the directions of the bodies and rays of the planets come to be in such a way, with the Lords of the bounds partnering. We move even the Lots and likewise the particular twelfth-parts through up to the end of the man's life. But often, some diverse things come about in the bound of a planet, or in the disposition of a planet's body or its ray. And if the dispositor or steerer of them were a benevolent, it signifies goods according to its nature. But if a malevolent, contrary [things]. And if the dispositors were diverse, you should make a commingling of their signification.

---

[15] This should be a square.
[16] The Hermetic Lot of Necessity (attributed to Mercury), from Mercury to the Lot of Fortune by day (and the reverse by night), projected from the Ascendant. The Lot should be at 8° 53' Taurus.

Chapter III.2: On the signification of the good and bad planets appearing as the Lords of the bounds, and of those who partner with them, whether by body or by rays

Distributors (both benevolents and malevolents) have their own proper signification in the disposition of the distribution, and likewise those partnering with them by body and also rays, for they even have a certain power and more effective signification than the Lord of the Year:[17] for the Lord of the Year signifies accidents for a [single] time,[18] but the distributor [signifies] the passions which are signified in diverse times, and likewise the planet which partners with it, with the sign of the profection and its Lord and the Moon testifying to it, and the rest of the things which we said before.

Therefore it is good to look at the place of the distribution, and to consider whose bound it is, and the condition of its Lord, both according to the nativity and according to the revolution, and if it is oriental or occidental, or if quick in course or retrograde, and if it were of a good condition or bad, and in what place the bound is from the Ascendant in the nativity, even in what sign in the figure of the profection, and in which one from the Ascendant of the revolution, and whose domicile or exaltation it is, or triplicity or decan, even the sign to which the distribution arrived, and which of the benevolents or malevolents will be in it according to the nativity and the revolution, and the way in which each one has strength or weakness, and which it had according to the nativity, which according to the revolution, and [whether] it signified good or bad things, and is it a benevolent or malevolent. Likewise one must consider which ones of the planets are ejecting [their] rays, and in whose ray the distributor appears, and which of the planets was in their bounds, both in the nativity and in the revolution.

The seven kinds of distribution should even be considered:

[1] Of which the first one is if the distributor were alone and a benevolent;

[2] Second, if it were alone and malevolent;

---

[17] Omitting *inopinabilem*, following Schmidt.
[18] Reading *tempori* for *termino*.

[3] Third, if the distributor were malevolent and its partner a benevolent;

[4] Fourth, if the distributor were benevolent and its partner a malevolent;

[5] Fifth, if the distribution were of a benevolent and malevolent together;[19]

[6] Sixth, if the distributor and its partner were both malevolent;

[7] Seventh, if they were both benevolent.

[1] If therefore the distributor were a benevolent alone, and well disposed in the nativity and also the revolution, and the Lord [of the Year] and the Moon [and the Lord of][20] the Ascendant of the year were unencumbered by the bad ones, they signify good things and manifest and famous prosperities. Moreover, if the distributor were a benevolent and it were of a bad condition according to the nativity, in a contrary place, and the Lord of the Year and the Moon and [the Lord of] the Ascendant of the revolution were impeded, it signifies contrarieties in those years. But if the place of the distribution were unfortunate according to the nativity, but fortunate according to the revolution, the good things will be moderate in that year. But if it were fortunate according to the nativity but unfortunate in the revolution, the goods will be diminished, but they will not be wholly pointless on account of the signification of the figure of the nativity being firmer and more certain than that of the figure of the revolution. And if it were partially of a bad condition, and partially a good one, the outcomes will be similar in kind. In the same way, it is good for you to consider the partners and dispositors and the rest of the significations of the planets having some relation[21] or dignity in the year.

[2] We stated that the second type of distribution was like if the distributor is a malevolent and it alone signifies the condition of the distribution, and it is well disposed in a good place according to the nativity, or in a sign in

---

[19] That is, if both benevolents and malevolents were in or aspecting the bound. See below.
[20] Adding with Schmidt, here and below.
[21] Reading *relationem* for *rationem*.

which it has some dignity, or in the sign of its planetary friends, or in a benevolent sign, looked at by benevolent planets, and that he would be disposed in such a way in the revolution,²² inspected even by benevolents, and that the Lord of the Year and the Moon and the Ascendant of the revolution and its Lord are fortunate. Therefore, all of these being disposed in such a manner, that malevolent is made just like one denying its own proper nature, because of the victory and triumph and prosperity [it signifies]. But if the distribution belonged to a malevolent, and it were of a bad condition both in the nativity and in the revolution of years in which it distributes, and a benevolent did not aspect the bound itself (whether in the nativity or in the revolution), [and] in addition to these even the Moon were impeded in the Ascendants of the revolutions of years, the Lords [of the Ascendants] being inspected by malevolents by the opposite or the square, the native will die in that distribution, namely in that year in which all [figures] of this kind will occur. Indeed as we stated, the figures of nativities are stronger than the figures of revolutions, and [have] a greater possibility for doing good (and *vice versa*) than they do.

[3] We have stated the third type: if the distributor were a malevolent, but the one which partnered with it by rays or by body [is] a benevolent, [the benevolent] will rescue him whose revolution it is from death, but the malevolent will subject him to dangers, and his condition will be commingled with goods and evils, and sometimes he will be afflicted, but sometimes it will be made easier and he will be expanded; sometimes also he will be sick, but sometimes he will rejoice in good health, and sometimes he will be saddened, and sometimes he will rejoice, and at some time adversities will rush in, in another he will be saved, and he will be prospering. For example, Saturn was the distributor in a certain nativity, but Venus was partnering with him in the division by rays, and both were of equal power: on account of the nature of Venus and her benevolence, he who had the revolution will find riches and be conjoined to a wife, and will beget children; but on account of Saturn's nature his children and wife will die, and he will cry much, and he will be saddened over these things. But if Venus were stronger, it does not indicate death.

Moreover, if it were the distribution of some malevolent, and the body or ray of a benevolent partners with it, and it were inspected by some malevolent according to the nativity, and it happened [that] the sign of the

---

²² Omitting *amisit*.

profection and the Ascendant of the revolution and all of [their Lords were][23] impeded by a malevolent of this kind according to the nativity, and the [malevolent] were going to be restored [to its natal place] at the time of the revolution,[24] [and] if even the Moon and the bound in which the distribution is were found to be in contrary places or impeded in those years, and deprived of the testimony of benevolents, a figure of this kind will be very vicious, and he will either die or will approach death.

And if it were the distribution of a malevolent, nor were there the body or ray of a benevolent according to the nativity, and that malevolent or its ray happened [to be there] in the revolution, it signifies the most difficult misfortunes. But if in addition the sign of the profection and the Ascendant of the revolution and their Lords were of a bad condition, [and] were even the Moon inspected by malevolents, the danger will be greater, and he will either die in that year or he will be close to death.

[4] We have stated the fourth type: if the distributor were a benevolent, but its partner a malevolent. And if it were such a figure, it signifies the commingling of his condition, and the mediocrity of goods and evils, joy and sorrow, illness and health. But if it were the distribution of a benevolent, and a malevolent partnered with it, and the malevolent were configured with a malevolent according to the nativity, and the malevolent fell in the sign of the profection or in the Ascendant of the revolution, or their Lords were made fortunate by that benevolent, and the Moon and the bound in which the distribution is, were[25] in benevolent places, it signifies many goods, and manifest prosperities, or the goods will be moderate on account of the partnership of the malevolent. And if it were the distribution of a benevolent, and a malevolent or the ray of a malevolent fell in it at the time of the revolution, it signifies prosperity on account of it being the distribution of a benevolent, but adversities on account of the ray of the malevolent, and especially if the distributor and their Lords and the Moon were of a bad condition and not in their own places.

[5] We have stated the fifth type: if it were the distribution of a benevolent or malevolent planet, and the distributor[26] according to the nativity were in a place not its own, and [there were] a ray or body of a malevolent in [the bound] (from whatever aspect the ray is), nor were the bound inspected by

---

[23] Adding with Schmidt.
[24] Reading with Schmidt.
[25] *Applicuerit*.
[26] Reading *divisor* for *divisio*.

some benevolent appearing in a strength,[27] or if it is being inspected by a benevolent [but] vaguely, [and the benevolent] were in fewer degrees than the malevolent, and the malevolent occurred in signs in which the distribution is according to the nativity, at the same time impeding the distributor according to the nativity or the sign of the profection or the Ascendant of the revolution (or at two of those times),[28] and it were restored in the revolution when the distribution reached the body or ray of the planet, the man will inevitably be killed.

But if it were the distribution of a benevolent or malevolent, and the body or ray of a benevolent were in it, [and] even the body and ray of a malevolent, and the Lords of those years happened to be of a good condition [and] likewise with the distributor[29] and the Moon, he will incur dangers, nevertheless he will be safe; but if the good figures were weak and the contrary ones stronger, he will not be safe. And if the aforesaid figures bore themselves in such a manner and there were a malevolent in the bound (or the ray of a malevolent) at the time of the revolution, he will not be saved but he will die in an honorable manner.

[6] We have stated the sixth type: if it were the distribution of a malevolent, and another malevolent partnered in it by body or ray. And if it were such a figure, it indicates great misfortunes and the illnesses of bodies, and impediments with respect to mundane cycles,[30] and it must be feared lest he die in that year in which the distributor and the Moon and the Ascendant of the revolution and its Lord, and the Lord of the Year, were of a bad condition, and especially if the sign in which the distribution was is the place of a malevolent according to the nativity or according to the revolution (namely, at the time of the revolution).

And if the distributor were a malevolent and a malevolent partnered with it (whether by body or by ray), and at the time of the revolution a benevolent sent its ray to it, the man will not be liberated from death, but he will be honorable in his illness, and his condition will be prosperous up to the time of his death. But if at the time of the revolution a malevolent hurled its own ray, he will suffer compulsion before his death, and he will be tormented in illness, and it will be difficult for those who cured him of the infirmity, and he will die a perverse death. And if the aforesaid significators were in their

---

[27] This must mean that it is in one of its own dignities.
[28] Reading with Schmidt. The Latin reads "two of their Lords."
[29] Reading *divisore* with Schmidt for *divisione*.
[30] *Mundanas conversiones.* Not in the Greek.

own proper places, his death will be in his own fatherland among his blood-kin; but if in alien ones, it will be in alien ones among strangers.

[7] The seventh type was if it were the distribution of a benevolent, and a benevolent partnered with it by body or by ray, and both were of a good condition; and if it were such a figure, those years will be prosperous and famous for good things, and especially if the distributor and the sign of the profection and its Lord, and the Ascendant of the revolution and the Moon, were of a good condition, and particularly if the distributor and its Lord sent rays to the bound itself. But if [one] is being made unfortunate [but] the [other] will be made fortunate, the determinations of the outcomes will be commingled.

And if it were the distribution of some benevolent, but a benevolent co-partnered with it by body or by ray according to the nativity, and a malevolent or the ray of a malevolent happened [to be] in the place of the distribution at the time of the revolution, he will indeed attain good things, but he will not delight securely in these, but he will be thrown into confusion according to the nature of the malevolent.

[Six places or planets in the distribution][31]

Often indeed it happens that the distribution is a bound of some planet, and that planet partners by body or by ray in certain years, and [then] the distribution in some year changes over to another distribution, and the distributor hands over the disposition to another distributor. And six ways are established for this: [1] The first bound which is called the first distribution; [2] second, the one which is called the first distributor, handing or pushing the distribution; [3] third, the bound into which the distribution is transferred; [4] fourth, the second distributor; [5] fifth, the one which partners by body or by ray. [6] [Sixth, the second partner.][32]

[Twenty-four benevolent-malevolent combinations]

These six ways at the time of the partnership, handing over, and reception are distributed in twenty-four other ways, of which four belong particularly

---

[31] This should be compared with the brief account by 'Umar in *TBN* II.2. But Abū Ma'shar almost seems to be describing a change of bound *during* a year which has already begun.

[32] Conjecturally added by me, based on *TBN* II.2.

to the distributors: and [1] the first is the crossing of its own distribution from the bounds of benevolents [to a benevolent]; [2] the second, the crossing from bounds of malevolents and into the bounds of malevolents; [3] the third, the bound of benevolents into the bounds of malevolents; but [4] the fourth, from the bounds of malevolents into bounds of benevolents.

But another four ways are composed of the benevolent or malevolent distributors, and their handing-over or reception. And [5] the first is when a benevolent hands over to a benevolent; [6] the second, when a malevolent hands over to a benevolent; [7] third, if a malevolent hands over to a malevolent; fourth, [8] when a benevolent hands over to a malevolent.

And[33] another eight ways are taken from the distributor and the malevolent or benevolent co-distributors or ones partnering with them, by body or by rays: of which [9] the first is that the distribution would be changed over from the bounds of benevolents [to one of benevolents], with benevolents partnering; [10] second, the changing of the distribution from the bounds of benevolents into the bounds of benevolents, with a malevolent partnering; [11] third, the crossing over of the distribution from the bounds of malevolents into the bounds of benevolents, with a benevolent partnering; [12] fourth, the changing of the distribution from bounds of malevolents into the bounds of benevolents, with a malevolent partnering; [13] fifth, the changing of the distribution from the bounds of benevolents into the bounds of the malevolents, with a benevolent partnering; [14] sixth, the changing of the distribution from the bounds of benevolents into the bounds of malevolents, with a malevolent partnering; [15] seventh, the changing of the distribution from bounds of malevolents into the bounds of malevolents, with a benevolent partnering; [16] eighth, the changing of the distribution from the bounds of malevolents into the bounds of malevolents, with a malevolent partnering.

Eight other ways are put together from the benevolent and also the malevolent distributors, by body or by ray, in the handings-over and receptions: of which [17] the first is the changing of the distribution from a benevolent to a benevolent in the bound of a benevolent; [18] second, the changing of the distribution from a benevolent to a benevolent, in the bounds of a malevolent; [19] third, the changing of the distribution from a malevolent to a benevolent in the bounds of a benevolent; [20] fourth, changing from a malevolent to a benevolent in the bounds of a malevolent; [21] fifth,

---

[33] I have changed some of the wording slightly to match the Greek, as there are ordering mix-ups in a few items in the Latin.

changing from a benevolent to a malevolent in the bounds of a benevolent; [22] sixth, changing from a benevolent to a malevolent in the bounds of a malevolent; [23] seventh, changing from a malevolent to a malevolent in the bounds of a benevolent; [24] eighth, changing from a malevolent to a malevolent in the bounds of a malevolent. Therefore the changes come to be according to these twenty-four ways.

[Four pairs and eight double pairs][34]

Twelve ways and their significations are even put together through a conjunction [by pairs]: of which [1] the first is the changing of the distribution from the bounds of a benevolent to benevolent bounds, or a pushing or handing-over of the body or ray of a benevolent to the body or ray of another benevolent: for these signify lasting prosperity and changing from luckiness to luckiness; [2] second, the changing of the distributor or distribution from a malevolent to a benevolent: and it signifies changing from misfortune and humility to exaltation and glory; [3] third, the changing of the distribution or distributor from a benevolent to a malevolent: and it signifies changing from goods to evils, and the fear of death; [4] fourth, the changing of the distribution and the distributor from a malevolent to a malevolent: and it signifies that in that year he will be wrapped up [in misfortune, changing] from evil to evil, and from dangers to dangers, and the fear of death. And these four ways of conjunction are of the simple [kind].

But the other eight [ways] of conjunction are of a double [kind], of which the first is [5] the changing of the distribution from the bounds of a benevolent into the bounds of a benevolent, with a benevolent partnering, and the pushing of the disposition[35] of a benevolent to another benevolent in the bounds of a benevolent: for it signifies prosperity in that year, and an abundance of goods.

[6] Second, the changing of the distribution from bounds of benevolents into benevolent bounds, with a malevolent partnering, or the pushing of the disposition of a benevolent to a benevolent in the bounds of a malevolent: for it signifies prosperity in that year on account of the disposition[36] of

---

[34] The significance of these combinations, as opposed to the previous ones, is unclear to me.
[35] Reading *dispositionis* as below for *divisoris*.
[36] Reading *dispositionem* for *dispositionum*.

goods, but not [wholly] pure and without stain on account of the nature of the malevolent.

[7] Third, the changing of the distribution from the bounds of malevolents into the bounds of benevolents, with a benevolent partnering, or the pushing of a malevolent to a benevolent in the bounds of a benevolent: for it signifies changing from adversity to prosperity in a year of his kind.

[8] Fourth, the changing of the distribution from the bounds of malevolents into the bounds of benevolents, with a malevolent partnering, or the handing over or pushing of a malevolent to a benevolent in the bounds of a malevolent: indeed it signifies the mediocrity of both fortune and misfortune in that year, and both in goods and in evils, but the goods will be more powerful.

[9] Fifth, the changing of the distribution from bounds of benevolents into malevolent bounds, with a benevolent partnering, or the handing over of a benevolent [to a malevolent in the bounds of a benevolent]: and it signifies the mediocrity of both goods and evils in that year, and the evils will be more powerful.

[10] Sixth, the changing of the distribution from the bounds of benevolents into bounds of malevolents, with a malevolent partnering, or the handing over of a benevolent to a malevolent in the bounds of a malevolent: and it signifies adversities and many harms and dangers in that year, and the fear of death.

[11] Seventh, the changing of the distribution from the bounds of a malevolent [to the bounds of a malevolent] with a benevolent partnering, or the handing over of a malevolent to a malevolent in the bounds of a benevolent: and it signifies great dangers in that year, and fears of death.

[12] Eighth, the changing of the distribution from the bounds of a malevolent into the bounds of a malevolent, with a malevolent partnering, or the handing over of a malevolent to a malevolent in the bounds of a malevolent: and in [situations] of this kind it signifies the appearances of many adversities, and the terrors of death, and that the evil is greater, and all [things] are malevolent.

Indeed the kinds of goods and evils is known [*a*] from the nature of the planet and from [*b*] the nature of its domicile and [*c*] even [its] place, both that of the nativity and of the revolution. But of these three, the distributor has the stronger power, the one which partners with it by body [has] the second-[strongest power], but partnership by rays is the last. Also, of the aspects, the opposite is stronger, after that the square, then the trine, but the sextile is most weak. But it is not necessary to take these things which we have stated about the one partnering according to the revolution, but [only] according to the nativity.

If the direction both from the Ascendant and from the rest of the *hīlājes* reached some one of the fixed stars signifying prosperity,[37] but that star was signifying prosperity before (according to the nativity), it will show its operation on the spot. And if it had no signification in the nativity, it brings in some portion of prosperity according to the nature of that planet to whose complexion the star is likened. Moreover, if the direction reached some malevolent fixed star signifying the blinding of the eyes or violent death, or homicide, some part of the operation of that star will appear immediately.

But whatever we have said before in our present treatise that signifies death for him whose revolution it is, both in distributions and in directions, they then come to be when those years will agree with the number of the years of life (or near it) which the *hīlāj* of the nativity signified. Let it be understood likewise in the death of parents, brothers, and others. But if the revolution of the year signified death and destruction, but the full amount of years did not happen then (namely, [the years] which the *hīlāj* signified), death will not touch [him], but [rather] a great and dangerous impediment.

Chapter III.3: On the signification of Saturn if he were the dispositor by distribution, and on the signification of the partnership of the planets in the distribution

If you made the direction of some one of the *hīlājes* (namely of the Sun or Moon or the Ascendant or the Lot of Fortune or the degree of the conjunction or the degree of the prevention), know the planetary distributor and the one which partners with it (whether by body or degree): for each one has its own proper signification, whether of good or bad things. And indeed the stronger of [them] is the distributor, which is said to be the dispositor of the *hīlāj* [by bound]; after that, the one which partners with it; but the rest are weak in power.

---

[37] For a list of these, see *BA* III.2.1 pp. 75-81, and Appendix D in *Persian Nativities* Volume I (p. 346).

If therefore Saturn disposes, with no planet sending a ray to those bounds nor aspecting Saturn, the signification in that year [signifies] long illnesses from coldness and thicker phlegm, and an attack of the belly, the disease of stones, with a cutting fissure[38] and swelling,[39] and melancholic illnesses; it even signifies worries, griefs and gloom, and regrets, and confusions[40] and violence, and the idleness of advantageous workings, not to mention a multitude of things being unsettled,[41] [and] anxiety over some past and badly-managed matters.

And if Saturn, as the distributor, himself aspected the bounds, it signifies the death of him whose revolution it is, namely in that distribution.

But if Jupiter partnered with him, it signifies the dissolution of evils, and harm to the native from parents or children.

And if Mars partnered with him, it signifies impediments and harms from brothers. But if Mars aspected Saturn with the benevolents not aspecting them, it signifies death and certain illnesses, and an attack on the brain and nerves, and he will be overcome by his enemies.

But if the Sun, being free from the bad ones, is partnering with Saturn, it signifies that that man is rescued from death, but he will suffer sorrows and perhaps his father will die, and he will endure diverse sorrows.

And if Venus partnered with him, he will be conjoined to a woman, and a child will be born to him, and he will suffer tribulations, and some one of his own children will die, and even [one] of his wives.

And if Mercury partnered with him, it signifies detriment from slaves and on account of teachings and computations and writings and giving and receiving, and purchases and sales. But if Mercury sent his own rays to the place itself and were inspected by Mars, it signifies harm on account of lying and false writing, and on account of deceptions and frauds and on account of certain statements and workings.

And if the Moon partnered with him, it signifies a multitude of worries and anxieties, and the disquiet of [his] life, and a multitude of upheavals in things and estate management, and he will be impeded in everything he will handle, and either his mother or sisters will die, and if they do not die they will endure serious dangers, and in a time of this kind he will be impeded in all of [his] workings.

---

[38] Reading *incisione fissura* with the Latin marginal comment. The Greek has "wasting."
[39] Or, a tumor (*tumore*).
[40] Reading *confusiones* for *configurationes*, with Schmidt.
[41] Or perhaps, things being undone or turned around (*revolutionum*).

But if Saturn, disposing in revolutions, were unencumbered by the bad ones according to the nativity, and in a good place, and inspected by Jupiter, it signifies that the native will be assisted on account of treasures and on account of buildings and habitations, and by all matters of which Saturn is the significator.

And then the signification of the planets will particularly come to be when they send their rays to that bound, as we have said before.

Chapter III.4: On the signification of Jupiter by his disposition, and on the planets partnering [with him]

If Jupiter disposed, with none of the planets partnering with or aspecting him, and he were in a good place according to the figure of the nativity, it signifies he is going to be conjoined with the best wife at the time of the distribution, and will have affectionate[42] children, and he will speak with kings and princes, and with noble fellow-citizens of his, and his dignity and honor and glory will be increased. And if he were born of a middling fortune, he will have a position of first place over those who are of his rank, and he will dominate over his compatriots, and he will attain riches. But if he were of a superior fortune, he will obtain dignity over cities and peoples and their habitations, and his glory and riches will be added to, and a child will be born to him, or a child to his child.

And if Saturn is partnering with him, it signifies that he will corrupt or destroy the paternal riches, and the patrimony of his forefathers, and his child and parents will be harmed, and he will be saddened, and he will suffer a breakdown of the soul; he will even cry and be slow in his works, and he will be impeded in his petitions,[43] and in business matters he will be not well manageable, and he will be sick with a different disease, and [afterwards] he will be restored or improve.

And if Mars partners with him, it signifies the confusion of the good things which we said (whose significator is Jupiter), and their diminution and being taken away.

And if the Sun partners with him, it signifies he will rule in some dignity or work, and his riches and prosperity will be augmented, and [his] dignity

---

[42] Schmidt reads: "legitimate."
[43] Lit., "in what he seeks for" (*petitionibus*).

and glory, and speaking with kings and princes, and many will arrive at his gate, and plead with him, and he will be respectable, and superior in every harmful thing, even blessed, and he will be glad with his parents and grandparents and blood-kin, and in diverse matters, and he will get the paternal inheritance.

And if Venus partners with him, it signifies he is going to be conjoined to an honest wife, a blood-relative or noble, and he will have a good child, and will rejoice in women, and he will have advantage through them, and he will persevere in songs and games and delights, and he will obtain renowned prosperities. And if Jupiter were configured to Venus according to the nativity, his prosperity will be increased, and he will acquire riches, and acquire renowned riches, and his garments increased, and he will be clothed in royal garments, and he will be adorned with royal dress, and his happiness will be multiplied. But if he were a man of mediocre fortune, he will obtain the aforesaid in a middling way.

And if Mercury partners with him and he were of a good condition, it signifies cheerfulness and advantage on account of doctrine and teaching and an increase of eloquence and wisdom, and he will befriend noble and illustrious men and the administrators of things, and he will be fortunate and prudent in his estate management and workings, and he will be prospering in his occupations, and he will be glad regarding his children, and his prosperity will be increased, and he will be improved in his [religious] tenets. But if he were of a bad condition, the aforesaid good things will be decreased, and he will get [something] of this kind, but he will suffer confusion because of them.

And if the Moon partnered with him, it signifies the soundness of the body, and a good bearing, and glory and prosperity, and he will rejoice over [his] sisters and mother, and he will obtain things hoped for, and he will be praised by many, and he will be an intimate of kings, and he will be ready in his works.

Chapter III.5: On the signification of the disposition of Mars and of those planets partnering with him

If Mars distributed in the disposition without the partnership or testimony of some planet, and he were of a good condition according to the nativity, look: and if the native were of an illustrious fortune, it signifies great offices and a lofty position of first places; and a multitude of soldiers and ordinary persons will be gathered together at his gate, and his strength will be added to, even arms and draft-animals, and he will engage in riding, and he will dominate over his enemies, he will get gold and silver, he will acquire abundant riches, and he will be triumphant in battles, he will even employ rashness and injustice. And if the native were of a mediocre fortune, it signifies his familiarity with powerful men from whom he will obtain advantages and his riches will be increased, and he will be in charge over some and be distinguished among his equals. And if he were of a small fortune, he will be friendly to certain princes and will be made fortunate through them. But if [Mars] were of a bad condition, it signifies an illness of the body by heat, from abscesses and the flowing of blood, even more so sorrows and contentions and useless foreign journeys, and especially if Mercury were the Lord of the Year and were of a bad condition.

But if Saturn partnered with him, and he aspected him by a contrary aspect, it signifies a long illness and the bad state of the body, and the motion of humors, and idleness in workings, and a multitude of [worried] thoughts, and flight from his own home, and perhaps he will fall into his enemies' [hands], and he will be connected to diverse misfortunes, or he will die. And if Mars and Saturn were impeded at the same time, perhaps he will meet with a violent death or shameful murder.

And if Jupiter partnered with him, and Mars were of a good condition according to the nativity, and in a domicile of Jupiter, aspected by him, he will reach greater fortune with it being great in extent, and prosperity, and he will direct his operations, and will use justice and [have] the best rank, and good works, and particularly if the Sun aspected Jupiter in the nativity by a concordant aspect: for then it signifies that he will serve kings. And if Jupiter were of a bad condition, he will suffer adversities from administrators and officials or powerful men, and illustrious persons will be inimical to him, and he will be harmed on the occasion of children.

And if Mars partnered with himself[44] and were of a bad condition, he will fall into the hands of his enemies, and will be connected to robbers and bad men in every way, and there is fear lest perhaps he might die.

And if the disposition belonged to Mars and the Sun partnered with him, he will be harmed by his parents, and kings and magnates, and he will suffer

---

[44] Reading with Schmidt for "Jupiter."

detentions and prison, and illnesses from heat and burning. But if they were impeded, there is fear lest perhaps he might die.

[But if Venus partnered with him, the native will be harmed by his relatives and children, or on account of them.]⁴⁵

But if Mercury partnered with him while Mars is disposing, he will suffer diverse dangers and disgraces, and many will accuse him, and he will suffer harms from his enemies, and from certain secretaries, and on the occasion of letters and lies and false writing, and contentions, and his own workings.

But if the disposition belonged to Mars and the Moon partnered with him, he will suffer illnesses and the drying out of the body, and diverse contentions, and he will be saddened on account of some estate management, but even more so on account of some legations and announcements and reputations, even the mother and sisters.

Chapter III.6: On the signification of Venus and of the planets partnering with her

If Venus alone disposes, with no planet partnering with her or configured with her, and she herself were of a good condition, it signifies the best and unencumbered marriage-union, and cheerfulness with women, and advantage from effeminate men (namely eunuchs and the like), and from kings and the children of kings, and the obtaining of diverse prosperities, and especially in the times in which Venus was the Lady of the Year or in a time in which the year arrives at the sign where the Lot of Marriage-Union was [in the nativity]. And if he were born of the highest fortune, in that distribution⁴⁶ he will have much food, having an abundance of the means of livelihood, and women and friends will be added to him, and he will rejoice in them, and they will rejoice in him, and he will persevere continually in melodies and songs and dancing and cheerful things. And if he were of a mediocre fortune, he will be conjoined to a wife, and he will obtain many goods from effeminate men and women, and he will speak with excellent men, he will even speak personally with them in assemblies [devoted to] teaching.

And if Venus disposed [the time] and Saturn partnered with her, it signifies impediments with respect to workings, and the contempt of women, and

---

⁴⁵ Adding based on Schmidt.
⁴⁶ Reading *in divisione* with Schmidt for *in dispositione illius fortunae divisionis*.

sorrows on account of them, and the illness or death of the wife, and he will have contentions and diverse discords. And if, while Saturn partnered with her, he aspected her and impeded [her], it signifies that he will rejoice in women for a middling amount of time, [but] afterwards [a woman] will die, and afterwards he will have the greatest grief, and he will cry and sigh continually.

And if the disposition of the distribution belonged to Venus, and Jupiter partnered with her, if the native were of a superior fortune it signifies he is going to be conjoined to a respectable and wealthy wife having treasures or diverse necklaces, and he will be anointed with good-smelling ointment, and he will converse with composers employing songs and jokes. And if he were of a mediocre fortune, he will be made moderately fortunate in [matters] of this kind.

And if Venus disposed [the time] and Mars partnered with her, it signifies a vicious and acute illness like madness[47] and [things] of this kind, and some one of his wives will die or be sick, and he will suffer harm because of them, and he will have contentions with them, and will be involved in lust and sexual intercourse, and will be corrupted[48] because of things of this kind. But if Mars aspected Venus and Mercury by a contrary aspect according to the nativity or according to the revolution, it indicates enmities and diverse quarrels, even threats and shameful situations.[49] But if Jupiter aspected Mars in the two times, it dissolves the impediments.

And if the Sun partnered with Venus, it signifies glory and favor from kings and princes, and advantage from them and from parents.

But if Venus partnered with herself, it indicates he obtains prosperity according to the nature of Venus; and if she were impeded, adversity.

And if Mercury partnered with her, he will be aided on the occasion of teaching and hidden documentation, and he will obtain usefulness because of women, and he will be delighted in them but he will suffer reprimands with them on the occasion of prostitutes.

And if the Moon partnered with her, he will be conjoined to a woman [who is] a blood-relative, most beautiful and the best, and he will go to bed with diverse beautiful women, and he will be aided on the occasion of women, and he will arrive at dignities and riches.

---

[47] Schmidt: "inflammation of the brain."
[48] Reading with Schmidt for *coinquinabitur*.
[49] Schmidt: "accusations" (Lat. *causas*).

Chapter III.7: On the distribution of Mercury and of the planets partnering with him

When Mercury disposes [the time], with Jupiter partnering with him or configured in that [year], it signifies the addition of knowledge, instruction, prudence and riches, and he will cling to writings and business dealings and contracts, and he will rejoice over some Mercurial dealings or actions or workings. But if he were of a bad condition, he will suffer evils from causes of this kind.

And if Saturn partnered with him, he will be weak in body and he will be sick with the worst and long-lasting illness, and his workings will be impeded, he will even be lazy and difficult, immovable,[50] and will meet with diverse dangers and contentions. And if Mars aspected him or the bound in some revolutions of the distribution, the native will be very much harmed, and he will be fined and suffer dangers on account of statements and quarrels and unsuitable estate management. And if in addition to what we said before the Moon aspected the bound by a contrary aspect, the impediment will be greater, and especially if the Lord of the Year were a malevolent.

And if Jupiter partnered with him, it signifies the increase of knowledge and doctrine through which he will be assisted, and he will attain advantage and riches from kings and princes.

And if Mars partnered with him, it signifies the worst illness, and false accusations and quarrels, and his mind will be fatigued over the attacks of certain people, and he will be blamed by many, and a certain disease will come about in his head, and especially if Mars were configured to Mercury by a contrary figure[51] according to the nativity. But if Saturn aspected Mars or the bound, or if the Tail were in the sign of the distribution, he will fall into the hands of his enemies and they will overcome him, and he will be sick with an illness about which the doctors will have fear, and he will have a poorly-tempered head and body. But if Jupiter aspected, it dissolves the evils.

And if the Sun partnered with him, it signifies the obtaining of dignity and the increase of glory, and he will have a position of first place over many [people], and he will be made especially fortunate, and his riches will be increased, and he will be industrious, and the secrets of knowledge will be revealed to him.

---

[50] Reading *immobilis* for *mobilis*.
[51] Schmidt: "opposite."

And if Venus partnered with him, it signifies teachings and friendships and familiarity towards some princes and people who know, and a child will be born to him, and he will rejoice over brothers and sisters, and he will be sweet in statements, and manageable, and he will speak with women, and rejoice with them.

And if Mercury co-partnered with himself, and he were of a good condition, it signifies manifest prosperities according to his nature. But if he were impeded, the contrary.

And if the Moon partnered, his knowledge and teaching will be increased, and he will think about divine and heavenly matters, and prophetic knowledge and astronomy, and he will be prosperous and manageable in all things which he undertook; he will have advantage from them, and his riches and treasures will be increased.

[Further instructions about the distributors and partners]

However, we have stated these things before about the distributor and [its] partner: they are certain foundations and general rules. And there are certain others which signify particular accidents: for if a benevolent or malevolent planet aspected some one of them at some time, [the benevolent] will add to good things and take away from bad things, or [the malevolent] adds to bad things and takes away from good things. For if some planet signified fortune, then were another planet to impede it, it turns that fortune to misfortune, and especially if it were in an angle. But if it fell away,[52] it does not have much power, and especially if it were in a tropical sign. And if some planet signified harm, but a benevolent planet aspected it, it signifies those things which were said before.

However, it is good for you to inspect both places in which [the distributor and the partner] are, and to make a determination with them. For example, it happens that, were Mercury in the Ascendant, free from the bad ones, but [he were] the Lord of the place of enemies and [also] the Lord of the Lot of Fortune, but the distribution reached him, it signifies impediments from enemies, and contentions on account of riches. Moreover Saturn and Jupiter, [if] one was the distributor but the other partnered in the distribution, [and] they were enemies at the beginning of the nativity, it signifies contentions and disagreements with parents and blood-kin. Moreover, Venus

---

[52] I.e., if it were cadent.

and Mars, [if] one was the distributor but the other the partner, [and] one was being impeded by the other, and [each] one was in the places of the other, on account of that they signify quarrels with the wife, and an accusation of fornication.

But if the planets signified lasting good or evil according to the nativity, a transfer and change of bounds does not change [something] of this kind, but at a certain time[53] [it can signify it] with a certain moderate alteration then. For each one of the planets shows its own operations which it was signifying according to the nativity, [more] openly when the distribution manifests them; and if that planet were[54] in a firm sign in the nativity, the goods or evils at the time of the distribution will be unchangeable. But if in a double-bodied sign, they take on intensification [or relaxation];[55] and if in a tropical sign, the accidents of the distribution will be at certain times.[56]

Likewise, at the beginning of the distribution it is good to consider where the distributor has arrived.[57] For, were it in a fixed sign in these two times, the goods or evils will be more lasting [and consistent];[58] in a like way, more changeable in double-bodied and tropical ones. And it often happens that the distributor shows its own operation at once, [but] often twice, whenever it disposes. (However, it is good to understand the same for the partner[59] [as for] the distributor.) For if the distributor were in a firm sign in the nativity, and it did not aspect the place of the distribution, the operation of the planet comes to be once, namely when the distribution agrees with the ascension of the sign in which it is according to the nativity, or [according to] the number of the greater or middle or least years. And if the distributor or partner were in a double-bodied sign according to the nativity, more often their significations are renewed. And if they were in a movable sign, their significations will be through individual distributions and partnerships, according to the power of the planet.

In those times which pertain to the dispositions of a man, in every distribution or partnership it will be according to the diversity of the figures of the planetary dispositors or those co-partnering with them. However, their

---

[53] Reading *alteras* for *altera*.
[54] Omitting *non*.
[55] Adding with Schmidt.
[56] Perhaps this means they are somewhat unpredictable or take place suddenly and in many changing circumstances.
[57] By transit at the time.
[58] Reading with Schmidt for *divisibiliora*.
[59] Adding with Schmidt.

operations come to be more intense when their figures are concordant with the figures of the beginning of the nativity, and when they aspect the place of the distribution and the Lord of the sign in which the distribution arrives, [and they aspect] the Ascendant of the beginning [of the nativity] and its Lord, if the distributor and the Lord of the Year were the same, or if the year reached [that planet's] place according to the nativity or according to the revolution. But if [the things] of this kind were discordant, the outcome of the judgments[60] will be infirm. If however the significations of the planet were concordant with the ascension of the sign in which it had been in the nativity, or its years, then the outcomes of the judgments will be strong.

Chapter III.8: On the partnership of the Lord of the Year and its distribution, [with] the distributor and the Ascendant according to [their combined] signification

If the distribution and its Lord were in a good place according to the nativity and according to the revolution, and the distributor were a benevolent, it signifies the greatest prosperity.

And if the year reached the fourth place [by profection], with no malevolent aspecting it, or the Lord of the Year happened to be in the fourth place of the nativity, in a sign in which it has some dignity, and the distributor were a benevolent and in the bounds of the distribution, and free of the bad ones according to the nativity, and the Moon aspected the Lot of Fortune, and she were conjoined to Jupiter, and both were of a good condition, he whose revolution it is will find many riches and prosperity because of inheritance and management and treasure. But it is good to look at the figure of the nativity: and if it signified the discovery of treasure or an inheritance, he will find [things] of this kind, and he will be suddenly enriched. And if Saturn were the distributor, it shows land and fields and inheritance from fathers and grandfathers and ancient men. And if it were Jupiter, it shows gold or silver from rulers and powerful men. But if the Lord of the Year and the distributor were malevolents, and they were found in alien places at the time of the revolution, and a benevolent were configured with them, it signifies good things, but moderate ones. And if the distributor were in a sign of the

---

[60] Reading *infirmus erit eventus iudiciorum* (as below) for *infirma erunt eventus iudicia*.

likeness of men in the eleventh, conjoined to the Lot of Fortune, it signifies a multitude of benefits and donations toward paupers.

Moreover, if at the time of the revolution there were some fixed star (of those which signify luckiness) in the Ascendant of the revolution or in the Midheaven, or in the degree of the sign of the distribution, or with the same degrees, or with one of the luminaries,[61] it signifies prosperity in that year. Moreover, if some fixed star having the nature of one or two of the planets were in some one of the aforesaid places, when that planet (or two) whose nature it has disposes through the distribution, they show their own proper operation immediately.

Likewise, if some one of the comets appeared in the Ascendant of the nativity or in the sign of the profection, or in the Ascendant of the revolution, or in the sign in which the distribution has arrived, or in the bounds of the distribution, or with the Lords of places of this kind, if those whose revolution it is were kings, they will be afflicted in battles, and certain people will turn away from them, and they will appear to their enemies and will be sick and will labor and be saddened, and they will do unjust things to the people, and perhaps they will be destroyed. But if they were of mediocre [or] inferior fortune, their enemies will be multiplied and they will suffer evils.

And if the Sun and Moon were eclipsed in some one of the aforesaid places, and their Lords were in the sign of the eclipse, they signify worries and anxieties, and illnesses, and [his] enemies' overcoming [him], and especially if the sign and the Lord of the sign were impeded.

Moreover,[62] if the Ascendant of the revolution were a sign in which there was a malevolent in the inception or at the beginning of the nativity, or the sign of the profection [was also in such a place], take the malevolent as both the Lord of the Ascendant or the Lord of the Year, because it is stronger than they are. And likewise for benevolents.

However, after these, look at the Lord of the Year and at the distributor and [its] partner. If however a malevolent were in some sign according to the nativity,[63] and that sign were the Ascendant of the revolution,[64] and accord-

---

[61] See these natal indications of prosperity in *BA* III.2.0-2.1, *JN* Ch. 6, and Abū Bakr II.2.0.
[62] See a very similar formulation in II.24 above. This sentence seems mainly to reinforce the idea that a natal configuration is more important for the themes of the year than locations and rulerships by transit alone at the revolution.
[63] Schmidt has the malevolent as the domicile Lord of the sign, which does not seem to be right, given the statements immediately preceding and following this sentence.
[64] Reading with Schmidt for "profection."

ing to the nativity that malevolent [harms] the distributor or the sign of the profection or its Lord, the judgment is contrary, and will very much impede.

Moreover, if the malevolents in the revolution aspected the sign of the profection or the Moon, with no benevolent aspecting, it signifies great detriment according to the nature of the Lord of the Year and of the distributor.

Likewise, if none impeded the Lord of the Year at the beginning of the nativity, and both the Lord of the Year and the distributor were malevolent, and some one of the benevolents were conjoined with the Lord of the Year or aspected it by a square, it will not harm, on account of the nature of the benevolent (it is the same for the distributor).

Moreover, if the Lord of the Year and the distributor were malevolents, and they were impeded in the revolution throughout the whole year, they signify inactivity and upheavals.

Likewise if the distribution and the distributor were of a bad condition, even being cadent from the Ascendant of the revolution, it signifies dangers and many necessities.

And if Mercury were the Lord of the Year, and it fell [to him to be] with Mars in the revolution, it signifies his being replaced in [some] duty, and especially if he had authority over the year.[65] And if [Mercury] were inspected by Jupiter, and he happened to be in a benevolent place with the Lot of Work or of the Kingdom,[66] his being replaced will be talked about, but someone will not succeed him.

Moreover, if the Lord of the Year were with some planet, it is good to unite with it the signification of the planet with which it is. In the same way it is good for you to look at the planet appearing[67] with the distributor: if it were a malevolent, it signifies illnesses and detriments and the dispersal[68] of riches. But if a benevolent, beneficence and prosperity according to its own proper nature.

Likewise if some planet were impeding the nativity at the beginning of the nativity, and in the revolution it was in the sign of the Ascendant of the nativity [by transit], or in the Ascendant of the revolution, or in [the place of]

---

[65] Reading with Schmidt for "if he were the Lord of the Year." I take this to mean that he is both the Lord of the Year and the distributor.
[66] See footnote to II.20 above.
[67] From this point, reading *cum divisore et cum malevolus fuerit* with Schmidt for *et cum divisor signo malevolus fuerit* ("and if the distributor were malevolent by sign").
[68] Reading *dispersionem* for *dispositionem*, with Schmidt.

the Moon in the nativity or the revolution, or in the place of the distribution, or with the Lords of places of this kind, they signify the greatest harm. Moreover if some planet signified [good fortune] according to the nativity [and were in these places], it signifies prosperity.

Moreover if the distributor were benevolent, [and] even the Lord of the Ascendant of the revolution and the Lord of the Moon, they perfect good things.

Likewise if the Lord of the sign of the profection and the sign itself were impeded, they signify harm and diminution.

Moreover, if the Lord of the Year and the distributor were benevolents, but placed in a bad place at the time of the revolution of the year, or retrograde, and one of the two [malevolent][69] planets were in the Ascendant or in the Midheaven in the revolution, it signifies the malice and difficulty of the year, and the victory of the enemies, and a wound from iron, or a fall from a high place, and loss.

Likewise, if the Lords of the Year were malevolent and at the time of the revolution they happened to be in the western angle, or in the place of a malevolent impeding the distribution[70] (either in the place of a malevolent impeding the Lord of the Year, or in the place of a malevolent impeding the sign of the profection), and Venus and Mercury were with that malevolent in the revolution, there will be harm concerning blood-kin and children. And if the Sun and Moon were with the malevolent, the parents will be harmed either in their body or in their riches, or in their power or in dignity.

Moreover, if the Lord of the distribution were a malevolent and it was in the place of diseases according to the nativity, and in the revolution it reached a bad place with a malevolent, and the Moon were impeded, it signifies impediments and necessities.

Likewise, if the Lord of the Year were a malevolent, and at the time of the revolution it was in a bad place, slow in course, or under the rays, or the distributor and the Moon in the two times were in a bad place, with malevolents aspecting [the Moon], with the Lord of the Year or the distributor appearing in the sixth[71] place, they signify impediment in that year, and harm; it signifies the same if the Lord of the Year were a benevolent and it was of a bad condition both in the nativity and in the revolution.

---

[69] Adding with Schmidt.
[70] In this case, the profection.
[71] Reading with Schmidt for *bono*.

Moreover, if the year reached the Ascendant of the nativity [by profection], and if the malevolents impeded it in a moderate way, they signify the greatest harm, especially if a benevolent did not aspect the Lord of the Year, and the distributor were of a bad condition.

Likewise, if the Lord of the Year [and] the distributor were malevolents, and were in a bad place in the revolution, and in the opposite of malevolents, with the benevolents not aspecting the Ascendant of the year, [and the Lot of Fortune][72] of the revolution were of a bad condition, it signifies the difficulty of the year and impediments and harms. But if Jupiter and Venus were in the conjunction of the Moon, or they aspected her, they signify liberation from the evils.

Moreover, if the year reached the Ascendant of the nativity [by profection], and a malevolent aspected it by an opposite in the revolution of the year, and both the Lord of the Year and the distributor were malevolents, and they impeded the Moon, and even the Sun and Moon and Mercury appeared in the Ascendant, and all happened to be of a bad condition, they signify fears and prison and contentions and quarrels with enemies.

Likewise if the Lord of the Year and the distributor were a malevolent, and both the Sun and Moon happened to be under the earth at the time of the revolution, not inspected by the benevolents, they signify the illness of him whose revolution it is, and harm on the parents, and the corruption of their riches. But if Jupiter aspected the Lot of Fathers at the time of the revolution, the [parents] will be saved and the harm will abate.

Moreover, if the Lord of the Year or the distributor were Jupiter, and at the time of the revolution he was with Saturn under the earth, it signifies the death of the children. Likewise if the distributor were benevolent (or malevolent)[73] and removed[74] according to the revolution and according to the nativity, and not inspected by the benevolents, and the distributor and the Moon happened to be impeded by the bad ones, with even the Lord of the Year being impeded, and in a place not its own,[75] it signifies death.

Likewise, if Saturn were the distributor and both he and Mars impeded the place of the distribution in the revolution, with the benevolents not aspecting the place itself, they signify death.

---

[72] Adding with Schmidt.
[73] Adding with Schmidt.
[74] That is, "declining" or cadent (Schmidt). Also omitting *super revolutionem*.
[75] Following Schmidt and reading *proprio* (as below) for *non primo*.

Moreover if the year reached the Ascendant of the nativity [by profection], and both the Ascendant of the revolution and the Ascendant of the nativity happened to be one sign, and the distributor and the Lord of the Year were malevolents, and in places not their own, and in the revolution the figures of the planets were such as that in the nativities of those who are not nourished,[76] it signifies losing hope for life in that year.

From the Ascendant up to the Midheaven is the eastern quarter, and it[77] signifies one-fourth of the year; from the Midheaven up to the seventh place[78] is the southern quarter, and it signifies [the second one-fourth] of the year; indeed from the west up to the angle of the earth is the western quarter, and it signifies [the third] one-fourth[79] of the year; but from the angle of the earth to the Ascendant is the northern [quarter], and it signifies [the last] one-fourth of the year. However, it is good to look at the Lord of the Year and at the distributor and at the benevolents and malevolents to see in what quarter they are, and to make a determination according to [the places] of this kind. If there were malevolents in the Ascendant or in the eleventh or in the Midheaven of the revolution, but benevolents under the earth, they signify severity at the beginning of the year, but good things in the last [part], especially if the sign of the year were movable.[80] Often the planets which are in the angles [signify things at the beginning of the year, while those which are cadent][81] signify those things which are at the end.

It is also good for you not only to make conclusions about[82] prosperous or adverse things with respect to the distributor and the partner and the rest, but to consider where they have reached, and [also] the Lots according to the nativity (whether [the Lots have reached] benevolents or malevolents), according to ascensions and according [to cycles or by profecting] one sign for a year.[83] Indeed, look at the Lord of the Year and at the distributor and the partner, to see of what Lot they are Lords, both according to the nativity and according to the revolution, and you should make a determination according to [matters] of this kind. For example, the Lot of Brothers and its

---

[76] See broadly *BA* III.1.3, *JN* Ch. 1, *TBN* I.3, and Abū Bakr I.12.
[77] Omitting *planeta*.
[78] Reading *locum* for *coelum*.
[79] Reading *quartam* for *tertiam*.
[80] A movable sign allows for changes from one thing to another.
[81] Adding with Schmidt.
[82] Reading *argumentari* for *augmentari*.
[83] Reading broadly with Schmidt in the preceding sentences. Schmidt's version only refers to the Lots, not where the other planets have reached. See also *BA* IV.1, p. 186.

Lord were in an unsuitable place in the nativity, with malevolents, and [a figure] of this kind was signifying that the native's brothers and sisters will be impeded in the time at which the malevolent distributes or partners; and if the Lord of the Lot in the nativity impedes the Lord of the Ascendant [of the revolution], the native will be impeded in that year.[84]

Chapter III.9: On the ninth-parts and their direction, and the third of their distribution, according to the opinions of the Indians

The Babylonians and the Persians and Egyptians use the distribution in the way we stated a little before. But the Indians and those bordering them, considering that diverse affections befall men in one [and the same] distribution, did not make the direction through the bounds just as the others did, but they made it through the *noupachrates*, in order that the judgments of the outcomes[85] may proceed more accurately. Therefore, in directions it is good to use these two methods, the one separately from the other, so that the knowledge of the accidents of the year might come to be more accurately. But the name of this method in the speech of the Indians is interpreted with the expression "ninth-part,"[86] and it [has a size] of 200', namely 3 1/3 degrees exactly:[87] therefore in every sign there are nine ninth-parts, of which each has its own significator.

---

[84] Presumably, the native will be impeded *because of* those matters signified by the Lot.
[85] Reading *eventuum iudicia* for *iudiciorum eventus*.
[86] *Novenarium*.
[87] *Directi*, but reading with Schmidt.

	0°00'– 3°20'	3°20'– 6°40'	6°40'– 10°00'	10°00'– 13°20'	13°20'– 16°40'	16°40'– 20°00'	20°00'– 23°20'	23°20'– 26°40'	26°40'– 30°00'
♈	♂	♀	☿	☽	☉	☿	♀	♂	♃
♉	♄	♄	♃	♂	♀	☿	☽	☉	☿
♊	♀	♂	♃	♄	♄	♃	♂	♀	☿
♋	☽	☉	☿	♀	♂	♃	♄	♄	♃
♌	♂	♀	☿	☽	☉	☿	♀	♂	♃
♍	♄	♄	♃	♂	♀	☿	☽	☉	☿
♎	♀	♂	♃	♄	♄	♃	♂	♀	☿
♏	☽	☉	☿	♀	♂	♃	♄	♄	♃
♐	♂	♀	☿	☽	☉	☿	♀	♂	♃
♑	♄	♄	♃	♂	♀	☿	☽	☉	☿
♒	♀	♂	♃	♄	♄	♃	♂	♀	☿
♓	☽	☉	☿	♀	♂	♃	♄	♄	♃

Figure 4: Ninth-parts

And if it were the sign Aries or Leo or Sagittarius, in signs of this kind the Lord of each first ninth-part will be [thus]: namely, Mars is the Lord of the first ninth-part of Aries, Venus (namely the Lady of Taurus) will rule the second one, Mercury (the Lord of Gemini) the third one, the Moon (the Lady of Cancer) the fourth one, the Sun (the Lord of Leo) the fifth one, Mercury (the Lord of Virgo) the sixth one—and in so doing you will find the Lord of the ninth ninth-part to be namely Jupiter (the Lord of Sagittarius).

And if it were the triplicity of Taurus and Virgo and Capricorn, the Lord of the first ninth-part will be Saturn (namely the Lord of Capricorn), of the second one Saturn [again] (the Lord of Aquarius), of the third Jupiter (the Lord of Pisces); and in so doing you will find the Lord of the ninth ninth-part in each of one those signs to be Mercury (the Lord of Virgo).

And if you took Gemini and Libra and Aquarius, again you will make Venus the Lady of the first ninth-part (since [she is] the Lady of Libra), Mars of the second one (since [he is] the Lord of Scorpio), and in so doing you will find the Lord of the ninth ninth-part to be Mercury (the Lord of Gemini).

And if you examined Cancer, Scorpio and Pisces, the Lady of the first ninth-part will be the Moon (the Lady of Cancer), of the second one the Sun (the Lord of Leo), and using the same rule you will find the Lord of the ninth ninth-part to be Jupiter (namely, the Lord of Pisces).

And there is another such way, more abbreviated. If you want to know the Lords of their ninth-parts, look to see of what triplicity it is: for you will always find the Lord of the movable sign to be that same Lord of the first ninth-part in each of the three signs, but the Lord of the following sign to be that same Lord of the second ninth-part, and the third of third; and using that same rule you will find all of the ninth-parts in the individual signs. But we have laid out the reason for this method of discovering the ninth-parts well and excellently in the astrological *Introduction* which we have published.[88]

But the Indians used to hold onto the direction of the ninth-parts of this type, both in nativities and in other [things], and the distribution of them into three, as though as a secret; [thus] they did not reveal [procedures] of this kind [except] only to those who had reached the end-point of knowledge, first receiving a whispered communication[89] from them, and they held the teaching in secret, nor did they share it with ignorant people, but only with those knowing the [significance] of the teaching (and how greatly does the experienced man stand out from other men!); after this, those receiving a teaching of this kind confessed great thanks to the teacher. We, however, wanting to adorn our respectable book with every method, have published this same method. Therefore it is good to use it in such a way: for every ninth-part you will enter the ascension of the clime, and you will make every degree of the ascensions into a year; then you will divide what you have assembled into three equal parts, and you will make the Lord of the first distribution the Lord of that ninth-part, and the Lord of the second part the Lord of the fifth sign from it, and the Lord of the third distribution the Lord of the ninth [sign] from that sign.[90] And you will take the Lord of the first distribution as the first significator, but the second Lord as that of the fifth sign from the sign[91] of the ninth-part. And if you wished to work [with] those which are of the third distribution, you would begin from the Lord of the ninth sign from the sign of the ninth-part.[92]

---

[88] That is, the *Gr. Intr.* V.17.
[89] *Susurrandum*.
[90] Thus each ninth-part is also subdivided into three parts, each ruled by one member of the triplicity. See the table below, which reflects the divisions of the sub-ninths by longitude for the first 10° of Aries. As Abū Ma'shar will now explain, these ought to be converted into ascensions in order to make a primary direction.
[91] Reading *domino* for *signo*.
[92] Omitting "Lord of."

BOOK III: DISTRIBUTIONS   165

♂ 0°00'-3°20'			♀ 3°20'-6°40'			☿ 6°40'-10°00'		
♂	☉	♃	♀	☿	♄	☿	♀	♄
0°00'00"-1°06'40"	1°06'40"-2°13'20"	2°13'20"-3°20'00"	3°20'00"-4°26'40"	4°26'40"-5°33'20"	5°33'20"-6°40'00"	6°40'00"-7°46'40"	7°46'40"-8°53'20"	8°53'20"-10°00'00"

Figure 5: Subdivisions of the ninth-parts

For example: a certain man was born in the fourth clime, in a certain place having a latitude of 36°.[93] But the Ascendant was the beginning of Aries, [and] we converted the first ninth-part into ascensions, and we made 2° 03' 20" of the 3 1/3 degrees of the ninth-part, which are 2 years, 20 days. We divided them into three parts, and they turned out to be 8 months, 6 days, 16 hours for every part. Therefore we gave this first distribution to Mars (namely the Lord of Aries), who will signify the things which pertain to this distribution; then after Mars, the Sun (namely the Lord of Leo) becomes the Lord of the second distribution, and he disposes 8 months, 6 days, 16 hours, which, put together are 1 year, 4 months, 13 days, 8 hours. Afterwards, Jupiter (namely the Lord of Sagittarius) rules the third distribution, and he disposes 8 months, 6 days, 16 hours, which are 2 years and 20 days in total. And[94] if the Ascendant or the work had been in the second distribution of the ninth-part, we would have begun without fail from the Sun (the Lord of Leo), then from Jupiter (the Lord of Sagittarius), then from Mars (the Lord of Aries and the first ninth-part). And if the Ascendant or work had been in the third distribution, we would have begun without fail from Jupiter (the Lord of Sagittarius), then from Mars, and then from the Sun, and those things which belong to the first distribution of the ninth-part come to be, as is said before.

Moreover, if the Ascendant or work had been in the second ninth-part of Aries, namely in the first distribution [of it], we will divide it without fail into

---

[93] Reading with Schmidt for "26." Abū Ma'shar seems to be using a chart with a calculated Ascendant but only rough ascensions based on the clime—unless perhaps the number is incorrect in the Greek. Strictly speaking the latitude should be closer to 39° N.

[94] The rest of this paragraph (and the corresponding instructions below) does not make sense to me, and may reflect two different methods. The normal distributor-partner method (see below, III.10) should make the Ascendant pass directly from its current sub-ninth into the next one, and forward into the next ninth. But the instructions here make it seem as though the direction begins in the relevant sub-ninth, but then cycles through the other two sub-ninths no matter where it begins, and only then moves into the following ninth.

three, and we will attribute the first distribution to Venus (namely the Lady of Taurus), but the second one to Mercury (the Lord of Virgo), but the third to Saturn (the Lord of Capricorn). And if the Ascendant or work had been in the second distribution of that ninth-part, we would have begun without fail from Mercury the Lord of Virgo, then from Saturn the Lord of Capricorn, then from Venus the Lady of Taurus. And if the Ascendant had been in the third distribution, we would have begun without fail from Saturn the Lord of Capricorn, then from Venus the Lady of Taurus, then from Mercury the Lord of Virgo, and thus the second ninth-part of Aries [is] a complete distribution.

We do it in the same way in the third [ninth-part]. And [thus for the] fourth ninth-part of Aries, dividing the fourth ninth-part itself into three, and making the Lord in the first distribution the Moon (namely the Lady of Cancer),[95] then the Lord in the second distribution Mars (the Lord of Scorpio), then the Lord of the third distribution Jupiter (the Lord of Pisces). And if the Ascendant or work had been in the second distribution of the ninth-part, we would have begun without fail from Mars, then from Jupiter, then from the Moon. And if the Ascendant or the work had been in the third distribution of that same ninth-part, we would have begun from Jupiter, then from the Moon, then from Mars, and these are the Lords of the fourth ninth-part of Aries.

And if we had wanted to perform the work of the fifth ninth-part of Aries, we would have divided it into three, and we would have given the first distribution without fail to the Sun (the Lord of Leo), but the second one to Jupiter (the Lord of Sagittarius), [and] the third to Mars (the Lord of Aries). And if the Ascendant or work had been in the second distribution of this fifth ninth-part, we would have begun without fail from Jupiter, then from Mars, then from the Sun. And if the Ascendant or work had been in the third distribution of the ninth-part, we would have begun without fail from Mars, [then from the Sun], then from Jupiter.

However, once the ninth-parts of Aries are disposed in this way, the direction [is] changed for Taurus. And we divide the first ninth-part into three, [and] after the conversion of the degrees into the ascensions of the clime, the Lord of the first distribution comes to be according the aforesaid treatment: Saturn (the Lord of Capricorn), but of the second one Venus (the Lady of Taurus), but the third one Mercury (the Lord of Virgo). And if the

---

[95] Reading *Cancri* for *Tauri*.

Ascendant or work had been in the second distribution of [this ninth-part],[96] we would have begun without fail from Venus (the Lady of Taurus), then from Mercury (the Lord of Virgo), then from Saturn (the Lord of Capricorn). And if the Ascendant or work had been in the third distribution of [this ninth-part],[97] we would have begun without fail from Mercury, then from Saturn, then from Venus. And we make the direction of the ninth-parts of all the signs in the same way, knowing the Lords of each distribution of a ninth, whether the ninth-part is in the Ascendant or the direction arrives at it.

But the affections and ends of the outcomes are known through [a procedure] of this kind, thus: it is good to look at the Lord of each distribution to see how [it is] according to the nativity, and how it was according to the revolution,[98] and if it is inspected [by the Moon][99] and a benevolent or malevolent, and again if it is being looked at by its partners, and if it is in strength or weakness. For if both were of a good condition, and they received each other, and one is near the other or in one sign, or in one degree, or they happened to be in the place of the Moon or in the places of benevolents or in their rays, they signify prosperity. Moreover if the Lords of one ninth-part were aspecting each other by a trine or sextile aspect, and they were unencumbered, they signify advantage and the greatest prosperity. But if in addition [they were inspecting each other][100] and with the Lords of their own domiciles, what the outcomes determine will be more certain, and [there will be] more goods. But if they were impeded and they aspected each other, the impediment will be less. And if one (or all) of them were in that ninth-part (and especially if it came out that the distribution would belong to it) or the rays of that planet [were in it] according to the nativity, he whose revolution it is will have advantage in it. But if the planets were of a bad condition and they aspected malevolents, and appeared in bad places, and [have relationships to] the place of death,[101] they signify adversities and deaths. But the impediment of a distribution of this kind is like if it is being inspected by the bad ones or it arrives at their places or their rays, both [in] the nativity and the revolution, or their Lords are in [their own] descension.

---

[96] Reading for "Taurus."
[97] Reading for "Taurus."
[98] Following Schmidt and omitting "even how it is in the two times."
[99] Adding with Schmidt.
[100] Filling in with Schmidt for *inspectus*.
[101] Reading with Schmidt and reading *mortis* for *martis*.

But it is good to inspect at the same time the places of the distributions, and their Lords, and the dispositions of the Moon. Likewise it is good to inspect the partner, whether by body or by ray. And if it were good, it signifies prosperity and good things; but if bad, it signifies destruction and misfortune according to the nature of the malevolent, just as we said before in the distribution of the bounds and of those who partner with their Lords. But if the distributor and the one which partners with it were of the same nature, and they aspected each other from an agreeable figure, [and] they even aspected the place of the distribution, they signify good things; but the contrary if they were disposed contrarily.

Therefore, in every matter it is good to look at both the Lord of the ninth-part and at the one which partners with it, whether by body or by a ray pushing it, and at the one taking [it], and to work out the determination of the outcomes in the same way.

Chapter III.10: On the knowledge of the Lord of the Year from the ninth-parts, according to the opinion of the Indians

If the year[102] reached some sign, the Indians take the Lord of the Year to be the Lord of the first ninth-part,[103] whether the revolution applied to the beginning of the sign or in the end, and they look at the Lord of the Year of this kind to see how it was according to the nativity, and how it was in the revolution, and whether it is in its own domicile or exaltation, or in the bounds, or in its own proper ninth-part, or in an alien sign, or it were in a good place with a benevolent, or with the Moon, and they determine the condition of the whole year according to their disposition. And if the Lord of the Year of this kind (namely the Lord of the first ninth-part) were of a good condition in the two times, it signifies good things; but if it they were impeded, the contrary.

---

[102] Omitting "Lord of the," with Schmidt.
[103] In other words, the profected Lord of the Year will be identical to the Lord of the first ninth-part, which is always the domicile Lord of the movable sign of that triplicity. Abū Ma'shar points this out particularly because his profections do not seem to go by whole signs but in 30° increments as with 'Umar: thus the degree of the profection would most often fall on the degree of a ninth-part other than the first. But note that this Indian method would make only Mars, Saturn, Venus and the Moon could be Lords of the Year.

For example: the year arrived to the twentieth degree of Taurus, more or less; the Lord of this degree is Saturn, the Lord of the first ninth-part;[104] and if perhaps the year had reached Gemini and to whatever place of it, Venus will be the Lady of the Year, for the reason that she is the Lady of the first ninth-part of Gemini. And if the year had reached Cancer, the Indians likewise would have taken the Moon as the Lady of the Year, because she is the Lady of the first ninth-part of Cancer.

But the reason why they used to take the Lords of the first ninth-part as the Lords of the Year, is this: because they considered how many ninth-parts had passed from the day on which the native was born, and they projected these from the ninth-part of the Ascendant of the nativity, at 108 [per year], then again 108; and through every revolution they held onto one year and one sign. And where it arrived, there was the sign to which the year had arrived, namely in that place where the ninth-parts were ended. We will describe in what follows below regarding the monthly and daily determinations of the ninth-parts, in the way the Indians thought about them.[105]

---

[104] Again, because he rules the movable sign in the earthy triplicity (Capricorn).
[105] See my summary of IX.7 below.

BOOK IV: ON THE *FIRDĀRIYYĀT*

Chapter IV.1: On the *firdāriyyah* of the Sun

Each one of the seven wandering [stars, and] even the Head and Tail of the Dragon, have certain determinate years, and every planet disposes the native according to its *firdāriyyah*. Indeed the *firdāriyyah* of the Sun is 10 years, but that of Venus 8, Mercury 13, the Moon 9, Saturn 11, Jupiter 12, Mars, 7, the Head 3, and the Tail 2, which all together are 75 years of life. In diurnal nativities the Sun has the disposition of the first *firdāriyyah*, whenever it was,[1] then Venus, then Mercury, then the Moon, then Saturn, then the others according to the order of their circles. But in nocturnal nativities the Moon has the first *firdāriyyah*, then Saturn, then Jupiter, then Mars, according to the prior order. However, when the disposition of this kind reached some one of the planets, that planet itself disposes exactly one-seventh of the years of its own *firdāriyyah*, then the rest of the planets unite to it in the signification of good or bad things, according to one-seventh of the years of each *firdāriyyah*. And the beginning will be from the planet having the *firdāriyyah*, but it unites itself to the first one which [is] nearest after it, then the next which [is] after it, and subsequently it will be understood thusly for the others. But the reason for the fellowship of the rest of the planets with [the first] one is for the reason that the years of the *firdāriyyah* of each planet were taken from the dignities which the planets have in the signs;[2] but the Head and Tail alone dispose according to their own disposition (not uniting to any planets), namely after the full amount of years,[3] for the reason that they do not have domiciles. But they have other reasons for this year, of which we will make mention in another book. But in this one we will declare the significations of the dispositions of the years of the planets' *firdāriyyāt*.

Therefore, whoever was born in the day, he is steered by the Sun from the hour at which he was born until the tenth year, and the Sun disposes only so

---

[1] Schmidt says the Greek can read "wherever" or "whenever," and favors "wherever," since in some techniques the Sun can only be the time lord if he is positioned in a particular way. But his ability to be a time lord in the *firdāriyyāt* is unaffected by his natal position.
[2] See footnote to I.8 above.
[3] Unlike some other medieval interpretations, Abū Ma'shar clearly puts the Nodes at the very end, and not in between the *firdāriyyāt* of two other planets. See also IV.8.

much as 1 year, 5 months, 4 days, 6 hours: namely close to one-seventh of his years. Then the individual planets dispose according to one-seventh of his years. Therefore, with the Sun disposing, it signifies the best change coming to be for the native if the Sun were of a good condition according to the nativity; but in the first and second month his parents will be saddened; afterwards their sorrow will pass, and it will be turned into joy and happiness. And if the Sun disposed according to his *firdārīyyah* with the native being a young man, he will find good things from princes, and he will rule over his own blood-kin, and his riches and joy will be added to. But the Sun disposes through the *firdārīyyah* in youth[4] when the nativity is nocturnal. But if he disposed in old age, he will rejoice in [his] blood-kin and in children, and praiseworthy prosperities will come about for him. (However, the Sun disposes in old age when the nativity is diurnal, and 75 years have passed.)[5]

For once the Sun has disposed, and he were in his own proper domicile or in the bounds of Jupiter or in the bounds of Venus,[6] whether the native is in the youthful or old age, it signifies luckiness and good welfare, and liberation from serious things, and his prudence and dignity will be added to, and men will heed his counsel about their workings, and he will be welcome in discussions, and [his] rule will pass over to his own fatherland, and he will benefit his own citizens, and he will be involved in good things, and he will get gold and silver, and precious stones, and royal favors, and wherever he is he will be honored, and kings will desire him and his statements, and many of the magnates will approach his gate, and he will rule over lands and towns, and his trees will be multiplied, and he will have children. And if he had a father, he will obtain those goods. But if the Sun in the nativity were [in] the Ascendant or with a Lord of the Ascendant [who] appeared oriental, it signifies the greatest prosperity.

Then Venus receives the distribution in the *firdārīyyah* of the Sun for 1 year, 5 months, 4 days, [and] about 6 hours. And she signifies that in a distribution of this kind his vestments and monies will be added to, and he will engage in discussions about nuptials or he will be conjoined to a wife (if the beginning of his nativity signified some such thing), and perhaps he will

---

[4] That is, what we would call adulthood. In a nocturnal nativity he will be the primary ruler of the *firdārīyyah* for ten years when the native is 49.
[5] The cycle of the *firdārīyyāt* will come back to the Sun at age 85 in a diurnal nativity.
[6] For the Sun there is no distinction between his position in the nativity at the revolutions; but for other planets one should look at both their natal condition as well as their transit at the time they take over the subdivision of the *firdārīyyah* and indeed throughout.

go on a foreign journey and will have a hidden disease. And if the nativity were nocturnal, he will be rescued from sorrow and his riches will be multiplied, and he will rejoice over women and children, and he will renovate remarkable buildings, and he will buy many things, he will even be liberal and travel[7] on account of some justice;[8] and he will go on a pilgrimage [for] divine propitiations. But he will have illnesses in certain hidden limbs of the body. But if Saturn and Mars and the Tail of the Dragon were with Venus or they aspected her by a contrary aspect,[9] it will not only take away things of this kind, but they will even harm on the occasion of them.

Then Mercury disposes [1] year, 5 months, 4 days, [and] about 6 hours in the *firdārīyyah* of the Sun (which together come to be 4 years, 3 months, 11 days, [and] near 20 hours). And it signifies that in a disposition of this kind he will lose certain of his monies, and some one from his blood-kin will harm him, and he will fall from a high place or come into danger of falling, he will even hurt in [his] eyes, and he will quickly be liberated from the pain. But if it were a nocturnal nativity, in a disposition of this [kind] he will destroy many riches and have contentions, [and] be afflicted in labors. And if he were in [any] public offices he will be fined, and his profit will be diminished, and he will be saddened on account of false writing; he will even fall from some house, and he will not be wounded, and he will suffer hemorrhoids[10] and be freed of them.

Then the Moon disposes through 1 year, 5 months, 4 days [and] about 6 hours in the *firdārīyyah* of the Sun (which together are 5 years, 8 months, 17 days, and about 3 hours). In a disposition of this kind he handles harmful business matters, and he will have advantage in other things, and he will suffer loss from thieves, and will delight in looking at waters, or he will sail [them], he will even hurt his head and eyes. But if it were a nocturnal nativity, he will handle business matters never thought of,[11] and he will attain riches, and his revenues and advantages will be increased, and gifts will be given to him secretly, and he will become a businessman of the sea, and he will use up immense riches, and he will speak to princes and acquire friends, and he will

---

[7] Adding with Schmidt.
[8] In the medieval West, "justice" also referred to the legal powers of a lord to decide disputes.
[9] Undoubtedly by transit.
[10] According to Schmidt the Greek reads "bleeding."
[11] Reading with Schmidt for *finienda*.

delight in erecting buildings,[12] and a headache will come over him in the last part of the distribution.

Then Saturn disposes 1 year, 5 months, 4 days [and] about 6 hours in the *firdārīyyah* of the Sun (which together come to be 7 years, 1 months, 21 days and about 10 hours. And it signifies he is saddened in a distribution of this kind, and suffers harm by his own blood-kin, and a pain of the belly, and he suffers burning (whether by fire or by hot water), he will even hurt his eyes, and he will be liberated from the pain and take a long journey, and he will suffer harm by water. But if it were a nocturnal nativity, he will be saddened and will have an infusion[13] around the eyes, and he will hurt in the belly, and he will handle business by sea, and he will suffer harm through water, and likewise by fire or boiling water, on account of the nature of the Sun and Saturn.

Then Jupiter disposes 1 year, 5 months, 4 days, [and] about 6 hours [in] the *firdārīyyah* of the Sun (which together come to be 8 years, 6 months, 25 days, 17 hours). It signifies that in a disposition of this kind his monies and treasures will be added to, and he will have advantage from his parents, but still he will fall from a high place. But if it were a nocturnal nativity, his dignity and glory and prosperity will be added to, and he will rule over those like him according to fortune;[14] he will even manage buildings and increase his riches, and he will find treasure, or he will earn many riches without labor, and he will be elevated over his enemies, but still around the end of a distribution of this kind he will fall from some house or from horseback.

Then Mars disposes 1 year, 5 months, 4 days, [and] around 6 hours in the *firdārīyyah* of the Sun (which come to be 10 years in total). And it signifies that in a distribution of this kind he will be changed from disposition to disposition, and he will go on a foreign journey and perhaps will be conjoined to a wife, but he will suffer evils from a poisonous bite or [he will suffer] a fall or beating, and a flowing of blood will come to be from this, and these things will be in the first four months. But if the nativity were nocturnal, he will be changed from one working to another, and he will go on a foreign journey, and he will suffer much labor and he will exert[15] himself regarding women and sexual intercourse and about fornications, because of which he will suffer evil; he will even be injured by certain people,

---

[12] Omitting *pravis*.
[13] Schmidt has: "cataracts."
[14] That is, according to *their* level of prosperity: of the same as or lower than his.
[15] Reading *exercitabit* for *certabit*, with Schmidt.

and suffer harm from them, indeed iron will touch his body, he will even be bitten by a dog and will be sick for 11 days. And however often the Sun and Mars were impeded,[16] he will be harmed that often.

Chapter IV.2: On the *firdārīyyah* of Venus

However, Venus disposes 8 years through her *firdārīyyah*, of which she herself alone disposes one-seventh, even 1 year, 1 month, [and] near 20 days. And it signifies that in a distribution or disposition of this kind, the native will rejoice and be glad and will have advantages, and perhaps he will be conjoined to a wife. But if the nativity were nocturnal, he will rejoice in a distribution of this kind and will be glad about diverse matters, and in his own proper wife, or he will be conjoined to an alien wife, and a fortunate child will be born to him, and he will join his sons and daughters in marriage, and he will manage buildings and the planting of trees, and his riches will abound to the extent that he will make treasures of them, and he will even make friends of those who excel in dignities, and the greatest office will be committed to him, and kings will give him vestments. But as Hermes says, the first 5 months and 25 days of this distribution are better than the rest.

Then Mercury disposes 1 year, [1 month], 20 days, and [about] 10 hours in the *firdārīyyah* of Venus (which are 2 years, 3 months, 12 days, [and] about 20 hours in total). And it signifies that in a distribution of this kind he will suffer thievery and will lose substance, and he will suffer harm and be sick and will cross from place to place. But if the nativity were nocturnal, he will destroy very many things acquired, and he will be overcome by his enemies, and he will flee from them, and he will be saddened to a degree that he will abstain from food and drink; illness from drinking poison or from the taking of some food will even happen to him.

Then the Moon disposes 1 year, 1 month, 20 day [and] about 10 hours of the *firdārīyyah* of Venus (which together are 3 years, 5 months, 4 days, [and] about 7 hours). And it signifies that in a distribution of this kind his condition will be prosperous, he will speak with some princes, and perhaps he will be conjoined to a wife. But if it were a nocturnal nativity, it signifies that he will be liberated from misfortunes and his condition will abound in prosperity, and he will walk to the gates of greater people, and he will be honored by

---

[16] That is, by transit *while* they rule this period.

princes and will rule over his blood-kin, and he will assemble sufficient riches; and if he does not have a wife, he will take [one].

Then Saturn disposes 1 year, 1 month, 20 days, [and] about 10 hours in the *firdārīyyah* of Venus (which are 4 years, 6 months, 25 days, [and] about 10 hours in total). And in a distribution of this kind it signifies that he will be very much full of labor, and he will suffer[17] from miseries, and he will harm some woman, and will be harmed by women. But if it were a nocturnal nativity, his worries and labors will be multiplied, and he will have confusion, nor will he have usefulness from his works, he will also invite his relatives[18] for food and drink, he will be saddened about them, and his wife will die or he will have a quarrel with her, and perhaps his wife will suffer a miscarriage (if she will be pregnant), and he will be mixed up with a fornicating woman or slave-girl, and he will harm his own child or the child of another.

Then Jupiter disposes 1 year, 1 month, 20 days, [and] about 10 hours in the *firdārīyyah* of Venus (which are 5 years, 8 months, 17 days and 3 hours in total). And in a distribution of this kind it signifies that his condition is prosperous, and his father will be made fortunate and his riches will be multiplied. But if the nativity were nocturnal, he will be rescued from misfortunes and will be praised by many, and his immovable substance will be increased. And if the beginning of the nativity signified prosperity, he will reach the greatness of glory. And if Venus were with the Head or Jupiter in an angle, he will rule over many by sea and land.

Then Mars disposes 1 year, 1 month, 20 days [and] about 10 hours in the *firdārīyyah* of Venus (which together are 6 years, 10 months, 8 days and near 13 hours). And it signifies that in a distribution of this kind he will labor often, and will harm his brothers, and perhaps he will take a wife. But if the nativity were nocturnal, he will be very much fatigued and full of labor, and he will injure certain people, and his brothers will suffer harm, and he will take a noble wife.

Then the Sun disposes 1 year, 1 month, 20 days [and] about 10 hours in the *firdārīyyah* of Venus (which likewise come to be 8 years). And it signifies that in a distribution of this kind he will grow terribly ill, and he will be conjoined with some preeminent people, and his glory and riches will be increased, and he will take an educated wife. But if it were a nocturnal nativity, he will fall into some vicious illness, and his male and female

---

[17] Reading *patietur* with Schmidt for *lucrabitur*.
[18] Adding with Schmidt.

servants will be added to, and he will wear the adornment of kings, and he will live with kings, and he will rule over his enemies, and he will be conjoined to a most skilled and learned wife. But if Venus or the Sun had the rulership of the year[19] and they were of a good condition, he will attain the greatness of glory. And if Venus were of a good[20] condition, his advantages will be multiplied and he will speak with kings.

Chapter IV.3: On the *firdāriyyah* of Mercury

The *firdāriyyah* of Mercury is 13 years, namely after the *firdāriyyah* of Venus. Indeed he disposes one-seventh [of the whole], namely 1 year, 10 months,[21] 8 days, [and] about 13 hours. And it signifies that in the first half the native will obtain good things but he will incur evils [in the last half],[22] and he will go on a foreign journey from region to region; and everything which he did, they will[23] come about prosperously for him; one of [his] men or a horse will even die, and he will be sick with an illness in which he will not be helped by the medicines of doctors. And if Saturn were of a bad condition and aspected him, there is fear lest he should die. But if Mercury were of a good condition, it takes away the evils.

Then the Moon disposes 1 year, 10 months, 8 days, [and] around 13 hours in the *firdāriyyah* of Mercury (which are 3 years, 8 months,[24] 17 days [and] about 2 hours in total). And it signifies that in a distribution of this kind he will have a turbulent life, having no delight in food and drink, but [involving himself in bad things].[25] And if he will sell a slave he will flee, and if he will handle business he will be fined.[26] And if he undertook to build, he will not complete the building, and if he had a wife he will kick her out or he will have discord with her; and if he did not have [a wife], he will seek [one] and complete nothing; and he will be sick with an illness, and he will fall from a house or horse, and he will approach death.

---

[19] Probably as the Lord of the Year.
[20] Reading *boni* for *mali*.
[21] Reading *decem* for *sex*.
[22] Adding with Schmidt.
[23] Omitting "not" with Schmidt.
[24] Reading *octo* for *quattuor*.
[25] Reading with Schmidt for *[unclear] ipsum illa quae habebit malis*.
[26] *Damnificabitur*. This term appears several times in the text. It refers to financial loss generally, but especially fines.

Then Saturn disposes 1 year, 10 months, 8 days, [and] about 13 hours in the *firdārīyyah* of Mercury (which together come to be 5 years, 6 months, 25 days [and] about 18 hours). And it signifies that in a distribution of this kind his friends and riches will be added to, he will even be liberal and he will acquire sufficient benefits,[27] and his wife will be sick with a vicious illness, or she will die and he will be saddened over it, and he will go on a foreign journey, and he will endure labor on his foreign journey.

Then Jupiter disposes 1 year, 10 months, 8 days, [and] about 13 hours in the *firdārīyyah* of Mercury (which together are 7 years, 5 months, 4 days, [and] about 7 hours). And it signifies that in a distribution of this kind he will earn resources from diverse efforts, and he will assemble gold and silver, and he will make many expenditures, and be in opposition to excellent persons, and he will suffer harm by them, and some low-class people will contend with him, but in the end he will be liberated from [things] of this kind, he will even be engaged in an illustrious office, and he will build a distinguished inn, he will employ lies and will befriend liars.

Then Mars disposes 1 year, 10 months, 8 days, [and] about 13 hours in the *firdārīyyah* of Mercury (which together come to be 9 years, 3 months, 12 days, [and] about 20 hours). And it signifies that in a distribution of this kind he will be opposed to those lesser than him, and he will have refuge among some persons worthy in reputation, and he will fall from misfortune to misfortune, and he will escape from that, and he will rule over his enemies, and take a sad journey, and if he will handle business he will be fined, and if he contracted a partnership with someone, he will pass by it;[28] he will even suffer detriment from fire, and he will fall from a high place or he will be close to falling, and he will be sick with a vicious illness through which he will suffer harm in the head, but he will get well. And if he took a wife she will die in that year, his mother will even die and his father will be incarcerated, and his parents will fall into wicked sufferings.

Then the Sun disposes 1 year, 10 months, 8 days, 13 hours in the *firdārīyyah* of Mercury ([which together come to be 11 years,] 1 month, 20 days [and] about 10 hours). And in a *firdārīyyah* of this kind, he will be pleasant and cheerful, and prospering every day, and his servants will be multiplied, and he will take on a secretary and a provider or administrator, and he will get riches from kings and from others. He will remunerate his

---

[27] The Greek text adds that he will squander much of it.
[28] *Supercedebit.* Schmidt tentatively reads "he will neglect it."

own domestics, and all of his household intimates, and some one of his brothers will die, and perhaps he will go to bed with the wife of his brother or father.

Then Venus disposes 1 year, 10 months, 8 days, [and] about 13 hours in the *firdārīyyah* of Mercury (which together come to be 13 years). And it signifies that in a disposition of this kind he will have enmities with some, and he will be befriended [by women][29] and be glad in that, and he will be likened to them both in vestments and in the anointing of ointments; his wife will even conceive and suffer a miscarriage. And if she[30] did not have a child, she will see the death of some of those whom she has in place of children.

Chapter IV.4: On the *firdārīyyah* of the Moon

Also, the *firdārīyyah* of the Moon is 9 years, [and] she disposes her own one-seventh, which is 1 year, 3 months,[31] 12 days and about 20 hours. And it signifies that he will be changeable, in joy and sorrow too, even in riches and prosperity, and he will have quarrels with his wife, and will go on a foreign journey, and be incarcerated, and suddenly he will be raised up to an honor and glory in which he will attain riches which are renowned and worthy in reputation. Then on the other hand, after a while he will fall from that glory, and he will return again to it, and in the end of a distribution of this kind he will suffer danger from iron or the sword, or be shut up.[32] But if the nativity were nocturnal, and the Moon were impeded, he will suffer illness and prosecution.[33] But if she were of a good condition, he will have dignity and be esteemed by his parents, and he will have advantage from them.

Then Saturn disposes 1 year, 3 months, 12 days [and] about 20 hours in the *firdārīyyah* of the Moon (which together come to be 2 years, 6 months, 25 days, [and] about 14 hours). And in a distribution of this kind, he will have contentions with kings, and whatever he says will be thought to be lies, and he will suffer detriment from his slaves, and they will flee from him, and his animals will be lost, and he will spend many resources and will grow ill, and

---

[29] Adding with Schmidt.
[30] Reading "she" with Schmidt, but it could refer to the native losing someone like a child.
[31] Reading *tres* for *decem*.
[32] *Concludetur.* That is, put away. Schmidt reads "shut out."
[33] Schmidt has "abuse."

he will suffer harm by fire or heat or the cutting of iron three times; after this he will be healed. And if his wife were pregnant, she will suffer a miscarriage. But if it were a nocturnal nativity, he will be sick from heat and will suffer harm from fire or boiling water, and he will be cured through iron, and he will cross from place to place in his travels, and he will be endangered and suffer thievery, and he will suffer trouble from one of those serving him, and some of his treasures will be snatched by thieves.

Then Jupiter disposes 1 year, 3 months, 12 days, [and] about 20 hours in the *firdāriyyah* of the Moon (which together come to be 3 years, 10 months, 8 days, [and] about 14 hours). Therefore in this distribution he will exercise a great office, and his name will be exalted, and he will earn riches worthy in reputation from that office, and he will be elevated over his own enemies, and he will have advantage from a faraway land, and from flat and mountainous possessions, and he will plant plants, and sell male and female slaves. But if the nativity were nocturnal, his vestments will be multiplied and he will serve someone.

Then Mars disposes 1 year, 3 months, 12 days [and] about 20 hours in the *firdāriyyah* of the Moon (which together come to be 5 years, 1 month, and 20 days, [and] about 10 hours). And in a distribution of this kind it signifies that he will be very much saddened and be wrapped up in evils, and he will lose[34] some of his possessions, and he will be fined great losses for which he will be tormented. But if he will go on a foreign journey he will be bitten by a serpent or he will suffer detriment on a ship, or from fire or from water, and he will approach death, and he will have harm in the eyes and will have a pain in the genitals. But if Mars aspected, the evils will be multiplied. And if the nativity were nocturnal, he will be sick in the worst way, in the eyes too and the belly, and perhaps he will be bitten by an animal, or he will suffer harm by fire or water, and he will endure thievery by one of the people serving him.

Then the Sun disposes 1 year, 3 months, 12 days, [and] about 20 hours in the *firdāriyyah* of the Moon (which likewise come to be 6 years, 5 months, 4 days [and] about 6 hours). And it signifies that in a distribution of this kind he will remunerate many, and he will distribute his resources among strangers, and he will be exalted and cheerful in his works, and he will rule over some, and either he himself or his wife will be sick, and he will be liberated from the illness after 30 days. And if his wife were pregnant, she will suffer a

---

[34] Schmidt has "destroy."

miscarriage, and afterwards will conceive [again]. But if the nativity were nocturnal, he will be sick and will change from place to place, and his instruction will be added to.

Then Venus disposes 1 year, 3 years, 12 days, [and] about 20 hours in the *firdārīyyah* of the Moon (which together come to be 7 years, 8 months, 17 days, [and] about 3 hours). Indeed in a distribution of this kind he will engage in singing and dancing and sexual intercourse, and certain pains will surround him, and he will be praised at the beginning of this distribution, he will rejoice over his slaves, and his glory will be increased.

Then Mercury disposes 1 year, 3 months, 12 days, and about 20 hours of the *firdārīyyah* of the Moon (which together come to be 9 years). And in a distribution of this kind he will be promoted into an office three times, and another will succeed him three times, he will have contentions with certain people, and he will lie against some, and maintain hidden frauds, and he will spend remarkable resources, and he will fear water and fire. However, at the beginning of this distribution it is good to be observant of [things] of this kind for 17 days; [and] his child will even be sick from black choler. But if the nativity were nocturnal, he will be accused and struck,[35] and will suffer thievery, or water or fire will harm him.

Chapter IV.5: On the *firdārīyyah* of Saturn

The *firdārīyyah* of Saturn is 11 years. Indeed he disposes in the first one-seventh of his years, which is 1 year, 6 months, 25 days, 17 hours. And it signifies that in a distribution of this kind he will do something for which he will be denounced and considered foolish or defamed; he even contends in vain and will endure censure on account of daughters, and he will be saddened over them, and what goes out [as expenses] will be more than his revenues, and his riches will be diminished and his glory annulled, and he will be sick in the worst way. And if Mars inspected him, he will suffer harm from fire or cutting by iron. But if the nativity were nocturnal, he will have advantage from certain occasions, or he will be saddened over diverse matters, and a certain one of his own blood-kin will die, and foolishness and insanity and inactivity will rule over him.

---

[35] Omitting a redundant "by water and fire."

Then Jupiter disposes 1 year, 6 months, 25 days [and] about 17 hours in the *firdārīyyah* of Saturn (which together come to be 3 years, 1 month, 21 days, [and] about 10 hours). And it signifies that in a distribution of this kind he will be honored and will have advantage from kings and he will climb from honor to honor, and at the end of the distribution he will go on a foreign journey and be sick. But if it were a nocturnal nativity, he will have advantage on some occasions and he will have certain knowledge through which he will have advantage, and he will be sick. Nevertheless, male and female slaves will be added to him or he will take a wife.

Then Mars distributes 1 year, 6 months, 25 days [and] about 17 hours in the *firdārīyyah* of Saturn (which together come to be 4 years, 8 months, 17 days, [and] about 3 hours). And it signifies that in a distribution of this kind he will handle his condition badly, and he will endure necessities, and perhaps he will fall from a house or horse, he will be discordant toward his wife, he will bear himself inimically with many, and certain ones of his blood-kin will have an illness, or his child will die. But if the nativity were nocturnal he will suffer sorrows and diverse contentions, and perhaps he will fall from a high place.

Then the Sun disposes [1] year, 6 months, 25 days, [and] about 17 hours in the *firdārīyyah* of Saturn (which come to be 6 years, 3 months, 12 days, 20 hours). And it signifies that in a distribution of this kind his glory will be added to and judgments over certain people will be committed to him, and he will judge among many and will rejoice over some matters, and he will take a journey and hurt his head, and he will be sick and will have contentions against someone exceeding him in age, and he will overcome him.

Then Venus disposes 1 year, 6 months, 25 days [and] about 17 hours in the *firdārīyyah* of Saturn (which together comes to be 7 years, 5 months, 8 days, [and] about 13 hours). And it signifies that in a distribution of this kind certain people will lie against him, and they will present false testimony, and he will have a long contention and be saved from it, and he will rejoice over the death of his enemies or over their greatest misfortune, he will even hurt his belly or a hidden place and he will be cured, and his wife will die and his child will be ill.

Then Mercury disposes 1 year, 6 months, 25 days [and] about 17 hours in the *firdārīyyah* of Saturn. And it signifies that in a distribution of this kind he will labor and go on a laborious foreign journey, and his wife will be ill, and he will be saddened about some women and about the death of a certain one, and his riches will be added to, and he will lose part of them, and he will be cheerful about his friends, and he will have a care about slaves and those mounted on beasts,[36] and even more so about children and disputations and associations in which he will suffer good and bad things.

Then the Moon disposes 1 year, 6 months, 25 days [and] 17 hours in the *firdārīyyah* of Saturn (which together are 11 years). And it signifies that in a distribution of this kind he will be saddened and his child will be sick and he or his child will die; he will be in the middle between greatness and humbleness, and he will go on a distant foreign journey in which he will get resources, and perhaps he will be on a foreign journey though the whole time of this distribution, and at its end he will acquire riches.

Chapter IV.6: On the *firdārīyyah* of Jupiter

The *firdārīyyah* of Jupiter is 12 years. However, at the beginning he himself disposes one-seventh of those years, namely 1 year, 8 months, [and] about 17 days. And it signifies that in a distribution of this kind he[37] will pass from every experience of evils to an experience of good things, and from every anxiety to every pleasantness, and his prosperity and riches will be increased, and he will be praised by kings, and business matters will be committed to him, with a worthy reputation. And if Jupiter were in his own proper bounds or those of Venus at the beginning of the nativity, or in his own triplicity (that is, in Aries, Leo, Sagittarius) the signification of prosperities will be greater. And if he were born of a superior fortune, he will rule over cities, and the class [of people] subordinated to him will be multiplied, and he will take a distinguished wife, and he will accept the favors of the kings, and he will have diverse [revenues] coming in, and he will remunerate many and will establish great buildings. But if Jupiter were in his own exaltation, the condition of the fortune will be greater.

Then Mars disposes 1 year, 8 months, 17 days [and] about 3 hours in the *firdārīyyah* of Jupiter. And it signifies that in a disposition of this kind he will be saddened, and he will provide a certain service to some official on account of which he will become frightful; nevertheless on account of business of this kind he will suffer vicious dangers, and he will have a fear of water and

---

[36] Schmidt has "beasts under the yoke."
[37] Omitting "he will either be changed or arrive."

will be sent on a distant foreign journey, and he will very much esteem women, and a child will be born to him.

Then the Sun disposes 1 year, 8 months, 17 hours [and] about 3 hours in the *firdāriyyah* of Jupiter (which together come to be 5 years, 1 month, 20 days, [and] 10 hours). And it signifies that in a distribution of this kind his prudence will be increased, and he will be able to rule, and his resources and prosperity will be added to, and he will discover treasure and will attain riches without labor, and he will be honorable in all things, and he will wield the greatest office, and a fortunate child will be born to him.

Then Venus disposes 1 year, 8 months, 17 days [and] about 3 hours in the *firdāriyyah* of Jupiter. And it signifies that in a distribution of this kind he will frequent the halls of kings and will befriend them, and he will find glory and prosperity and riches without pain, and his enemies will die. But if Jupiter were impeded by Saturn and Mars, all of the aforesaid will be diminished.

Then Mercury disposes 1 year, 8 months, 17 days [and] about 3 hours in the *firdāriyyah* of Jupiter (which together come to be 8 years, 6 months, 25 days [and] about 17 hours). And it signifies that in a distribution of this kind he will be compliant and [idle and][38] he will have many enemies and his friends will be inimical to him, and he will suffer jeering by many, and will be conjoined to a wife, and will be bitten by a dog or by another animal, and his home will be destroyed (or part of it), and he will fall from a house or another place.

Then the Moon disposes 1 year, 8 months, 17 days [and] about 3 hours in the *firdāriyyah* of Jupiter (together they come to be 10 years, 3 months, 12 days, [and] about 20 hours). And it signifies that in a distribution of this kind his glory will be added to, and he will rule over many, and he will attain unexpected things, and sometimes he will be cheerful but sometimes saddened, and someone greater than he will die,[39] from whom he will inherit an inheritance;[40] he will even go on a distant foreign journey and will happen upon robbers, and these things will be in the first year.

Then Saturn disposes 1 year, 8 months, 17 days [and] about 3 hours in the *firdāriyyah* of Jupiter (which together come to be 12 years). And it signifies that in a distribution of this kind he will make diverse donations, and his friends and those near him will be distanced from him, and they will handle

---

[38] Reading with Schmidt and *BA* IV.22.
[39] The Greek identifies this as an older brother.
[40] This can include real estate (*haereditatem*).

themselves in an unfriendly way with him, and those who at first established a friendship with him will be against him, [and] perhaps certain ones of them will go on a foreign journey; the native will even suffer a fear of kings and dangers on account of children, and he will have a loss from his home,[41] and if he lent to[42] someone, he will never receive it back, and if he received it, [it will be only] in part and with much labor, [and] sorrows and worries [will come to those] in his house for 30 days, at which [time] he will come close to danger.

Chapter IV.7: On the *firdārīyyah* of Mars

The *firdārīyyah* of Mars is 7 years, and indeed from the beginning he disposes one-seventh of these, namely 1 year. And it signifies that in a distribution of this kind he will be unfair and thoughtless, and he will fall into a great offense and a long fight, and his enemies will rise up against him, and they will defame him in the presence of princes and rulers, and he will suffer harm from his parents and he will be saved, and he will endure the fear of a wild animal or fire or iron or boiling water, or from hanging, or from someone hanged and those half-dead; in that year his seed will be harmed by water or submersion, he will even go on a distant foreign journey, and he will suffer a headache and pain in the eyes. But if Mars were with Jupiter or Saturn in the bounds of Mars, or in the bounds of Venus, he will be harmed by enemies and be saved.

Then the Sun disposes 1 year in the *firdārīyyah* of Mars (which together come to be 2 years). And in a distribution of this kind it signifies that his brothers will be disposed inimically against him, and he will suffer harm from some one of his associates for 11 days, and he will have a pain in some hidden limb, and he will fall from a high place, and his wife will die, and one of his children will be insane or die.

Then Venus disposes 1 year in the *firdārīyyah* of Mars (which together come to be 3 years). And in a distribution of this kind he will persevere in singing and pleasant things, and he will live with prostitutes and will quarrel with his wife, and he will have familiarity with robbers and advantage from them.

---

[41] Reading with Schmidt for *domi [unclear] planeta unius*.
[42] Reading with Schmidt and *BA* IV.6 for *mutuabit* ("exchanged").

Then Mercury disposes 1 year in the *firdārīyyah* of Mars (which together come to be 4 years). And in a distribution of this kind he will have harms and he will go on a foreign journey and will be saddened on account of thievery or loss, and he will be inimical to his friends, and perhaps he will perish from some misfortune.

Then the Moon disposes 1 year in the *firdārīyyah* of Mars (which together come to be 5 years). And it signifies that in a distribution of this kind he will be confined, and he will fall into adverse things, then he will suffer expenditures and costs in buildings; and if he bought [a slave],[43] he will die or flee; and if his father were living, he will die.

Then Saturn disposes 1 year in the *firdārīyyah* of Mars (which together come to be 6 years). In a distribution of this kind he will suffer evils and losses, and a quartan [fever] will come over him, and there will be a divorce between him and his wife.

Then Jupiter disposes 1 year in the *firdārīyyah* of Mars (which together come to be 7 years). And it signifies that in a distribution of this kind he will overcome his enemies, and he will despise everyone, and he will have advantage on the occasion of contentions, and his revenues will be multiplied, and a child will be born to him, and he will rejoice in all things.

[Chapter IV.8: On the *firdārīyyāt* of the Nodes][44]

The Head of the Dragon disposes 3 years. And it signifies prosperity and riches from a contention, and friendship toward superior persons, and he will embrace judges, and will obtain good things, and his speech will have authority, and he will rule over many and will obtain advantage from an inheritance, and he will suffer harm by magic, and he will be healed.

Then the Tail disposes 2 years. And it signifies that in these years he will suffer evils, and he will be inimical with his own friends, and both he and his wife will be fined,[45] and they will fall into the worst illness, and he will be healed of it.

---

[43] Adding with Schmidt.
[44] The first few paragraphs of this section originally appeared near the end of the Latin passages on transits, but they properly belong here in parallel with BA IV.24-25. I have used them to replace the text on the Nodes which originally appeared here in the Latin and Greek editions, and have moved the latter to Appendix A.
[45] Or perhaps, "condemned."

And if the Head were[46] in the Ascendant according to the root, the man himself will have a royal life in [those] three years. And if Jupiter or the Moon or Venus[47] were with it, his glory will be added to. And if the Tail were in the Ascendant, he will fall down into wicked things.

And if the Head were in the second,[48] he will get rich. And if the Tail were there, he will be impoverished.

And if the Head were in the third place, he will rule over his own brothers; but if it were the Tail, he will be the least of his brothers.

And[49] in diurnal nativities the aforesaid Nodes dispose after Mars, but in a nocturnal one after Mercury. But once the 75 years are completed, the distribution of the *firdārīyyāt* is restored to the planet from which the *firdārīyyah* at the beginning of the nativity began, according to the above-stated order, and the determinations of the outcomes proceed just as we have made clear before. And if the his life passed beyond 75 years, or the number reached [something] less than that number, his death will be in the *firdārīyyah* of that planet which it touches according to the teaching laid out for you before.[50]

☋ ☊ ☿

And these are the significations of the planets in their *firdārīyyāt*, in themselves and in association with the others. But in addition to these it is good to consider their significations according to the nativity (if they were of a good condition or a bad one), and according to the dispositions[51] which they had at the beginning of the nativity, and to make a determination concerning the particular significations of the outcomes.

---

[46] Reading *fuerit* for *Veneris*.
[47] *BA* IV.25 adds "or the Sun."
[48] Reading *secundo* for *Ariete*, following *BA* IV.25.
[49] The inserted section ends, and the Latin edition continues.
[50] This might mean that death will be more certain if it is indicated in both the *firdārīyyah* and in a direction of the Ascendant.
[51] Schmidt understands this to indicate house positions (and probably house rulership) in the nativity, to make the indications more specific.

BOOK V: ON INGRESSES

Chapter V.1: On the ingress of the planets

The ingress of the planets (in a revolution of years) to their places according to the nativity will have certain hidden significations, namely of good and bad things. Indeed it is good to consider their places, for oftentimes a planet in a revolution of the year reaches its degree according to the nativity and oftentimes to the sign but not to the degree. But if in a revolution of the year it reached the degree in which it was according to the nativity, or to the bound in which it was, then its signification will be perfected. And if the planet itself in a revolution of the year were in some sign, [and] then it will go retrograde to its place according to the nativity, so does it have a certain signification. But when it will reach the place of another planet, it will have to be considered in a three-fold way:

And firstly it is good to consider or commingle the significations of each of the stars when they aspect each other.

Then [secondly] to consider the natures, just as when a benevolent reaches the place of a benevolent, [it indicates great benevolence]; and a benevolent [reaching] the place of a malevolent makes the operation of the malevolent fortunate. But if a malevolent will reach the place of a benevolent, it corrupts the operation of the benevolent. But if a malevolent [reaches] the place of a malevolent, it increases its malice.

Thirdly, it is good to consider the sign in which the planet was according to the nativity, and to make it just like the Ascendant, and to determine the qualities of the outcomes according to it. For example,[1] Jupiter was in some sign according to the nativity, and that sign was his domicile (or the domicile of another), but Venus entered into the place of Jupiter in the revolution of the year: therefore we made each of the domiciles of Jupiter into an Ascendant, then we looked at the domiciles of Venus to see in which places they are touching from those

---

[1] This example departs from the definition just stated, since he now treats the places ruled by the planets as Ascendants, not their places in the nativity.

places. Therefore, looking at Taurus (the sixth from Sagittarius), we said that he will be sick. Moreover, seeing Libra (which is the eleventh place from Sagittarius), we said that he would acquire friends. Then we made Pisces just like an Ascendant, and, finding Taurus to be the third from it, we said that he will go on a foreign journey; and since Libra is the eighth from Pisces, he will attain resources on the occasion of an inheritance, and someone of those known to him will die, and he will prosper from inheritances.

And if one [planet] had many dignities in the [profected] sign of the year, we make its domiciles to be just like Ascendants, and we count from them up to the domiciles of Jupiter [in the example above].

But the time of the completion of the outcome will then be when a planet restored [to that place] will dispose the months or days in that year.

And if a planet reached the place of another planet, then it shows an operation if it were associated to that planet by a figure.[2]

And if you wanted to know how long the signification of the outcome will last, look: if a malevolent reached its own proper place, double its orb[3] and say the signification of the outcome will last for that amount of time. And if the place in the revolution were not contrary, the signification will be once[4] according to the orb of the planet. For example, Saturn was in the seventh according to the nativity, but he happened to be restored [to that same place] in some revolution, and I found [him] within the seventh sign from the sign of the profection, or in the seventh place of the Ascendant of the revolution.[5] Therefore we say that he will make both his wives and his enemies unfortunate, according to twice the orb[6] of the planet. And if he had been in the Midheaven or in another good place, once would have sufficed according to his orb. Likewise if some benevolent returned in some year to its own place according to the nativity, it signifies good, and if it were in a good place both in the nativity and in the revolution, it will operate for a double orb. However, you will decide an orb of this kind thusly: if the sign were in a

---

[2] Probably in the nativity.
[3] Converting its lesser, middle or greater years into units such as days. See below.
[4] Schmidt reads: "for the entire period."
[5] Thus he would be doubly in the seventh place, since by making a return to his natal position he would already be back in the seventh of the nativity.
[6] Reading with Schmidt for "place."

movable sign, you would take the lesser orb of this [planet]; if in a double-bodied one, the middle; if in a fixed one, the greater.

But [there] is another manner of ingress: if a planet were in some place according to the nativity, and another planet goes into that place according to the revolution, it has certain significations. But if planets of this kind were associated through a figure, they make a very evident operation, and one will work in the orb of the other,[7] and especially if they were in good places. For example, Jupiter was in a movable sign according to the nativity, but in a certain revolution Venus happened to be in the place of Jupiter. However, that place itself was the sixth from the sign of the profection or [from] the Ascendant of the revolution: therefore Venus, entering into the place of Jupiter, signified that the native will have windiness, and an illness of the windpipe.[8] But if she had been associated [to Jupiter] through a figure, then we would have conjoined Venus to Jupiter, [that is], the orbs of the two planets, and we would have said that the danger would last twenty days.[9] And if they has not been associated, it will last through one orb. If however it will be in movable signs, perhaps they will signify hours or days, and especially if they were benevolents, for benevolents signify a quick escape from evils, therefore we will use the same doctrine for every planet restored to its own place in a revolution, or one entering into the place of another.

But if two or more planets will be entering into the place of one, or one planet will be entering into the place of two, the judgment will be the same. For example, the Moon was in Cancer according to the nativity, [and] Saturn and Jupiter have entered into the place of the Moon at the time of the revolution: we say that the ingress of Saturn introduces harm on the occasions of women, but that of Jupiter introduces a good bearing of the body and an increase of riches, and good morals, and perhaps he will beget a child; and the period of sorrows will be according to the orb of Saturn, or until Saturn goes out from the bounds in which it is. And likewise for Jupiter. But if Jupiter and Saturn were in Cancer according to the nativity,[10] and the Moon will be entering upon them at the time of the revolution, it signifies that, through the ingress of the Moon upon Saturn, he whose revolution it is will go to bed with extremely old or decrepit women; but through the ingress

---

[7] Or, they "will be active in the periods of both of them" (Schmidt).
[8] Schmidt suggests breathing problems like asthma.
[9] The lesser years of Venus are 8, those of Jupiter 12: added together but considered as days, makes 20 days.
[10] Reading *nativitatem* for *revolutionem*.

upon Jupiter it signifies that he will go on a foreign journey in certain watery places, and from them to others.

Chapter V.2: On the ingress of Saturn to his own places and those of the rest of the planets

Saturn being restored to his own proper place in the revolution, and well disposed in the two times, renews [his] operation for the native, and leads [the native] from dignity to dignity. And if he were in an angle in the revolution, [the native] will attain greater goods. And in the Midheaven, or with them having dignities, from powerful men; in the seventh, either from women or from enemies; and you will likewise make a determination concerning the [rest of the] twelve places.

If however in the revolution he reached the [natal] place of Jupiter, and it happened that Saturn is the Lord of the Ascendant according to the nativity or according to the revolution, or [he is] the Lord of the Lot of Fortune, or the Lord of the Moon in the night or the Lord of the Sun in the day, it signifies dignity and the addition of friends and money and successes. But if he has no dignity in these places, he will harm [his] riches and immovable things, and whenever[11] he will go retrograde in that sign, he will have discords with his friends.

And if Saturn at the time of the revolution will reach the [natal] place of Mars, and Saturn will have dignity in either the Ascendant of the nativity or in the Ascendant of the revolution, or in the Lot of Fortune, it signifies a foreign journey and need with respect to brothers and friends, and advantage from them. However, he will be deceived about his own operations and will be idle in [his] education,[12] and his thoughts will be unjust; and he will be of middling faith in his own tenets, and he will be accused on account of this. And if Saturn will have no dignity with the aforesaid, he will suffer evils and be saddened on account of brothers and friends, and he will jump at the chance for travel and will go on a foreign journey.

And if [Saturn] at the time of the revolution will be conjoined to the [natal] Sun, and he has dignity in the aforesaid places, he will be ill with an acute and dangerous illness, and a certain fear is introduced from some

---

[11] Reading *quotiens* with Schmidt for *quot*.
[12] Reading with Schmidt.

authority or from one who has dignity, and he will have quarrels with women. And if Saturn does not have dignity in the aforesaid places, he will suffer contentions and one of his women will die, and [his father][13] will come near to danger. And if [the native] served someone, his master will suffer harm; but if not, he will be impeded because of his dignity.

But if [Saturn] reached the place of Venus, he whose revolution it is will go on a foreign journey, and he will try to be conjoined to a woman, but he will be impeded and his sexual intercourse will be middling. And if the figure signifies the begetting of children, he will procreate and will fall in love.

And if Saturn in the revolution of the year will reach the [natal] place of Mercury, he will have a slow mind[14] and he will go on a foreign journey. And if he had children, he will be saddened on account of them; and he will be bold, of lofty business dealings, and he will have fear of certain actions, and he will suffer harm from his discourse, and he will be harmed in his work.[15]

And if Saturn at the time of the revolution will reach the place of the [natal] Moon, he will contradict and be contemptuous on the occasion of women. And if at the time of the revolution the Moon were in an angle, it will be the greatest harm according to the nature of the sign in which she is: which if she were of the signs of the likeness of men, [and] there will be impediment through men. But if [of] the likenesses of wild animals, through wild animals. And if in Scorpio, through venomous things; if in Cancer or Pisces, through things creeping in waters and the like. But if the Moon were in the Ascendant of the Revolution, he will be ill with a dangerous illness.

Chapter V.3: On the ingress of Jupiter to his own and to the places of the rest of the planets

And if Jupiter arrived to the [natal] place of Saturn, it will give prosperity and it will put in order those things which Saturn destroyed at the beginning; but he will be obliging and most faithful, and he will prosper in his business matters, and he will have good things from friends, and his enemies will make peace with him and esteem him.

---

[13] Adding with Schmidt.
[14] Reading with Schmidt for *cordi multis*.
[15] Reading with Schmidt for *ab equitaturis suis, & experientia & exercitium eius cadet*.

But if Jupiter were restored to his own proper place, it renews the prosperities which are indicated by the beginning of the nativity, and it also shows riches from an unexpected source.[16]

But arriving at the place of Mars, he will make a foreign journey, and it will show advantage even from powerful men and from soldiers,[17] or [from] those having power, and perhaps he will beget a child, and his brothers (or some whom he regards as brothers) will have advantage.

But when he will reach the [natal] direction[18] of the Sun and he will be under the rays, [and] he will have dignity in the Ascendant of the revolution or in the sign of the profection, one must fear his destruction so long as he were under the rays. And if he escaped, [then] until Jupiter were outside the rays he will only suffer fears from authorities, and he will be concealed from them, and he will be sick; and if Jupiter were outside the rays, he will have prosperity.

But if Jupiter in the revolution will reach the [natal] place of Venus, he will be ill and will lay his body down, and his dignity and glory will be increased, and his friends will be added to, and he will be praiseworthy. But if Venus were of a bad condition, one will have to fear for him.

However, if Jupiter will reach the [natal] place of Mercury, his knowledge and teaching will be increased, and he will attain good things. [And if Jupiter is out from under the rays, he will obtain many good things.][19]

But arriving at the [natal] place of the Moon, it signifies the worthiness of the body, and the increase of riches and children, and good rumors. And if Jupiter were associated with Moon [at the time] of the inception [of the nativity],[20] it rescues him from every evil. When[21] they happen to be ascending in [the native's] revolution, or in the fifth place, or with their Lords, or in the place of Venus, or with the Moon, or with the Lot of Children, it signifies the generation of a child.

---

[16] Following Schmidt's "journey" or "source" for *emolumento* ("effort, success").
[17] Reading *militibus* with Schmidt for *mulieribus* ("women").
[18] That is, the Sun's position.
[19] Adding with Schmidt.
[20] Reading with Schmidt for "revolution."
[21] Treating this paragraph as referring to Jupiter and the Moon, else it would not make much sense.

Chapter V.4: On the ingress of Mars

Indeed Mars, reaching the [natal] place of Saturn at the time of the revolution, makes a multiplication of brothers and friends, and he will take a nearby journey; and if Mars has dignity in that year, it signifies inactivity and idleness. But if Saturn has dignity in the year, he will be sick from a wound. If however Mars will be entering into the place of Saturn, and Saturn will be entering into the [natal] place of Mars, it signifies exile from the fatherland.

But Mars entering into the [natal] place of Jupiter signifies foreign journeys and advantages from those under the yoke, then [also] namely if Jupiter will be entering into the place of Mars.

But if Mars were established in his own proper [natal] place, and in [that] year he would [be well situated in the inception],[22] he whose revolution it is will have good things, and particularly from soldiers. But if he were cadent from an angle, and he inspected the Ascendant, it signifies foreign travel and the increase of those serving [him]. But if [Mars] declined [from] the sign of the profection or of the Ascendant,[23] and he had dignity in it, [the native] will find good things through iron and blood.

But entering into the [natal] place of the Sun, with the revolution being diurnal, he will be saddened by authorities, and he will be ill from heat. But if Mars were the Lord of the Year, and he were in a hot and dry[24] sign, one will have to fear about [someone] killing [him]. But if the revolution were nocturnal, the dangers will be light.

Indeed, Mars reaching the [natal] place of Venus signifies an increase of sexual intercourse, and very intense desire, and arousal or stimulation to things having to do with women, and he will be delighted in pleasures, and his glory and dignity will be increased, and he will be made unfortunate because of women, and his friends will be multiplied, and he will be praiseworthy. But if Mars has the dignity[25] in that year, he will be sick from an overflowing of food or an overflowing of sexual intercourse. And if Venus would have the dignity in that year, he will be ill from the drinking of poison and from a pain of the artery of the windpipe.[26] And if in addition Venus were impeded, there is fear lest perhaps he die.

---

[22] Adding with Schmidt.
[23] That is, if he were not configured with them.
[24] Schmidt reads, "moist."
[25] For example, by being the Lord of the Year.
[26] *Tracheae arteriae*. Schmidt has only "windpipe."

And if Mars applied to the [natal] place of Mercury, he will use false writings and a certain one of his younger brothers will die.

But, entering into the [natal] place of the Moon [while she is] appearing in a good place, he will find dignity and perhaps he will beget a child. But if Mars will have the dignity in the year, he will be sick and be saddened on account of blood-kin and wives; which if he had dignity, he will lose her.

Chapter V.5: On the signification of the Sun in the individual signs

If the Sun at the time of the revolution were in Leo, and he were in an angle, of a good condition, and had the dignity in the year or at the beginning of the nativity, [the native] will be sound in body and will have very many benefits. But if he were of a bad condition, he will fall into illnesses. And if he were cadent from the angle, the illnesses will be easier.

And if he were in Virgo above the earth, and he aspected the Ascendant, having some signification in the year, it signifies the struggle of him whose revolution it is with respect to riches and teachings; and if the benevolents would be presenting testimony, he will obtain what he intends. But if the malevolents [did so], he will be deprived of it.

And if he were in Libra above the earth, having the dignity in the year, it signifies a foreign journey which will be useful if the Sun were associated to a benevolent by a figure.

And if he were in Scorpio in an angle, and unencumbered by the bad ones, and especially in the Midheaven, and he had the dignity in the year, he whose revolution it is will find good things and will manage buildings.

And if he were in Sagittarius and he had the dignity in the year, and he were of a good condition in an angle, he whose revolution it is will find good things and be glad, and perhaps he will beget a child. And if he were of a bad condition, his sorrows will be multiplied and he will have fear about what is his own.[27]

And if he were in Capricorn, and he had the dignity in the year, it signifies illnesses, sorrows, misfortunes and needs.

And if he were in Aquarius, and he had the dignity in the year, it signifies nuptials and the addition of blood-kin and subordinates, [but if he were

---

[27] Schmidt has "for a child of his."

corrupted, it indicates the death of relatives and of subordinates],[28] and contentions and quarrels.

And if he were impeded in Pisces, it signifies sorrows and deadly worries. And if he were unencumbered, he will be saddened without any reason.

And if he were in Aries, of a good condition, and he had the dignity in the year, it signifies a good foreign journey. But if he were of a bad condition, it signifies sorrows on the foreign journeys, and a scarcity of faith.

And if he were of a good condition in Taurus, and he had the dignity in that year, he will be friendly with powerful men and will have advantage from them; and if he were of a bad condition, he will be saddened and made anxious, and especially if he were in an angle.

And if he were of a good condition in Gemini, and he had the dignity in the year, and he were above the earth, aspecting the Ascendant and the sign of the profection, it signifies the multiplication of friends, and perhaps a son will be born to him. But if he were of a bad condition, he will be saddened and his business matters impeded.

And if he were in Cancer and he had the dignity in the year, appearing below the earth, he will be overcome by his enemies, and especially if the Moon did not aspect him.

Chapter V.6: On the ingress of Venus into her own place and that of the other planets

When Venus will reach the place of Saturn according to the nativity, it signifies concern about venereal acts. And if she were of a good condition, he will embrace lawful sexual intercourse. But if she were of a bad condition, [it will be] illicit [kinds] on account of which he will often be denounced. And if Venus were under the earth, [things] of this kind will be in secret; if above the earth, the contrary. And if Venus had the dignity in the year, he will be saddened because of women; he will even love waters and purifications and playing with water. And if Saturn had the dignity in the year, it signifies foreign travel and sexual intercourse and perhaps a boy will be born to him, or a woman will conceive because of him.

And if she will reach the [natal] place of Jupiter it signifies very intense faith, and foreign travel to sacred[29] places, and he will inherit riches, and will

---

[28] Adding with Schmidt.

go on a foreign journey to friends, and he will acquire new friends [who are] magnates, he will even be sick and be healed. And if Venus had some dignity in that year, he will suffer in throat. But if Jupiter has some dignity in that year, he will be sick from black choler.

And if she will reach the [natal] place of Mars, it signifies diligence about venereal things and nuptials. And if they were configured to one another, he will obtain all of the things he seeks in matters of this kind.

And if she will reach the [natal] place of the Sun, and she had the signification in the year, and they were both in angles, he will suffer necessities and he will fear the rulers. But if they were cadent from the angle, he will be sick from heat. And if the Sun has testimony in the year, his glory will be multiplied, and he will attain dignity and will go on a foreign journey and [someone will] long for him.

And if Venus will return to her own [natal] place, it renews the things which she signified in the inception [of the nativity], and his treasure will be increased.

And if she will enter into the [natal] place of Mercury, it signifies the power of speech, and eloquence and teaching. And if Venus has the dignity in the year, he will keep company with flute-players and cithara-players and jokers. But if she were of a bad condition, he will suffer harm.

And if she will enter into the [natal] place of the Moon, and the Moon were of a good condition, and either of them would have the dignity in the year, it signifies the good condition both of him and of his blood-kin, and attendance[30] with powerful people, and he will gain some friend equal to a brother.

Chapter V.7: On the signification of Mercury when he enters into the places

When Mercury enters into the place of Saturn according to the nativity, and he will have the signification in the year, free from the bad ones, it signifies a useful foreign journey, and perhaps a boy will be born to him. And if Saturn has signification in the year, it signifies the death of children, and

---

[29] Reading *sacra* for *sicca* with Schmidt.
[30] Or perhaps, being a servant (*famulationem*).

the illness of the one having the revolution, and unfairness and unfaithfulness, and contempt for those who make legal decrees.

And if he will enter into the [natal] place of Jupiter and either of them will have the dignity, [he will have honor][31] from someone superior, and his knowledge and acts will be increased. But if they were impeded, it signifies harms and contentions with enemies.

And if he will enter upon Mars, it signifies that he will be adjusted to lies and false writings. And if either of them is retrograding, it signifies thieveries. And if Mercury has the signification in the year and he is being impeded by Mars, the year will be dangerous. And if in addition he were under the rays, it will have to be feared lest perhaps he be killed in a foreign place.

And if he will enter upon the Sun and they will be in the angles, he will find dignity and glory, and especially if they are in the Midheaven.

And if he will enter upon Venus and he has the dignity in the year, it signifies the search for stories and verses and melodies.

And if he were restored to his own proper [natal] place, and he would have the dignity in the year and he were in an angle, it signifies the addition of glory and riches. And if he were impeded, it signifies diverse impediments.

And if he will enter upon the Moon, and the Moon has the dignity in the year, it signifies foreign travel, and contentions on journeys, and the scoffing of enemies, and fear of them.[32] And if Mercury has the dignity in the year, he will find good things, and his friends will be multiplied, and he will be commendable. But if the Moon were of a bad condition, he will be saddened on account of the reasons which we said before.

Chapter V.8: On the signification of the ingress of the Moon

The Moon entering in upon Saturn at the time of the revolution, having signification in the year, signifies libidinous or passionate dispositions towards some very old or decrepit women. And if she were of a bad condition it signifies detentions and contentions; and if it is feared concerning the danger of life in that year, perhaps he will die. And if Saturn has the dignity in the year, it signifies diverse and sad rumors.

---

[31] Adding with Schmidt.
[32] Schmidt reads this as though the enemies are afraid of the native. Perhaps this delineation is related to the fact that Gemini (a domicile of Mercury) is the twelfth (enemies) from Cancer (the domicile of the Moon).

But reaching the [natal] place of Jupiter, if she were of a good condition it signifies foreign travel to watery places, and from these to other ones. But if she were of a bad condition, he will fall into adversities and be sick.

Indeed, entering into the [natal] place of Mars while she herself[33] is of a good condition, he will find dignity and will stick by soldiers, he will be sick from heat, and he will suffer a terrible sickness[34] and fears of authorities, and he will go on a useless foreign journey. And if the Moon were impeded both in the nativity and in the revolution, and she were conjoined to a Mars appearing in a bad condition, on that day [his] blood will be poured out by some means, and he will have quarrels and injustices or false accusations.

And if she reached the [natal] place of the Sun, and she had the dignity [in the year], he will suffer [because of] authority, or from those having bad power, or from greater persons. And if the Sun has the dignity in the year, he will acquire some dignity, and he will perhaps be deprived of his mother (or the father instead of the mother).

And if she will enter into the [natal] place of Venus, and she were of a good condition, it signifies impediments concerning movement, and he will be saddened on account of blood-kin, and he will be in rest and delight, and he will acquire immovable substance. But if she herself were the Lady [of the Year], he will obtain glory and his blood-kin will have advantage through him.

But, arriving at the [natal] place of Mercury, it signifies foreign travel and harm from enemies. But if Mercury had the dignity in the year, his condition will be prosperous, and he will acquire resources and be praised by many.

But the Moon arriving at any [place],[35] it being a nocturnal revolution, [the native] will be in health and safety, and he will obtain advantage from it. And if some planets aspected it,[36] the individual [planets] will show their operation. And if the Moon were impeded, and she reached [the square of][37] her own place according to the nativity, or to its opposite, he will have danger on that day.

---

[33] Reading *ipsa* for *ipse* ("he himself") with Schmidt.
[34] Reading with Schmidt for *enormia*.
[35] Schmidt has "if the Moon come to be near itself," which probably means to her natal sign.
[36] Schmidt reads "the Moon," but this probably means "her natal sign."
[37] Adding with Schmidt.

And[38] if a malevolent in the revolution reached the [natal] place of the Moon, and [no benevolent] aspected the Moon,[39] it signifies illnesses and sorrows and difficulties, and especially if the malevolent is the Lord of the Year and it is in a contrary place in the revolution. And if the Moon reached the place of a malevolent according to the nativity, the same thing happens.

But when the Moon in the revolution of the year is associated through a figure to a benevolent or a malevolent, when she will arrive to the body of that benevolent or malevolent, or to the ray of one of them, it signifies good or bad things according to the nature of the planet. And when she arrives at a planet signifying good or bad according to the nativity, it will show [its] operation on that day.

[Chapter V.9: General comments on transits]

And if some planet will enter at some time into the degree in which the distribution or distributor was, or to the degree of the Ascendant of the inception [of the nativity] or to the degree of the Ascendant of the revolution, or to the rays of some of the planets, or [to] the Lots or the particular twelfth-parts, or their Lords, it moves the signification according to its own proper nature.

And if a planet aspected the place of another planet from whatever aspect, it will renew its signification.[40]

And when the planet having the dignity in the year will enter upon the twelfth-part of a sign, or the twelfth-part of the planet to which it belongs, it signifies the same thing: the signification of the aforesaid planet and sign. For example: [if] the twelfth-part of the fourth place will fall on the second sign, we say that when a planet will enter into that [second] place, [the native] will handle those things which pertain to houses and resources; indeed the planets have other significations according to the distance of the domiciles of one from the other, about which we say nothing here for the reason that those learning [can] conjecture [the significations from what has been said].[41] For if the planets signified something, both according to the root [of the

---

[38] For this paragraph, cf. *BA* IV.14.
[39] Adding based on *BA* IV.14.
[40] I.e., if those planets were already configured in the nativity.
[41] Reading with Schmidt. See the beginning of the transit material in V.1 above.

nativity] and according to the revolution, the determinations of the outcomes will be more certain.

Indeed, in ingresses it is good to look and see to which of the planets (according to the nativity or according to the revolution) the entering planet is configured. And if the planets are configured according to the nativity, it signifies the outcome is from a preceding cause; but if the planets are configured according to the revolution [alone], they signify [it is] from a supervening cause.[42] And if [ingressing planets] are not configured to any [planet], either of those which are according to the nativity or the revolution, it signifies the outcome is from an unexpected cause.[43]

[Chapter V.10: Miscellaneous considerations][44]

However, in a revolution of the year it is good to look at the Moon and her Lord: if they were of a good condition and associated to benevolents through a figure, they signify a good bearing and health and prosperity. But if it were of a bad condition, there will not be good in that year. However, you should look at the twelfth-part of the Moon, and it will be worse if it is being aspected by malevolents. And if the Moon is not being aspected by any [planet], nor does she aspect the Ascendant, he will strive to acquire something in that year but he will not acquire it.

And know that the Sun burning up the planets is worse than a malevolent; and if he is being aspected by a bad one, it signifies combustions and exiles. And if he is being aspected by Saturn, he will suffer a long illness or death. But if by Mars, murder or flight.

And if Jupiter and Venus were in the angles or in the succeedents of the angles according to the nativity or according to the revolution, they signify goods and glory from men, and the compacts of friendship. However, Venus does not have the same power as Jupiter does, except for womanly things and for having advantages from noble women—even more so for delights.

And if Mars and Saturn were in places of this kind, they signify adversities for natives; in doing good he will be censured and men whom he has not

---

[42] That is, from a cause that comes to be only at that time. It is hard to know exactly how this is different from the "unexpected" cause in the next sentence.

[43] At this point a short section on the *firdārīyyāt* of the Nodes appeared in the Latin edition, but it has been moved to its proper place above.

[44] This chapter is not reflected in Pingree.

harmed will injure him. And if he were a king, the condition of his kingdom and blood-kin and house will be diminished, and he will fall into the greatest misfortunes, such as that he will be in need of necessities. And if he were of middling [people], the condition of his house will be handled [badly]. And if Saturn were in places of this kind, he will always be refuting himself in thoughts and worries, and be harmful[45] to others. But if it were Mars, he will be bold and worthless[46] and having his hands full in many matters.

And if Mercury were with Jupiter he will be skilled and fit to be consulted, and eloquent and intelligent, and delightful or loved by all, and praised by all; [when] speaking lies he will even be believed, and perhaps he will be a secretary of kings.

And if someone wanted to know at what time he will receive pleasant rumors, and when he will receive sorrowful rumors, he should look at Mercury according to his own nativity. For if the benevolents aspected [Mercury], or the ray of the Sun or Moon [were] appropriate,[47] a good rumor will reach him. But if the Moon were in that sign, and a malevolent with [Mercury], he will receive adverse rumors. And if Mercury were oriental [and] inspected by benevolents and malevolents, he will receive rumors less.[48] But whenever Jupiter and Venus reach the place of the Sun or Moon or to their squares, and the sign were one of the angles according to the revolution, and Mercury is not being aspected by a malevolent at the time of the nativity,[49] good and pleasant and useful rumors will reach [him].

Moreover, if the Lord of the Year were well disposed in the revolution, it signifies health and soundness of the body. Even the Lord of the Lot of Fortune [being well disposed signifies that] he manages [things] well and signifies riches and advantage. And if they were of a bad condition, you will make it the contrary, and even [make] a direction, taking it in the months and days.

When however the Sun arrives at the place where Mars was, but Mars happened to be where the Moon had been according to the nativity, you will say that blood has flowed out from the native.

---

[45] Or, "noxious" (*noxius*).
[46] *Vacuus*, but this may be an error.
[47] *Convenientes*.
[48] *Minus*. Or perhaps it should read "mixed" (*mixtos*).
[49] ...*et fuerit signum unum de angulis, et secundum revolutionem non aspicitur a malevolo tempore nativitatis Mercurius.* Or perhaps it should read, "and the sign were one of the angles according to the nativity, and Mercury is not being aspected by a malevolent at the time of the revolution."

And when the Moon will reach the place of Venus, with there not being a malevolent, it is the best. And if it will be with Mars, he will obtain venereal actions. And if Saturn aspected or is being conjoined, it signifies their frigidity.

And when Saturn arrives at his own bound it introduces advantages; but when the Moon arrives at the place of Mercury, you will make a determination according to the quality of the place.

And when she arrives at the [natal] Ascendant, it elevates thoughts.[50] But when she arrives at the Midheaven, it signifies according to the nature of the stars aspecting her; however, the figure will be appropriate to the one seeking the action. But when she arrives at the angle of the earth, there will be good with respect to things able to be hidden, and counsels, and thieveries, and incantations or magic,[51] and for the belief in secret things. [And in the seventh, it is good against enemies.][52]

---

[50] Or perhaps, "cares" or "worries" (*cogitationes*).
[51] Or, "poisoning" (*veneficia*), which was related to spells and magic in the medieval mind.
[52] Adding with the parallel Dorotheus text in Schmidt 1995 (p. 5), to which Abū Ma'shar evidently had access as opposed to 'Umar's version.

BOOK IX: DIVISIONS OF MONTHS, DAYS, HOURS

Chapter IX.7: On the indicators of the days and hours

N.B.: What follows is my own summary of the nine types of indicators from the surviving Greek text of Book IX, based on Robert Schmidt's translation. The indicator titles are my own. I myself have doubts about the interpretive value of some of these indicators, but identifying daily and weekly rulers might be useful for electional or magical practices.

Abū Ma'shar states that, for indicators 1-5, one should note the condition and transits of the daily/weekly rulers on the day of the revolution, since they will give indications for the whole year.

1. Weekly and daily rulers.[1]

Count the number of days which have passed since the first day of the nativity, including the birth day itself. Group these into cycles of seven days, with each planet ruling a complete week. The Lord of the Ascendant rules the first complete week, then the planet below it in the heavens, rotating back to Saturn after the Moon's turn. (Thus every 49 days or seven weeks will contain a complete cycle of all the planets.)

Continue counting off weekly cycles until you reach the time of the solar revolution/annual profection you want. The day will usually fall in the middle of an incomplete weekly cycle. The planet ruling that week will continue to rule until its week is completed, and will then hand the week over to the next planet as usual.

For any week, the ruler of the week will also rule the first complete day, with the next planet in order ruling the following day, and so on.

The ruler of any day will also rule the first 1/7 of that first day, again handing the rulership over to the next planet for the next 1/7, and so on.

---

[1] This indicator is the same as that given by Māshā'allāh in *BA* IV.16, and is based on al-Andarzaghar. But one may read the instructions differently depending on which text one consults. See also *Carmen* IV.1.57.

2. The Lord of the period.[2]

Find the Lord of the period for the year in question. The first week of the revolution will be allotted to it, with the rest of the planets (in descending Chaldean order) governing successive weeks in turn, in cycles throughout the whole year. Just as with Indicator #1 above, each ruler of the week also rules the first complete day and the first 1/7 of it.

3. The "greater weeks."

For any revolution you want, divide the entire year (about 365.25 days) by 7. This will yield periods of about 52 days and 4.25 hours, or a "greater week," each one being allotted to one of the seven planets. The first period is ruled by the Lord of the Ascendant of the revolution, and each one thereafter to the next planet in descending Chaldean order.

Then divide each greater week by 7, yielding smaller "weeks" of about 7 days and 10 hours. Each Lord of the greater week will also rule the first smaller "week," as before, with the rest being allotted to the remaining stars in order as above. One may also subdivide these smaller "weeks" as with Indicator #1.

4. Signs per week.

Just as with Indicator #1, group the days from the nativity (including the birth day itself) into weeks. But unlike #1, each week is attributed to a zodiacal sign (instead of a planet), beginning from the rising sign of the nativity. Each week will thus be ruled by a sign of the nativity in order, until you reach the revolution you want.

At the revolution, the sign which rules the current week will still rule the remaining days of that week (as with #1), and will also rule the first 1/7 of its own week (about 14 hours), with the following signs ruling the subperiods of that week as usual.

5. Signs per day.

Group the days from the nativity (including the birth day itself) into sets of 12 days, each day assigned to one of the signs in order, beginning with the natal Ascendant. At the solar revolution, the sign ruling that day will have relevance for the entire year, and it will also rule the first 1/12 (or 2 hours) of

---

[2] Abū Ma'shar refers us back to Book VI, which only exists in Arabic.

that day, with the rest of the signs ruling the successive 2-hour periods of that day. The following sign rules the following day, and so on.

6. The "greater condition" or "greatest days."[3]

Profect the natal Ascendant (or the Lots for the Father and Mother, if you want their condition) in 30° increments until you reach the year you want. If there is a planetary body or ray in the degree you reach, take it as the first governor; if not, use the bound Lord of that degree.

Convert the following 30° into ascensions, and treat them as equaling 1 year: thus every degree will on average equal 12 1/6 days of the revolution, starting on the day of the revolution. Track the passage of the Ascendant (or the Lots) through these degrees and convert the bounds, bodies and aspects to days throughout the year.

7. The "lesser condition" or "small days."[4]

Direct the degree of the Ascendant of the revolution around the entire circle for the year of the revolution, at a rate of 59' 08" per degree: these are the "small days." Just as with the "greater condition" above, track the bound Lords and the planetary bodies or rays encountered by the Ascendant throughout the year.

8. Monthly and daily profections.[5]

In a given annual profection, profect the four chief indicators[6] through the months at a rate of 30° per month. You will also profect these months from the Ascendant, the Lot of Fortune, and the Moon, and even all of the remaining eleven places besides the Ascendant.[7] For all of these, direct them

---

[3] Schmidt (1999, p. 79 n. 182) believed this was a straightforward distributor-partner direction from the Ascendant, as in Book III above. But based on certain key words (Abū Ma'shar says "greatest days") and the reference to the Lots of the parents, I believe it is really 'Umar al-Tabari's annual/monthly profection method for the "greater condition" from *TBN* II, but converted into ascensions instead of ecliptical degrees.

[4] Again, this must be 'Umar's "lesser condition," in which one directs points in the solar revolution around the entire circle for the period of one year.

[5] Assume that the annual profection by 30° increments is from 12° Taurus to 12° Gemini. That increment will also be the first month of the year, the first 2 ½ days of that month, and the first 5 hours of those 2 ½ days, with each successive 30° increment allotted to the following months, sets of 2 ½ days, and sets of 5 hours as desired.

[6] These are left unnamed.

[7] The text does not specify whether these are Equal Houses from the Ascendant, or quadrant-style houses such as Porphyry or Alchabitius Semi-Arc.

through the next 30° (representing one month) at a rate of one day per degree,[8] noting the planetary bodies and rays encountered.

For the days of the month, treat each monthly increment of 30° as the first 2 ½ days of that month, and so on around the whole circle, yielding a month comprised of 30 days.

For divisions of hours, treat the whole circle as a period of 2 ½ days, such that each 30° increment equals 5 hours.

Again, direct the points through these at the relevant rates, as before.

9. Ninth-parts.

N.B.: The instructions here do not quite make sense to me, since they suggest a continuous direction through the ninth-parts beginning where the 30° annual increment falls; but in Abū Ma'shar's own example, it is as though the year begins with the Lord of the first ninth-part in every case. I report the instructions as I understand them by continuous directions.

Indicators may be found for the following points:

(a) The sign of the annual profection (probably by 30° increments). The Lord of the Year will be the Lord of the first ninth-part of the sign, as described in III.10 above.[9] Then the following nine ninth-parts (by a 30° increment) will be assigned to the first month of the year: the Lord of the sign is the Lord of the initial ninth-part, the Lord of the next sign rules the following ninth-part, and so on. The next 30° increment will be the second month of the year in the same way. Each ninth-part may also be sub-divided into three equal parts (as in III.9-10 above), to yield sub-periods of 1 1/9 days. You could even divide each subdivision by 9 to get hourly divisions, and so on.[10]

(b) Do the same for the degree of the Ascendant of the revolution, beginning in the sign in which it as at the revolution.

(c) Do the same for the degree of the transiting Moon at the revolution, beginning the ninth-parts from the degree where she is.

---

[8] The text does not specify whether these are by ascensions or by simple ecliptical longitude.

[9] By definition the Lord of the first ninth-part can only be Mars, the Moon, Venus, or Saturn.

[10] In Abū Ma'shar's example, he has the profected Ascendant arriving at 20° Taurus, clearly the ninth-part of the Moon. Since it is an earthy sign, we should expect Saturn to be the Lord of the Year, but for the subdivisions of the year to begin with the Moon. However, Abū Ma'shar acts as though we begin with the first ninth-part of Taurus, assigned to Saturn.

APPENDIX A: ALTERNATIVE TEXT FOR THE *FIRDĀRIYYĀT* OF THE NODES

The following two paragraphs originally appeared at the end of IV.7 in *On Rev. Nat.* (now IV.8), but I have replaced them with this fuller version which had been incorporated incorrectly into the material on transits. This fuller version parallels Māshā'allāh's own use of al-Andarzaghar in *BA* IV.24-25, and has allowed me to correct the Latin text of Abū Ma'shar.

"Then the Head of the Dragon alone disposes 3 years, and it signifies that in a distribution of this kind he will be prospering, and will befriend princes and will rule over many, he will even buy male and female slaves, and he will have friendship with women.

"Then the Tail disposes 2 years. In a distribution of this kind he will become inimical to his friends, and he will be fined and saddened about his wife, and he will be defamed because of her, and he will be sick with a vicious illness."

Appendix B: Table of Egyptian Bounds for Distributors

♈	♃ 0°-5°59'	♀ 6°-11°59'	☿ 12°-19°59'	♂ 20°-24°59'	♄ 25°-29°59'
♉	♀ 0°-7°59'	☿ 8°-13°59'	♃ 14°-21°59'	♄ 22°-26°59'	♂ 27°-29°59'
♊	☿ 0°-5°59'	♃ 6°-11°59'	♀ 12°-16°59'	♂ 17°-23°59'	♄ 24°-29°59
♋	♂ 0°-6°59'	♀ 7°-12°59	☿ 13°-18°59'	♃ 19°-25°59'	♄ 26°-29°59'
♌	♃ 0°-5°59'	♀ 6°-10°59'	♄ 11°-17°59'	☿ 18°-23°59'	♂ 24°-29°59'
♍	☿ 0°-6°59'	♀ 7°-16°59'	♃ 17°-20°59'	♂ 21°-27°59'	♄ 28°-29°59'
♎	♄ 0°-5°59'	☿ 6°-13°59'	♃ 14°-20°59'	♀ 21°-27°59'	♂ 28°-29°59'
♏	♂ 0°-6°59'	♀ 7°-10°59'	☿ 11°-18°59'	♃ 19°-23°59'	♄ 24°-29°59'
♐	♃ 0°-11°59'	♀ 12°-16°59'	☿ 17°-20°59'	♄ 21°-25°59'	♂ 26°-29°59'
♑	☿ 0°-6°59'	♃ 7°-13°59'	♀ 14°-21°59'	♄ 22°-25°59'	♂ 26°-29°59'
♒	☿ 0°-6°59'	♀ 7°-12°59'	♃ 13°-19°59'	♂ 20°-24°59'	♄ 25°-29°59'
♓	♀ 0°-11°59'	♃ 12°-15°59'	☿ 16°-18°59	♂ 19°-27°59'	♄ 28°-29°59'

APPENDIX C: APHORISMS ON REVOLUTIONS

Following are some aphorisms taken from three well-known medieval centiloquies: the *Centiloquy* of pseudo-Ptolemy, that attributed to Hermes, and that attributed to al-Mansūr. I have also translated some of the medieval commentary by al-Ridwān to pseudo-Ptolemy's *Centiloquy*.

1. Pseudo-Ptolemy: Centiloquium

Aphorism 24:

An eclipse of the luminaries in the angles of nativities or the revolutions of years impedes according to the nature of the sign in which the eclipse comes to be: namely according to house. And the time in this is that there be a proportion which is between the ascending degree and the degree of the eclipse, up to that hour, to the total time which is signified from the total eclipse, with each hour [being] a month [in the case of lunar eclipses, but a year for solar eclipses].[1]

> *Al-Ridwān:* His intention is that as the Sun and Moon, if either of them is being eclipsed in the angle of a human nativity, or in the angles of his revolutions of years, something to shudder at will reach him in the place which belongs to that sign: for example, if it was the angle of the house of the kingdom, it will be in [his] kingdom; but if it were the angle of the house of life, it will be in his body. And speak in the rest of the angles according to this way, except that the angles of revolutions are easier than the angles of nativities. However, the hour at which it especially happens to be, [is] that you should look at the hours of the eclipse, to see how many they are. And if it were an eclipse of the Sun, I put a year for an hour of it, and the same proportion for a fraction of an hour. Then look at that whole time, to see how many years it is, and how many years the fraction is, and take from that according to the quantity of that which is between the ascending degree and the place of the eclipse, from 180°.

> *Dykes:* al-Ridwān now offers an example that conflates the chart of the eclipse with the nativity. My understanding of Ptolemy's method in *Tet.* II.6 is as follows. Cast the chart for the eclipse, at the location of the nativity. Measure how long the eclipse lasts, in "equinoctial" or standard 60-minute hours by the clock. The total number of hours (and fractions of hours) is equated to years for solar eclipses, and months for lunar ones. The 180° of the hemisphere where it takes place is made equivalent to that whole period, but the place of the eclipse

---

[1] Adding with 1550.

within that hemisphere determines when the effects will take place. So, suppose it is a solar eclipse that lasts one hour, and it occurs above the earth: then the whole upper hemisphere of the chart is equated to one year. Now suppose that the eclipse took place more towards the Ascendant of the eclipse chart: then the effects will happen in the first portion of the year, proportionate to its distance from the horizon; if it were nearer the Midheaven, then the effects would be expected closer to the middle of the period; and so on.

Aphorism 77:
Direct the ascending degree for accidents of the body, and the degree of the Lot of Fortune [for] his substance; but the degree of the Moon for the being of the body with the soul; and the degree of the Sun for the power of his princes; the degree of the Midheaven, however, for those things in which he works—[giving] a year to every degree.

Al-Ridwān: This statement is as plain as it appears: however, it renders doubts regarding the degree of the Ascendant and the degree of the Moon. For by the ascending degree we know about the condition of the body and its alterations and complexions—according to which it is repeated for this with respect to diseases and health. And we will direct the degree of the Moon for that which will be for the body in terms of cheerfulness and agility, and what obeys the soul; and they do those things which pertain to the soul. But the direction of the Lot of Fortune [is] for that which he will acquire or lose. And we will direct the degree of the Sun for the power or dignity which he will have from his own prince or king, for good or evil: because if the degree of the Sun encountered a fortune or its rays, his honor with respect to his master will be increased; but if to a bad one or its rays, his honor will be diminished. And the direction of the degree of the Midheaven does not come to be thus, because the direction of the Sun is for you, and all of those who rule over you; but the direction of the Midheaven is for you and all those whom *you* rule. And the direction is just as we have said. Which if [the direction] were in the Midheaven, you will direct by the ascensions of the right circle; if it were in the Ascendant, by the ascensions of your region. But if it were not in one of these, by the ascensions of these two.[2] Also, [direct] the degree of the Midheaven for that in which he busies himself, in terms of works; [but] direct the degree of the Sun for a dignity which he has from his king. These are in the last chapter of the book of the *Tetrabiblos*.[3]

---

[2] That is, by proportional semi-arcs, of which the Ptolemaic, Placidean, and Regiomontanan are examples.

[3] Lat. *alabra*, a mistransliteration for the Arabic.

Aphorism 87:
The time of the changing of signs in the revolution, initiated by the sign of the profection, are 28 days and 2 hours and approximately 18 minutes of one hour. But initiated by the Ascendant, namely in the hemisphere in the east, 28 days and approximately 1/5 of a day. But the solar month is from the changing of the Sun from the degree in which the nativity was, into the degree corresponding to it in another sign.

Al-Riḍwān: He wants to show us this: how many days one must note that the profection of the sign is in charge of, from the Ascendant, and from the observed Ascendant to the revolution. And what are the minutes of the degree of the Sun in the other solar months, near to the truth. And that the sign in which the solar year begins (namely, the one which we revolve in the Ascendant) will be the second from that one in which the concluded year began.[4] And it is that we should direct from the beginning of the sign up to its end, and the signs will be completed in the solar year, that is the signs in which the native will be changed: and his condition will be signified. Therefore once we have distributed the 365 and ¼ days through 13 signs,[5] they will come out as 28 days and 2 hours and 18 minutes of an hour, approximately. And this is the time in which the profection will stay in every sign, until it is moved from that one to the sign which succeeds it, and it is called the month of the profection:[6] wherefore however, the hour of its revolution is initiated by the Ascendant; wherefore [it is] a year which is of 365 and approximately ¼ days. If it were distributed through 13 signs and approximately 1/10 of one sign, from the observed minute of the Ascendant in the revolution, up to the Ascendant in which the following year began. To every sign fall 28 days and approximately 1/5 of a day. Indeed the times of the *solar* month are different: and they are from the ingress of the Sun into the minute in which it was at the hour of the nativity, up to where he reaches one like it in the following sign from it: and we have already made clear the property of each one of those parts in our books of judgments.

Aphorism 88:
If we wished to direct the Lot of Fortune in some revolution of years, we will take it from the place of the Sun in the nativity to the place of the Moon,

---

[4] This is simply a complicated way of saying that the year as marked by the sign of the profection and the solar revolution begins at the same time.
[5] That is, we assume 13 lunar months per year.
[6] So, Ptolemy (*Tet.* IV.10) is describing profections of *lunar* months, at a rate of 1 sign per lunar month, for a total of 13 signs/lunar months.

and we will project out from the degree of the Ascendant of the *revolution of the year*.[7]

2. Hermes: Centiloquium

Aphorism 87:

There will be an impediment around that part of the body which a sign which was impeded at the time of the nativity, signifies.

3. Al-Mansūr: Propositions

Proposition 63:

From the degree of the Ascendant are known the accidents of the body; from the degree of the Lot of Fortune, the being of substance; but from the degree of the Moon is observed the being of the body; from the degree of the Sun, however, his strengths, but masteries and works are distinguished from the degree of the Midheaven: give a year to each degree.[8]

Proposition 64:

He will be made fortunate, and will be of a good condition, not to mention powerful, whose revolution of the year[9] were similar to the root, and whose circle was in that same likeness in which it will be in that year of the root.[10]

Proposition 65:

The daily being of the native is taken from a direction, in one way from the motion of the Lord.[11] [But] the day-to-day being of the native is taken in another way: from the motion of the Lord of the sign of the profection of the year, in the bounds [which are] laid out (belonging to the Lord of the sign of the completion[12] of the year), to [other] bounds [which are] laid out.[13]

---

[7] Emphasis mine; this is an important variation.
[8] See Aphorism 77 of pseudo-Ptolemy above, and al-Ridwān's commentary.
[9] Reading *anni* for *annus*.
[10] The reference to the "year of the root" sounds like a profection. If so, then this passage is comparing the revolution, the nativity, and the sign of the profection.
[11] Perhaps the direction of the Lord of the Ascendant of the year, around the revolutionary chart.
[12] Or "terminal point" (Lat. *alynthiae*, Ar. *intihā'*), referring to the place of the current profection.
[13] The key to understanding this paragraph lies in the Arabic verb which is translated here as "laid out" (*expono*). But my sense is that it simply suggests that we take either the Lord of the Ascendant of the year, or the profected Lord of the Year, and direct it through the

Proposition 81:

If the infortunes reached a suitable place,[14] they will not harm, if there were not a signification of that in the root of the nativity; and likewise the fortunes will not be of benefit if there is not a signification of those things in the root.

---

bounds around the chart of the revolution for that year, starting from where it is by transit at the revolution.

[14] Probably a transit.

Appendix D: Study Guide to *Persian Nativities*

This guide will help students compare the natal teachings of the five astrologers in *Persian Nativities I-III*. References are listed by chapter based on their main content, so not every possible reference to every topic is listed. The division of questions for each topic is based mainly on those found in *BA*.

Book Abbreviations

Abū Bakr	Abū Bakr, *On Nativities*
BA	Māshā'allāh bin Atharī, *The Book of Aristotle*
JN	Al-Khayyāt, Abū 'Ali, *The Judgments of Nativities*
Nativities	Māshā'allāh bin Atharī, *On Nativities* (in *Works of Sahl & Māshā'allāh*)
On Rev. Nat.	Abū Ma'shar al-Balhi, *On the Revolutions of the Years of Nativities*
TBN	Al-Tabarī, 'Umar, *Three Books on Nativities*

1. Overview of questions and methods: Abū Bakr I.1

2. Rectification/namūdārs

	BA	TBN	Abū Bakr
1. Ptolemaic		I.2	
2. Hermetic	III.1.10		I.4.1-2
3. Other			I.4.3

3. Conception, gestation and birth

	TBN	Abū Bakr
1. Conception		I.2
2. Gestation	I.1	I.2-3, I.5
3. Birth		I.7
4. "Monsters"	I.3.1	I.8

4. Rearing/nourishment

	BA	Nativities	JN	TBN	Abū Bakr
1. Survival	III.1.2	§1	Ch. 1		I.12.0, I.14
2. No survival	III.1.3	§1	Ch. 1		I.12.0
3. Exposure	III.1.4				I.13
4. Birth type 1				I.3.1	I.12.1
5. Birth type 2				I.3.2	I.12.2
6. Birth type 3				I.3.3	I.12.3
7. Birth type 4				I.3.4	I.12.4
8. Prediction		§1	Ch. 1	I.3.1-3	I.12.2, 12.5-6

5. Longevity

	BA	Nativities	JN	TBN	Abū Bakr
1. *Hīlāj*	III.1.5	§2	Ch. 2	I.4.1	I.15
2. *Kadukhudhāh*	III.1.6	§3-4	Ch. 3	I.4.2-4	I.15
3. Prediction	III.1.7-10.	§4	Ch. 4	I.4.5-8	I.15

6. Character

	Nativities	JN	Abū Bakr
1. Overview			II.1
2. Lord 1st/Mercury	§5	Ch. 5	
3. Fear			II.1.1
4. Aggression		Ch. 34	II.1.2-3
5. Shame/modesty			II.1.4-5
6. Happy/sad			II.1.6, 1.25-27
7. Truthfulness			II.1.7-8, 1.17
8. Intellect/knowledge			II.1.12-16
9. Faithfulness			II.1.18-19
10. Taking/giving			II.1.20-24
11. Greed			II.1.28
12. Discord			II.1.29-30
13. Beauty			II.1.31
14. Calm/quick			II.1.32-33

7. Body/physiognomy

	Abū Bakr
1. Face	I.9-10
2. Body type	I.10
3. Family resemblance	I.11

8. Prosperity

	BA	Nativities	JN	TBN	Abū Bakr
1. Always high	III.2.1	§6	Chs. 6-7, 30-32	III.1.1, III.9	II.2.0-2
2. Always middle	III.2.3		Ch. 7		II.2.3
3. Always low	III.2.6	§6	Ch. 7	III.1.1	II.2.4-7
4. Rising	III.2.4	§6	Ch. 7	III.1.1	II.2.9
5. Sinking	III.2.2		Ch. 7	III.1.1	II.2.8
6. When	III.2.6	§6	Ch. 8	III.1.2	
7. Other			Chs. 10, 30-32		II.2.10

9. Wealth

	JN	TBN	Abū Bakr
1. Source	Chs. 9, 11	III.2	II.3.2-11
2. Abundance	Ch. 11	III.2	II.3.1
3. Scarcity	Ch. 11	III.2	
4. When	Ch. 11	III.2	

10. Siblings

	BA	JN	TBN	Abū Bakr
1. Older/younger	III.3.3	Ch. 13	III.3	II.4.1
2. Number	III.3.2-3	Ch. 12	III.3	II.4.1-2
3. Sex	III.3.2	Ch. 13	III.3	II.4.1
4. Half-siblings		Ch. 12		II.4.5
5. Concord	III.3.5-6	Chs. 13, 15-16	III.3	II.4.1, 4.3-4
6. Status		Chs. 12, 14	III.3	II.4.5
7. Death	III.3.4, 3.7			

11. Parents

	BA	JN	TBN	Abū Bakr
1. Legitimacy	III.4.2		III.4.1	I.6, II.5.10
2. Lineage	III.4.3-4			II.2.10, II.5.1
3. Status/when	III.4.1	Ch. 16	III.4	II.5.1-2, 5.6-7, 5.10-11
4. Love between			III.4	
5. Love with native	III.1.4, 4.5, 12.7		III.4, III.9	II.5.3-4
6. Death	III.4.6-4.7, 4.9	Chs. 17-19	III.4	II.5.8-13
7. Inherit?	III.4.8	Ch. 16		II.5.5

12. Children

	BA	JN	TBN	Abū Bakr
1. Fertility	III.5.2	Ch. 20	III.6	II.6.1-3
2. Number	III.5.3-4	Ch. 20	III.6	II.6.1-2, 6.4
3. Sex	III.5.5			II.6.1
4. Death	III.5.3	Ch. 20		II.6.10
5. Status				II.6.8-9
6. Love for native		Ch. 21	III.6	II.6.1, 6.6-7
7. When	III.5.3, 5.5	Ch. 21	III.6	II.6.1, 6.5

13. Illness

	BA	JN	TBN	Abū Bakr
1. Signs of illness				II.7.1-2
2. Eyes	III.6.2	Ch. 24	III.7	II.7.3-8
3. Various	III.6.3	Ch. 24	III.7	II.7.9-13, 7.15-22, 7.24, 7.28, 7.31-36, 7.38
4. Mind	III.6.4	Ch. 24		II.7.14
5. Sociality	III.6.5			
6. Sexual	III.6.6		III.5, III.7	II.7.23, 7.25-27
7. Height	III.6.7			II.7.11, 7.29-30
8. When	III.6.8	Ch. 24		II.7.37

14. Slaves/servants

	BA	JN	Abū Bakr
1. Concord	III.11.1	Ch. 22	II.8
2. Benefit/harm		Ch. 22	II.8

15. Animals

	JN	Abū Bakr
1. Benefit/abundance	Ch. 23	II.3.6
2. Loss/scarcity	Ch. 23	

16. Marriage

	BA	JN	TBN	Abū Bakr
1. Marry?	III.7.2	Chs. 25-26	III.5	II.9.2-3
2. Spouse age	III.7.4-5	Ch. 26		II.9.6
3. Appropriate/type	III.7.4, 7.6, 7.11	Chs. 25-26	III.5	II.9.0, 9.4-8
4. Benefit/harm	III.7.3	Ch. 25		II.9.13-14
5. Incest	III.7.7			II.9.6
6. Sexual misbehavior	III.7.8	Ch. 25	III.5	II.9.1, 9.5, 9.8-9, 9.15
7. Number	III.7.9	Ch. 25		II.9.17
8. Death	III.7.12	Ch. 25		II.9.16
9. Homosexuality	III.7.13	Ch. 25	III.5	II.9.1, 9.10-12
10. When	III.7.2, 7.10	Chs. 25-26	III.5	II.9.18

17. Death

	BA	JN	TBN	Abū Bakr
1. Cause	III.8.1	Ch. 37	III.13	II.10.2-12, 10.14
2. Suicide	III.8.1			II.10.13
3. Where		Ch. 37		II.10.15-17
4. Easy		Ch. 37		II.10.2
5. Violent	III.8.1	Ch. 37	III.13	II.10.3, 10.5, 10.8-12

18. Faith/Law

	JN	TBN	Abū Bakr
1. Type of law	Ch. 29		II.1.9, 1.11
2. Changes	Ch. 29	III.12	
3. Honesty	Ch. 29	III.8, III.12	II.1.10
4. When	Ch. 29	III.12	

19. Travel

	BA	JN	TBN	Abū Bakr
1. Travel?	III.9.2	Ch. 27	III.8	II.11 *passim*
2. Benefit	III.9.2	Chs. 27-28	III.8	II.11.1
3. Harm	III.9.2	Chs. 27-28	III.8	II.11.2, 11.4

20. Profession/trades[15]

	BA	JN	TBN	Abū Bakr
1. Unskilled?	III.10.2, 10.6		III.9	
2. Three sigs.	III.10.2	Ch. 33	III.9	II.12.2, 12.5, 12.46
3. Moon's application	III.10.3-4	Ch. 33		II.12.7
4. Lot of Work	III.10.4, 10.7			
5. Success	III.10.5	Ch. 33	III.9	II.12.1, 12.3, 12.6, 12.8
6. Misc. indications	III.10.8	Ch. 33	III.9	II.12.4, 12.9-45

21. Friends

	BA	JN	TBN	Abū Bakr
1. Synastry	III.12.1, 12.4, 12.8		III.10	
2. Prediction	III.12.3, 12.6			
3. Types	III.12.2	Ch. 35	III.10	II.13.1-2
4. Strength	III.12.3, 12.5	Ch. 35	III.10	II.13.3-5
5. Election	III.12.9			

22. Enemies

	JN	TBN	Abū Bakr
1. Have enemies?	Ch. 36	III.11	II.14.1
2. Status	Ch. 36	III.11	II.14.1
3. Who prevails	Ch. 36	III.11	II.14.2

---

[15] In the Persian method, one should determine first the level of prosperity, and thus whether the native will actually practice a trade.

23. Annual Methods

	BA	TBN	Abū Bakr	On Rev. Nat.	Al-Qabīsī
1. Ages of Man				I.7-8	
2. Profection	IV.1-7	II.4-6		II.1-22, II.24	IV.8
3. Distributor-partner	III.1.10, IV.8-13	II.2	I.17	III.1-8	IV.14
4. Solar revolution	IV.14-15			I.6, II.23	
5. *Firdāriyyāt*	III.17-25		I.16	IV.1-8	IV.20
6. Ingresses, returns	IV *passim*			V.1-9	IV.21
7. Moon	IV.1			II.22, III.8, V.10	
8. Directions in the revolution		II.3, II.5-6		II.1, III.1	IV.13
9. Ninth-parts				III.9-10	IV.16-17
10. Monthly, daily, hourly rulers	IV.16			IX.7	
11. Natal directions	II.17, III.1.10	I.4, II.1, II.5-6	I.15		IV.11-12

APPENDIX E: THE *ESSENTIAL MEDIEVAL ASTROLOGY* CYCLE

The *Essential Medieval Astrology* cycle is a projected series of books which will redefine the contours of traditional astrology. Comprised mainly of translations of works by Persian and Arabic-speaking medieval astrologers, it will cover all major areas of astrology, including philosophical treatments and magic. The cycle will be accompanied by compilations of introductory works and readings on the one hand, and independent monographs and encyclopediac works on the other (including late medieval and Renaissance works of the Latin West).

I. Introductions
- *Introductions to Astrology*: Abū Ma'shar's *Abbreviation of the Introduction*, al-Qabīsī's *The Introduction to Astrology* (2010)
- Abū Ma'shar, *Great Introduction to the Knowledge of the Judgments of the Stars* (2010-11)
- *Basic Readings in Traditional Astrology* (2011)

II. Nativities
- *Persian Nativities I*: Māshā'allāh's *The Book of Aristotle*, Abū 'Ali al-Khayyāt's *On the Judgments of Nativities* (2009)
- *Persian Nativities II*: 'Umar al-Tabarī's *Three Books on Nativities*, Abū Bakr's *On Nativities* (2010)
- *Persian Nativities III*: Abū Ma'shar's *On the Revolutions of Nativities* (2010)

III. Questions (Horary)
- Hermann of Carinthia, *The Search of the Heart* (2010)
- Various, *The Book of the Nine Judges* (2010-11)
- Al-Kindi, *The Forty Chapters* (2011)

IV. Elections
- *Traditional Electional Astrology*: Abū Ma'shar's *On Elections* and *Flowers of Elections*; other minor works (2011-12)

V. Mundane Astrology
- *Astrology of the World*: Abū Ma'shar's *On the Revolutions of the Years of the World* and *Flowers*, Sahl bin Bishr's *Prophetic Sayings*; lesser works on prices and weather (2011-12)

VI. Other Works
- Bonatti, Guido, *The Book of Astronomy* (2007)
- *Works of Sahl & Māshā'allāh* (2008)
- *A Course in Traditional Astrology* (TBA)
- Al-Rijāl, *On the Judgments of the Stars* (TBA)
- *Astrological Magic* (TBA)
- *The Latin Hermes* (TBA)
- Firmicus Maternus, *Mathesis* (TBA)

BIBLIOGRAPHY

Abū Bakr, *On Nativities*, in Dykes (2010).

Abū Ma'shar al-Balhi (attr. Hermes), *De Revolutionibus Nativitatum* (Basel: Heinrich Petri, 1559)

Abū Ma'shar al-Balhi, *Albumasaris de Revolutionibus Nativitatum*: see Pingree 1968.

Abū Ma'shar al-Balhi (Richard Lemay ed.), *Liber Introductorii Maioris ad Scientiam Iudiciorum Astrorum* (Naples: Istituto Universitario Orientale, 1996)

Abū Ma'shar al-Balhi, *On Solar Revolutions Part I*, trans. and ed. Robert H. Schmidt (unpublished)

Abū Ma'shar al-Balhi, *On Solar Revolutions Part II*, trans. and ed. Robert H. Schmidt (Cumberland, MD: The PHASER Foundation, Inc., 1999)

Al-Khayyāt, Abū 'Ali, *The Judgments of Nativities*, trans. and ed. Benjamin N. Dykes, in Dykes 2009.

Al-Mansur, *Almansoris astrologi propositiones, ad Saracenorum regem* (Basel: Johannes Hervagius, 1533)

Al-Qabīsī, *The Introduction to Astrology*, eds. Charles Burnett, Keiji Yamamoto, Michio Yano (London and Turin: The Warburg Institute, 2004)

Al-Tabarī, 'Umar, *Three Books on Nativities*, in Dykes (2010)

Boll, Francisco et al. eds., *Catalogus Codicum Astrologorum Graecorum* vol. 2 (Bruxelles: Heinrich Lamertin, 1900)

Bonatti, Guido, *Book of Astronomy*, trans. and ed. Benjamin N. Dykes (Golden Valley, MN: The Cazimi Press, 2007)

Burnett, Charles, and Ahmed al-Hamdi, "Zādānfarrūkh al-Andarzaghar on Anniversary Horoscopes," in *Zeitschrift für Geschichte der Abrabisch-Islamischen Wissenschaften* v.7, 1991/92, pp. 294-400.

Dorotheus of Sidon, *Carmen Astrologicum*, trans. David Pingree (Abingdon, MD: The Astrology Center of America, 2005)

Dykes, Benjamin trans. and ed., *Works of Sahl & Māshā'allāh* (Golden Valley, MN: The Cazimi Press, 2008)

Dykes, Benjamin, trans. and ed., *Persian Nativities I: Māshā'allāh & Abū 'Ali* (Minneapolis, MN: The Cazimi Press, 2009)

Dykes, Benjamin, trans. and ed., *Persian Nativities II: 'Umar al-Tabarī & Abū Bakr* (Minneapolis, MN: The Cazimi Press, 2010)

Gansten, Martin, *Primary Directions: Astrology's Old Master Technique* (England: The Wessex Astrologer, 2009)

Hephaistio of Thebes, *Apotelesmatics* vol. II, trans. and ed. Robert H. Schmidt (Cumberland, MD: The Golden Hind Press, 1998)

Hermes, *Hermetis centum aphorismorum liber* (Basel: Johannes Hervagius, 1533)

Māshā'allāh bin Atharī, *The Book of Aristotle*, in Dykes 2009.

Māshā'allāh bin Atharī, *On the Significations of the Planets in a Nativity*, in Dykes 2008.

Paulus Alexandrinus, *Late Classical Astrology: Paulus Alexandrinus and Olympiodorus*, trans. Dorian Gieseler Greenbaum, ed. Robert Hand (Reston, VA: ARHAT Publications, 2001)

Pingree, David, "Historical Horoscopes," in *Journal of the American Oriental Society* v. 82 (1962), pp. 487-502.

Pingree, David ed., *Albumasaris de Revolutionibus Nativitatum* (Leipzig: B.G. Teubner, 1968)

Pingree, David, *The Thousands of Abū Ma'shar* (London: The Warburg Institute, 1968)

Pseudo-Ptolemy, *Centiloquium*, in *Liber Quadripartitus* (Venice: Bonetus Locatellus, 1493)

Ptolemy, Claudius, *Tetrabiblos* vols. 1, 2, 4, trans. Robert Schmidt, ed. Robert Hand (Berkeley Springs, WV: The Golden Hind Press, 1994-98)

Schmidt, Robert trans. and Robert Hand ed., *Dorotheus, Orpheus, Anubio, & Pseudo-Valens: Teachings on Transits* (Berkeley Springs, WV: The Golden Hind Press, 1995)

Schmidt, Robert H., trans. and ed. *Definitions and Foundations* (Cumberland, MD: The Golden Hind Press, 2009)

Sezgin, Fuat, *Geschichte des Arabischen Schrifttums*, vol. 7 (Leiden: E. J. Brill, 1979)

Valens, Vettius, *The Anthology*, vols. I-VII, ed. Robert Hand, trans. Robert Schmidt (Berkeley Springs, WV: The Golden Hind Press, 1993-2001)

INDEX

This index is intended as a guide for students. Due to the overlaps between different annual techniques, I have not, for instance, listed every occurrence of the term "Lord of the Year," but have confined myself to the chapters and sections with primary discussions of each topic. Other technical terms and names of authors are listed as usual.

Above/below the earth 60, 80, 86, 103, 108, 127, 160, 161, 194, 195, 210
Abū Bakr........2, 5, 33, 59, 73, 157, 161, 214-21
Ages of man 61–65
al-Andarzaghar...25, 37, 42-43, 65, 203, 207
al-Kindī 1
al-Manṣūr 209
al-Qabīsī 1-2, 5, 59, 69, 133, 221
Al-Riḍwān, ʿAlī 209, 211
al-Sijzī 2
Anubio 45
Ascendant of the year ... 27–28, 60, 123–31, 156–62, 209, 212
  its Lord 28–29
Awj 60
Bonatti, Guido 2
Combustion 102
Comets 157
Cycle of the year (solar revolution) 203
Decimation 48, 49, 48–51
Distribution .. 29–34, 132–62, 210-12
Eclipses 38-39, 157, 209-10
Firdāriyyāt 37–41, 170–86, 207
Fixed stars 33, 59, 146, 157
Gansten, Martin 133
Ḥalb 60
Ḥayyiz 60
Head/Tail of the Dragon 3, 38-40, 58-59, 71, 127–28, 134, 153, 170, 172, 175, 185–86, 200, 207

Hephaistio 48
Hermes .42, 53, 174, 209, 212, 222
Hīlāj (releaser) 4, 26, 29-30, 33, 72, 108, 110, 121, 132-33, 146
Hugo of Santalla 2, 4, 52
Jārbakhtār .... See Distribution
Kasmīmī (ᶜazīmī) 60, 102, 110
Lots. 1, 4, 19, 22, 27–28, 30, 36–37, 36–37, 58-60, 72, 74, 76, 78, 90, 94, 100, 103, 108, 110, 113, 115, 118-19, 122, 132-36, 161, 199, 205
  of Brothers 161
  of Children 79, 94, 119, 192
  of Courage 135-36
  of Fathers 160
  of Fortune. 6-7, 29, 59, 78, 135-36, 146, 154, 156-57, 160, 190, 201, 205, 210-12
  of Marriage 13, 36, 79, 83, 101, 115, 151
  of Necessity 136
  of Slaves 79
  of the Father 82, 94, 205
  of the Kingdom 119, 158
  of the Mother 94, 205
  of Victory 135-36
  of Work 79, 119, 158
Māshāʾallāh 1-2, 4, 6, 10, 25-26, 29, 34, 37, 49, 51, 58, 65, 70, 71, 133, 203, 207, 214, 221-22
Monthly, weekly, daily, hourly rulers 36, 47–48, 203–6, 211
Moon (in revolutions) 34–36
Neighboring 32

Ninth-parts 47, 162–69, 206
Overcoming 48–51, 157
Paul of Alexandria 42–43, 135
Peregrine/alien signs.. ..... 7, 60, 75, 78, 80, 87-89, 91, 93, 100-03, 113-14, 142, 156 168
Pingree, David 2
Profections .. 17–21, 74–130, 156–62, 200–203
　Lord of the Year (special instructions).. 21–27, 75–76, 85–87
pseudo-Ptolemy 209, 212
pseudo-Valens 42
Ptolemy, Claudius 4, 7, 42, 57, 209
Pythagoreanism 38, 72
Quadruplicities
　common signs 17, 80, 155, 189
　fixed signs 17, 155, 189
　movable signs 17, 154, 155, 161, 164, 189
Retrogradation.. 14, 23, 41, 44, 58, 60, 75, 76, 78, 80, 88-89, 91, 93, 98, 102, 106, 115-16, 120, 126, 128-29, 131, 134, 137, 159, 187, 190, 197
Revolution
　defended 53–58
　defined 53, 58–59
　features 60–61
　general approach 7–17, 64–68, 69–74
　what 4–6

Sahl bin Bishr 214
Salio of Padua 2
Schmidt, Robert 49, 203
Sect .. 13, 20, 22, 28, 38, 39, 40-41, 44-45, 52, 60, 75, 77, 80-82, 86, 88, 97, 100, 102-04, 106, 109, 119, 135, 170-75, 178-81, 186, 193, 198
Signs
　agreeing in journey 74
　ascending equally 74
　four-footed 7, 82
　hateful 52
　inimical 52
Stations 14, 44-45, 102, 126
Sālkhudāy *See* Profections, Lord of the Year
Transits, ingresses, returns. 41–47, 187–200, 213
Triplicities
　fiery signs 101
　watery signs 7, 82, 100
Twelfth-parts 19, 27, 34, 58-60, 71, 74, 76, 78, 81, 90, 94, 100, 103, 108, 110, 113, 115, 118, 122, 132-33, 135-36, 199-200
'Umar al-Tabarī 1-2, 6, 10-11, 18, 35, 71, 73, 133, 142, 168, 202, 205, 214, 221
Under the rays 23, 60, 75-76, 80, 82, 91, 93, 102, 105, 109-11, 115, 127-28, 130-31, 159, 192, 197
Valens, Vettius 6, 17, 42-44, 132

www.ingramcontent.com/pod-product-compliance
Lightning Source LLC
Chambersburg PA
CBHW070548160426
43199CB00014B/2424